D1256023

THE
GILDED
GHETTO

THE GILDED GHETTO

*Women and Political Power
in Canada*

SYDNEY SHARPE

A Phyllis Bruce Book
HarperCollins*Publishers*Ltd

THE GILDED GHETTO: WOMEN AND POLITICAL POWER IN CANADA
Copyright © 1994 by Sydney Sharpe.
All rights reserved. No part of this book may be used or reproduced in any
manner whatsoever without prior written permission except in the
case of brief quotations embodied in reviews.
For information address HarperCollins Publishers Ltd,
Suite 2900, Hazelton Lanes, 55 Avenue Road,
Toronto, Canada M5R 3L2.

First Edition

Canadian Cataloguing in Publication Data

Sharpe, Sydney
The gilded ghetto : women and political power in Canada

"A Phyllis Bruce book".
Includes index and bibliographical references.
ISBN 0-00-255276-0

1. Women in politics — Canada. I. Title.

HQ1236.5.C2S5 1994   305.43'32'0971   C94-930699-1

94 95 96 97 98 99 ❖ DWF 10 9 8 7 6 5 4 3 2 1

Printed and bound in Canada

*To all those who overcome adversity,
and especially to Norah Hutchinson,
Jim Stanton and Don Braid*

CONTENTS

ACKNOWLEDGEMENTS

M any people offered me unselfish help and co-operation while I was preparing this book. First, I would like to thank the scores of women politicians who gave their precious time, often for lengthy taped interviews. Many men also supported the project by granting interviews, including Prime Minister Jean Chrétien and former prime ministers Brian Mulroney and Joe Clark.

Various libraries and resource centres were of immense help, including the magnificent Library of Parliament and Elections Canada, whose friendly and co-operative staff disprove every day the myth that anything connected with government is slow and unwieldy. The offices of the Speaker and clerks of the Senate and House of Commons were also very helpful. In provincial capitals, I had assistance from several legislatures, especially the resourceful staff at the Alberta Legislature Library, whose readiness to search out material from across the country I will always remember with admiration and gratitude.

The Alberta Foundation for the Arts provided invaluable assistance, as well as the wise counsel of senior consultant Scot Morison. Many friends provided insight and support, especially Patricia and

Richard Gariepy, Holly and Jerome Slavik, Sheila Pratt, Cathy Cavanaugh, Norah Hutchinson, Jim Stanton and Lisa Grand. Thanks also to my mother, Norma Sharpe, and to Helen and Hugh Braid. And the book would never have been started (or finished) without the friendship and wise advice of my publisher and editor, Phyllis Bruce. My husband, Don Braid, and our two children, Gabriel and Rielle, were more patient than a writer has any right to expect.

Finally, a word of gratitude to Miss Piggy, who gives the ultimate advice to a writer chained to the keyboard for months on end: "Never eat more than you can lift."

PARTIAL LIST OF PEOPLE INTERVIEWED

POLITICIANS

Diane Ablonczy
Lise Bacon
Pam Barrett
Monique Bégin
Dawn Black
Ethel Blondin-Andrew
Marion Boyd
Jan Brown
Catherine Callbeck
Iona Campagnolo
Kim Campbell
Pat Carney
Sharon Carstairs
Jean Charest
Jean Chrétien
Mary Clancy
Joe Clark
Mary Collins
Sheila Copps
Dorothy Dobbie
Gary Doer
Ann Edwards
Joyce Fairbairn
Ellen Louks Fairclough
Ron Ghitter
Evelyn Gigantes
Deborah Grey
Lynda Haverstock
Céline Hervieux-Payette
Chaviva Hosek
Janis Johnson
Frances Lankin
Marjory LeBreton
Peter Lougheed
Flora MacDonald
Preston Manning
Paul Martin, Jr.
Grace McCarthy
Elaine McCoy
Alexa McDonough
Barbara McDougall
Janice McKinnon
Audrey McLaughlin
Anne McLellan
Lyn McLeod
Val Meredith
Brian Mulroney
Tony Penikett
Jean Pigott
Bob Runciman
Judi Tyabji

OTHERS

Sheila Arnopoulos
Sarah Band
Maude Barlow
Don Braid
Alvin Cader
Stevie Cameron
Catherine Cavanaugh
Miro Cernetig
Aline Chrétien
Anne Marie Decore
Dale Eisler
Allan Fotheringham
Roger Gibbins
Frances Henry
Norah Hutchinson
Rosemarie Kuptana
Michelle Landsberg
Kathleen Mahoney
Sandra Manning
Patrick Nagle
Wanda O'Hagan
Jock Osler
Vaughn Palmer
Francine Pelletier
Sheila Pratt
Peter Raymont
Judy Rebick
Glenda Simms
Sunera Thobani
David Thomas
Graham Thompson
Linda Trimble
Jodi White

FOREWORD

"There are fifty-six whooping cranes in Canada, and one female federal politician."

Barbara Frum, *writing in*
Chatelaine, *in October 1971*

Ask Canada's women politicians a few simple questions— "What's your life like?" or "Is it harder for you?"—and the result is a remarkable torrent of anger, resentment, satisfaction, regret, shrewd perception, and guerilla humour. These women have hoarded a storehouse of feelings whose contents come pouring out as soon as the door is pried open a crack. Some of the interviews for this book, especially with pioneers like Monique Bégin and Iona Campagnolo, were deeply emotional experiences for the interviewer and, I suspect, for the subjects. Sometimes they wondered almost plaintively why nobody had ever asked them before about their trials as women in politics. Their conclusions are virtually unanimous: yes, political life was harder for them, and it is still difficult for women today, although progress in the past decade has been encouraging.

Most women were eager to have their story told—the full story of their struggle, and that of their predecessors, for political equality in Canada. They also wanted it told by a woman. When I faxed a request for an interview to Iona Campagnolo, the former Liberal cabinet minister, she fired back an angry response: Why would a man presume to write such a book? How dare I? How could I really *know*? After I told her of my strange lot—to go through life as a woman named Sydney—she readily agreed to talk, and she demonstrated an impressive depth of humanity, intelligence, and humour.

Most of all, I was struck by how well all these women understood the male political system, and by how completely they were forced to disguise their knowledge. This is less true today, but it still applies to many women in politics. They are travellers in a strange and alien culture that was created by and for men. Women are socialized to be the wives and handmaidens of power, while men *are* power, and the brave women who cross this psychological divide take a giant leap into a strange world of prejudice and misunderstanding. To survive and prosper, they often need a disguise of some sort; their solutions range from taking on a manly bluster or "battle armour" (high-heeled shoes, power dresses and make-up) to excessive weight gain.

Often they find their core values as women wildly out of sync with the win-or-die male system. The resulting compromises and forced duplicity can be deeply conflicting. And yet, in spite of the many barriers thrown up against their participation in politics, they have achieved astonishing things for women and for all Canadians. Because of these pioneers, the day when all women will enjoy equality in political life is at last in view.

The women I spoke to covered the full ideological range, from the convinced feminists of the NDP to Reform Party women who reject institutional feminism entirely while still advocating gender equality. I have been an ardent feminist for more than twenty years, but I came to respect *all* these women for what they have brought and continue to bring to politics. In well over a hundred interviews, I did not find one political woman who was not working, in her own way, toward equal representation for her gender.

As I spoke to them, I became convinced that they deserved a book that recounts both the long struggle for women's equality in politics and the personal experiences of those who live in the political world every day. After toiling in the shadows of history for generations, they are entitled to the spotlight. I hope that in this book they see themselves revealed clearly and honestly.

THE
GILDED
GHETTO

1

THE GILDED
GHETTO

"The eyes of Stalin, the voice of Marilyn Monroe."
French president François Mitterrand
on Margaret Thatcher

When Jean Pigott was a Conservative MP in the 1970s, most Canadians considered her to be part of the small band of lofty legislators who run the country and always get their way. But she and a few other elected women knew how far the public impression was from the daily reality. The belief that only men should be politicians was so deeply rooted that when she won a by-election in Ottawa-Carleton in 1976, the CBC in Vancouver announced that a francophone man named *Jean Pigott* had carried the riding.

This misunderstanding persisted for years, Pigott recalls. Once she was waiting in the office of a prominent Chief

Executive Officer in Calgary after announcing herself and giving the receptionist her card. "Finally this secretary came out and said to the receptionist in a loud voice, 'Where's this gentleman from Ottawa, this *Jean Pigott?*' We had a laugh about it. I got used to this after a while. It was just part of the landscape."[1]

And yet, from the perspective of most Canadians, elected women like Pigott were and are among the most visibly privileged people in the country. When they reach cabinet status they enjoy all the daily trappings of influence: servile courtiers, eager audiences, limousines, waiting planes, and avid media pursuers. Every message tells them they are *important*. The words "Yes, Minister" follow them like a mantra. Even the most humble backbench parliamentarian, female or male, cannot be fired by anyone but the voters. As Nova Scotia NDP leader Alexa McDonough reminds herself when she feels frustrated, politics is one of the few areas where women get equal pay.

Women politicians, whatever their problems, know that they are far better off than an unemployed single mother with children to feed. When Kim Campbell spoke of the "unspeakable loneliness" of Ottawa, NDP leader Audrey McLaughlin sharply reminded her that thousands of Canadian women would love to trade places with her. According to the National Action Committee on the Status of Women, "The privileges available to a Kim Campbell . . . are far removed from the daily reality of food banks, welfare lines and unemployment rolls that are the lot of growing numbers of women."[2]

But even though they belong to a gilded elite, elected women also remain a ghettoized minority within parties, legislatures, and governments. Judy LaMarsh, a famous Liberal minister in the 1960s, aptly called her lonely world a "gilded cage." The bars have since moved outward to enclose a larger community—a privileged political neighbourhood with security guards and exclusive membership. But emotionally, intellectually, and culturally, women's political enclave remains a gilded ghetto surrounded by the larger, dominant world of male politicians. The best of those men now want to remove the bars and welcome the women into the larger world; others would like to run them back into the cage. But women always know that the main struggle for improving their lot falls to them.

Slowly, they are winning, although in historical terms the progress looks paltry. Agnes Macphail, the first female member of Parliament, was elected more than seventy years ago, in 1921. Yet the 1968 sweep that brought Pierre Trudeau to power, incredibly, still produced only one female MP, the incumbent New Democrat Grace MacInnis. Now there are fifty-three elected women in Ottawa (18 per cent of the total) and hundreds more in the traditional training grounds for the federal Parliament: provincial legislatures, local councils, school boards, and party executives. Canada has its first elected female provincial premier, Catherine Callbeck of Prince Edward Island, and Canadians saw Kim Campbell briefly at the pinnacle of power as prime minister. Gradually, they are getting used to the idea that women have a place in political life.

But there are still many stretches of barbed wire around the gilded ghetto. Deeply rooted in the Canadian psyche is the contrary notion that women should stick to the private sphere of home and family while men do the public work—"the big shiny jobs," in Judy LaMarsh's phrase. If women work outside the home, they are expected to do menial jobs that serve men. This private–public divide explains much of the backlash faced by women politicians when they begin to exercise real authority, as they have in Ontario. On the personal level, it colours perceptions of female politicians. Deborah Grey, the Reform Party MP, once sat beside a man on a plane who asked her what she did. When Grey said she was an MP, he responded, "Oh, you work for an MP. That must be interesting." Grey said, "No, I *am* the MP. But I do have a secretary, and his name is Robert."[3]

This powerful dichotomy can cause female politicians immense personal distress. Many feel guilty when they are forced to spend time away from their families, even if they have supportive husbands and children at home. Most women simply avoid this "role strain" by staying out of politics until their children are grown—or forever. In general, men seldom feel such social constraints as they ponder a career in the legislatures or Parliament of Canada.

When women do manage to clamber to the top rungs of leadership, they face an even more daunting challenge. How should they behave? What image, what style, does the public expect of a woman leader? That public gives wildly contradictory answers. If a woman behaves like a typical male politician, she is branded as "aggressive" or worse, "ambitious." (And women wonder, how could a leader not be ambitious?) But if she acts in a mild and conciliatory manner, she clearly isn't tough enough to do the job. This trap has confounded women leaders from Audrey McLaughlin to Kim Campbell. They find no escape from the double-edged jibes of editorialists, cartoonists, and columnists. One problem is that no Canadian woman has yet appeared with the charisma to set a style, a way of leading, that the voters can accept and that other female politicians can absorb and use.

In place of their own, Canadian women are forced to search abroad for successful role models. They see Margaret Thatcher, a uniquely British dominatrix whose style is alien to the Canadian context; Benazir Bhutto, who had an arranged marriage and rose to the prime minister's office in Pakistan through family connections; the surprising Tansu Ciller, elected on her own talent in Muslim Turkey; Ireland's popular figurehead president, Mary Robinson; America's Hillary Rodham Clinton, brilliant but controversial because she is not elected to any public office; Gro Harlem Brundtland, former prime minister of Norway, sensibly committed to women's rights and perhaps the most useful model for Canadians. Each of these women is admirable in her own way and well worth studying, but none holds the key to a woman's breakthrough in Canada. We will have to invent our own female leadership style from the raw materials of our own culture.

Even trickier is the vexing issue of sexuality. Women in politics face a series of unspoken (or sometimes snidely spoken) questions regarding their private lives. Is she married? If so, why isn't she home with the kids? If not, who is she sleeping with? If she isn't sleeping with a man, is she gay? Is there an abortion in her past?

Very few political women escape such speculation even as they approach retirement age. Too many men seem incapable of looking past a woman's sexual nature to see the potential political leader.

Female leaders, uncertain of what the public wants, frame their responses as they go along. Kim Campbell at first talked rather openly about her private life, perhaps in the hope that the media would lose interest. Instead, she unleashed a torrent of public abuse. During her disastrous election campaign, she was reduced to making pathetic jokes about her expanding body parts. B.C. politician Judi Tyabji flaunted her sexuality, found a new husband, and lost her promising career. Audrey McLaughlin simply ignored her sexuality. She presented herself as a divorced woman without romantic interests (or none that was anybody's business), so the media deemed her drab and boring, and abandoned her. Nobody has found a strategy that works to defuse sexuality as a political problem. The majority of Canadian men clearly have a use for sexually attractive female politicians, but it is not leadership.

When in office at any level, women carry an extra work burden that men do not share: they are expected to represent not only their constituents, but their gender as well. This involves a good deal of bone-crushing labour, attending socials, teas, and women's functions of all kinds. They are enlisted to fight for every woman's cause, attack every woman's enemy, and secure every woman's opportunity. They aren't paid for this work, and it adds hours to their days, but very few female politicians refuse to plunge in.

"I was always expected to be present when we had women's delegations attending upon the Cabinet," wrote Judy LaMarsh, who suffered more than most because she was the only female minister of her day. "I was, further, expected to be particularly diligent in attending conventions of the party's women, and to make regular rounds in speaking to any and every women's organization. . . . I was the usual invitee whenever any organization, anywhere in Canada, held its annual 'ladies night.' I was asked to fashion shows, award dinners and meetings of the professions in which women were a dominant group."[4] LaMarsh had a simple emotional reaction to this role: she hated it.

Today, Liberal Resources Minister Anne McLellan recognizes the same pressure. "I feel a tremendous onus to do the best I can," she says, "because it's also women I'm representing. And that gets real tiring. . . . Being a woman is tiring work. We juggle so many things. And there's the guilt. Guilt is tiring."[5]

The modern political woman's forced obligation is not just social but ideological as well. Female politicians are claimed—or attacked—by the various factions of feminism, women of the moderate centre, and those of the far right who believe they are traitors to their gender merely by being elected. Some feminist women feel that if a female politician isn't committed to feminist prescriptions for change, she is worthless. Indeed, she may even set back the cause of women by allowing the men to be complacent.

Kim Campbell lost this impossible battle on all fronts. Feminist groups branded her a sell-out for her 1991 attempt to recriminalize abortion and to award helicopter contracts while ignoring the need for a child-care program ("Choppers over Child Care," read the headlines), and for her support of free trade. Meanwhile, REAL Women mobilized to keep Campbell out of the Tory leadership. A spokesperson for an affiliate of this conservative women's group thundered: "We agree that she is left-wing, a captive of the feminist interest groups and pro-homosexual." Campbell's experience, and that of many other female politicians, shows that women are denied the privilege enjoyed by their male colleagues of simply representing all their constituents as best they can. Instead, they inevitably become cannon fodder in the battle of the sexes.

Does a woman have to be a declared feminist to accomplish anything useful? Many feminist women believe so, because, they say, a female politician who lacks the proper "analysis" will do no more good than a man. Nova Scotia's Alexa McDonough, for instance, doesn't see the slightest value in the election of Catherine Callbeck as premier of P.E.I., because Callbeck does not consider herself a feminist. Author and activist Maude Barlow once argued for the election of large numbers of women of all opinions, but now she believes that only strong feminists can make a difference.

The question is central to the whole issue of women's involvement in politics. Without doubt, strong feminists can generate beneficial change very quickly if they occupy key positions. In a few short years in office, NDP women in Ontario and British Columbia have brought significant social gains for women. But it's also true that the Tory women of Brian Mulroney's government, in their quieter way, stimulated startling advances toward acceptance of women's political authority. In many provinces, including hyper-conservative Alberta, women have inched closer to power by burrowing quietly within the system. Along the way, they have begun to introduce improvements for all women.

It is becoming increasingly difficult to define who is a feminist. At a "Winning Women" conference in Calgary in May 1994, a woman confided that though she supported the goals of feminism she was afraid to call herself a feminist. It was a big step, she said, just to participate in a political seminar sponsored by women. This feeling is widespread: a poll conducted in 1993 showed that only one-third of Canadian women call themselves feminists, but 80 per cent of all Canadians, women and men, agree that the women's movement has been good for society, and that more should be done to achieve its goals.

As Margaret Wente wrote in *The Globe and Mail:* "I don't feel like a victim and I think most men are pretty decent. I send money to a few women's causes but I'm not really political. Does that make me a feminist? Darned if I know." One thing is clear: many women who believe in some feminist goals do not care to call themselves feminists because the word has become too ideological and pejorative. Wente feels that "today you don't dare call yourself a feminist unless you're against free trade and helicopters, and for trees and whales. Dissent at your peril."

For the women who have considered themselves feminists for the last generation, it is important to remember why feminist goals remain crucial. But it is also vital to understand the reluctance of some women to label themselves feminist, especially when that label can seriously hinder relations with spouses, friends, and employers.

The term "women's issues" has become just as limiting, provoking an instant backlash among those who believe policies should be aimed at society as a whole, not at certain groups. Some strong feminists now suggest other approaches to the women's problems of violence, poverty, single-parent families, wage and job inequity, as well as many others. "We must do a gender analysis of why issues impact differently on women and men," says Glenda Simms, president of the Canadian Advisory Council on the Status of Women. "Don't call them 'women's issues' any more—there's a backlash against women's issues. Instead, show how various policies affect women differently than they do men."[6]

Maude Barlow urges an end to the common practice of appointing ministers responsible for women's issues. She believes this allows male ministers to ignore women's problems because somebody else is designated to look after them. "I would like women's issues to be addressed in all portfolios," she says. "They must be considered a key part of the economic and social departments. What's important is how seriously these issues are taken by the whole government."[7] Many women politicians have come to dread being named to the "women's ghetto" portfolios. It's the ultimate tokenism, they say, pushing women into one little corner of the operation. When Brian Mulroney made Barbara McDougall his minister for the status of women, she was appalled. Like many other women, she wanted to prove herself, and help women, in a tough economic department.[8]

There is certainly plenty to be done. In 1993, Canada's international ranking based on treatment of women slipped from eighth place to eleventh. Women's participation in the workforce is actually declining for the first time in twenty-five years; between 1990 and 1993, it dropped from 58 per cent to 57 per cent. According to one estimate, the real rate of women's unemployment is close to 20 per cent. Sixty-two per cent of single mothers have incomes below the poverty line and their incomes dropped by nearly $3,000 in two years.[9] Yet in the key task of getting women elected to solve such problems, "the rate of progress remains very slow and random." If that rate holds, it will take eight more elections, or nearly forty years, before an equal number of men and women are elected to the House of Commons.[10]

This poses the ultimate question: do women bring to politics a female style, a new, gentler way of doing business? Can women put an end to childish behaviour, partisan name-calling and other boyish pranks, even as they lead the world to equality for women? One point of view holds that once women are in the male world, some of them begin to act increasingly like the men. Ontario minister Frances Lankin says she has to fight this temptation constantly: it's like being dragged down into quicksand; some women sink.

Internationally, women leaders are as likely as men to bluster and use their armies. Corazon Aquino mercilessly put down coups in the Philippines, and Indira Gandhi successfully led a brutal war against Pakistan.[11] Margaret Thatcher sent British troops and warships to the Falkland Islands to fight Argentina in 1982. In some situations, women leaders will act tougher because they have more to prove. Certainly nothing in genetics, and precious little in Western culture, bars female leaders from being aggressive and even murderous. French President François Mitterrand, speaking in startled admiration, said that Margaret Thatcher had "the eyes of Stalin, the voice of Marilyn Monroe."

In the United States, a debate has raged for years over whether women bring an inherently different style to politics and business. Some scholars say they do: women think in terms of consensus and eschew hierarchies, these researchers claim. "They are intuitive, process-oriented, tolerant of ambiguity, and not invested in hierarchy. They think in webs of many factors, not in straight lines." Men, meanwhile, are "logical, hierarchical, goal-oriented, intolerant of ambiguity, and interested in power for power's sake."[12] Supporters of the "difference theory" claim reams of evidence; opponents say the research is loaded, and produce their own to show that there are no fundamental differences between male and female decision-makers.

In one sense, the claim that women bring a different style to politics is a limiting trap. One hundred and fifty years ago, the earliest feminists argued that the feminine virtues of nurturing, caring, and purity deserved a place in public life. It was the only argument available to them in their struggle to expand their world beyond the private confines of the home, and to a degree it worked. Gradually, women broke into politics with their mission to purify the nest that had been fouled by men for generations.

Today, political women are offering a modern version of the same outdated case when they say that their values and styles are more beneficial to the public. Hidden within their argument is the lingering assumption that because they are women, they need some extra justification to be in political life. They do not. It is time to recognize that they deserve full political equality with men simply because they *are* equal. No elaborate defences are required, and none should be demanded.

There is absolutely no question, however, that many of Canada's women politicians *believe* they bring different and useful qualities to politics, including a calmer, more consensus-driven style. One after another, they describe their shock at confronting the male-created system, their discomfort with confrontation, their desire to make a change, their almost instinctive efforts to do things differently.

These women know something else, too. In the struggle for women's equality in politics and society, only they can be counted upon to do the job. Men might follow the flag for a while if they see political advantage. And some elected men, like Alexa McDonough's two caucus mates in Nova Scotia, are active and convinced champions of women's causes. But in the end, only women know how it feels to live in the gilded ghetto. The one way for them to escape its confines is to flood the system with large numbers of women. Gradually, but with increasing momentum, they are succeeding.

2

TINKERBELL SPELL

"Her face was most feminine: exceptionally mobile and expressive, with the shadowed blue eyes widening and narrowing, the eyebrows rising and falling, the forehead wrinkling, the lips pursing, parting, often breaking into a sudden smile."

The Montreal Gazette*'s William Johnson*
comments on Kim Campbell, March 1993

"All that's missing is a reference to heaving breasts."
Liane Faulder *of* The Edmonton Journal *responds*

Kim Campbell caught Canadians with their stereotypes exposed as vividly as pink pantaloons in a Victorian windstorm. Politically, the country was ready for a woman prime minister in 1993, but psychologically we were still in need of mass therapy. Suddenly we had not only a woman prime minister, but an *attractive* one—a blonde, no less—someone who might still, on a good day, stir desire in the male populace. She was forty-six, twice divorced, and perhaps (who really knew?) still sexually active. Campbell even *talked* about her sex life, or lack of it, and made jokes about her body.

Very quickly, Campbell began to provoke peculiar reactions. The media, looking for fresh angles after a decade of male Tory rule, seized upon her as that priceless treasure, a fresh story. The responses of journalists in turn became fodder for more media analysis and criticism. William Johnson's column, appearing first in the Montreal *Gazette* and then reprinted many times across the country, was attacked as an astounding example of journalistic puppy love. Many Tory men, having initially supported Campbell while blinded by blondeness, were soon appalled at their choice, reacting as if their date had made the first move. What they had really wanted was another Margaret Thatcher, a woman who gave no credit to the pioneer females who preceded her, who was safely married, and who seemed beyond sex (although Thatcher still inspires whip-and-leather fantasies among many British men). There was even, perhaps, a Canadian market for a reborn Golda Meir or Charlotte Whitton: somebody tough and plain.

But there was still little space in the Canadian psyche for a national leader who was a modern professional woman, pretty, twice divorced, and childless, whose mother, a "free spirit," had left the family home when Kim was twelve. Could Canadians accept a woman who emerged from all this insecurity with a tough attitude and, as some men would say, "a real mouth on her"? (Campbell once wittily combined a joke about Mae West and gun laws: "Say, fella, is that a prohibited weapon with a barrel length of less than 18 inches, possession of which is grandfathered by those who satisfy the requirement of being a genuine gun collector on or before Oct. 1, 1992, in your pocket, or are you just glad to see me?"[1])

A similar life history, mixed with equal amounts of wit, might have made a man in Campbell's position appear energetic and resourceful, a worthy survivor. Many men have led unconventional lives and yet gained the respect of the country. Mackenzie King, unmarried, a patron of prostitutes, used a crystal ball to talk to his dead mother. Wilfrid Laurier was at various times rumoured to be impotent, homosexual, and the father of an illegitimate son. Pierre Trudeau was divorced amid worldwide scandal, while his troubled ex-wife was photographed *sans* panties with the Rolling Stones.[2] Yet King's private life was shielded from public view in his time, the Laurier rumours only added to his androgynous allure, and Trudeau's stoical poise won him a sympathetic press.

Not so Campbell. Her marital history was used to accuse her of "instability," her zigzag career produced as evidence of "flakiness," her very rise shown as proof that she was "crushingly ambitious."[3] Even before she ran for the leadership, *Frank* magazine pasted a photo of Campbell's head on a nude body with the headline: "Kim Campbell's naked ambition tour." The whiff of illicit sex hounded Campbell's election travels. When *Frank* discovered that she was involved with Montrealer Gregory Lekhtman,[4] the magazine needled her endlessly for "campaign coitus" and going "out with a bang." (To be fair, *Frank* is equally avid in its reporting of political males who go in for "horizontal jogging" and "exchanging briefs.") In earlier days, reporters routinely covered up the details of dalliance by male prime ministers and cabinet ministers, from George Hees to Pierre Trudeau.

It quickly became evident that there was no Canadian mould for a female prime minister; no model, no tradition, no guide for anybody to follow. Carried along by media hype, few people had really pondered their response to a youngish female baby boomer as leader. From coast to coast to coast (and gender to gender to gender), we fashioned our responses as we went along, and most of them were deeply revealing of our national confusion.

Sadly but understandably, one of the most confused people of all was Kim Campbell. Trying desperately to be herself, to show that she could both joke and take a joke, she began to make fun of her physique, perhaps in an unconscious effort to defuse the issue of her sexuality. Men tended to laugh, often with a touch of derision, but many women cringed. "People are wondering what to call my campaign plane," she said during a speech to the Calgary Chamber of Commerce on September 18, 1993. "I keep having the same problem. You have heard about the prime ministerial bottom. I am thinking people should call it derri-air." The same day she told people at an Alberta truck stop that her only exercise was getting into blue jeans. "I lost 300 calories trying to do up the zipper." Asked about the famous photo of her standing bare-shouldered behind judicial robes, she said, "I was fat when they took that picture. . . . The only part of me that looks good when I'm fat is my shoulders." Women have long known that if they demean themselves, others will invariably join in. It soon happened to Campbell: while Montreal's *La Presse* suggested that she could solve her problem by wearing loose, flowing clothes, the *Toronto Sun* recommended a red push-up bra. The day after the election, a newspaper in St. John's published a cartoon of an enormous Campbell-like posterior embossed with a male boot mark.

The urge to justify physical appearance simply never occurs to male politicians because their sexuality is not an issue. Perfect or flawed, handsome or plain, they are judged first as politicians. From the beginning, Campbell sensed that she was being sized up as a woman. One sure measure was the constant interest in her clothes, especially from male reporters. After the first Tory leadership debate, during an April 15 CBC Newsworld broadcast, host Don Newman and columnist Michel Gratton talked at length about Campbell's red dress, while Southam News correspondent Joan Bryden sat poker-faced through the exchange. Newman and Gratton didn't mention the other candidates' clothes.

Ironically, throughout the campaign, both Jean Chrétien and Preston Manning wore blue denim shirts for that man-in-the-street appeal, but journalists made little of this clever packaging. It's fascinating to note the change in cover photographs for the two editions of Chrétien's autobiography, *Straight from the Heart*. In the original 1985 edition, he wore a pinstriped suit, white shirt, and tie. For the 1994 reprint, he is photographed more intimately in a rugged denim shirt.

On occasion, Campbell was all too blunt about her personal life, freely answering questions that would probably not be posed to a male counterpart in a Canadian election. She told Quebec's *Oui* magazine: "My first husband (Prof. Nathan Divinsky) was quite simply the first man I felt comfortable with. That's why I married him. The second (Howard Eddy), he wasn't around long enough to have an influence on me. As for the third, there won't be one. I never again want to marry." And then, more forthright still: "I hope I never fall in love with a man who lives in Vancouver. Imagine the scenario: me at one end of the country, him at the other. I would rather do without, even if it cost me my sex life."[5]

On the subject of women, Pierre Trudeau confined himself to quips. Asked once if he planned to get rid of his Mercedes, he inquired, "The car or the girl?" At the height of his marital scandal, when his wife, mentally ill and confused, poured out her troubled soul to *Playgirl* magazine, Trudeau uttered not a word against her.[6] His sphinx-like silence made him a national hero and helped him win a fourth term in 1980. He had girlfriends while his marriage was breaking up (as Margaret had boyfriends), but everyone in the Ottawa press gallery dreaded asking him questions about his personal life. Each query was met with the same steely, poisonous glare.

Campbell's candour, intended to take the threat out of her sexuality, backfired badly. Tories began to whisper that she was "unstable," cartoonists lampooned her physique, and commentators felt free to discuss her life history. Respect for Campbell drooped like a wilted flower. Often, on hot-line shows, callers addressed her simply as "Kim," not "Ms. Campbell" or "Prime Minister." They were encouraged by other leaders, especially Reform chief Preston Manning. During the second televised election debate on October 4, he addressed Campbell as "Kim," and referred to NDP leader Audrey McLaughlin as "Audrey." "I've never felt so patronized by anybody or so put down as I was by Preston Manning during the debate," says McLaughlin. "He was lecturing me!"[7]

Campbell did little to discourage this trend when she chose the shortest, most vacuous campaign slogan in Canadian history—"Kim!" But female politicians all over the country notice this tendency toward familiarity. Alexa McDonough, Nova Scotia's NDP leader, says that when she is introduced with the male leaders of the provincial Tory and Liberal parties, "For them it's 'Mr. This' and 'the Honourable That.' Then they come to me and it's just 'Alexa.' They don't even get around to using my last name a lot of times."[8] In contrast, Alberta premier Ralph Klein, who insists that everyone call him just "Ralph"—and used the name as his campaign motto—often has to coax people to say it.

During the federal campaign, the media made a determined effort to dig up dirt on Campbell. Reporters researching a cover story for *Maclean's* asked people in Vancouver if she had ever had an abortion. The same question was still being posed by other journalists in early 1994, months after she had been defeated. The Liberals placed a campaign operative in charge of rooting out Campbell scandal, but the party was so far ahead that little needed to be used (or invented). Parties play the same game with male opponents, of course, but they tend to look as much for business and financial misdemeanours as sexual escapades. In Campbell's case, our national enquirers were after pure titillation and scandal.

She wasn't the first woman politician to face this double standard. In 1990, when *West* magazine was preparing an article on Audrey McLaughlin, an editor said in a memo to the writer: "it will be necessary . . . to talk to all manner of Audrey associates, obvious and otherwise: everyone from her image makers to her hairdresser to her plastic surgeon to her ex-husband to her current boyfriend (or girlfriend). . . ."[9]

Campbell perhaps headed off the scandal-mongers by being so frank about her past. The crushing Tory election defeat suggests that the voters were avenging the government's record and the party's utter lack of coherent policy. But more than that, they were also expressing uneasiness about this female leader, and proving that we still demand a higher standard of personal conduct from female politicians than we do from males. The stark reality is that a man with an active sex life is considered virile (a stud no less), while a woman who shows even a hint of similar tastes is considered a slut. Worse, in the intruding eyes of Ottawa, if a powerful woman is obviously not sleeping with a man, then she must be gay.

Campbell fell out of favour for many reasons, most of them connected to her party's record and her own mistakes. But one powerful sub-theme, even within her own party, was a growing uneasiness with her status as a "non-traditional" woman with two broken marriages and an undefined sex life. Canadians were perhaps ready for an unmarried female prime minister—as long as she was Mother Teresa.

The media's role in all this was fascinating, complex, and sometimes sordid. The coverage began, as Campbell expected, with excitement and adoration. The editorial moaning of the Montreal *Gazette*'s William Johnson, who wrote that the "V of her blouse framed her head and kept the viewer's attention on the face," was quickly eclipsed by the wilder excesses of the British press. Campbell was suddenly "dewy-eyed, sexy and powerful," a "Canadian Madonna," with an "overt, flaunting sexuality." The British quotes were published across Canada, along with endless reprints of the famous bare-shouldered photo by Barbara Woodley.[10] "Comparing her to Madonna . . . just shows that people are visually illiterate," Woodley fumed, perhaps unaware that she was hardly flattering Campbell. Once again, Campbell fed the frenzy with her own zany quip: "A comparison between Madonna and me is a comparison between a strapless evening gown and a gownless evening strap." Rick Salutin, *The Globe and Mail*'s perceptive media columnist, captured the absurdity of the British comments, and Canadian acceptance of them. "Is this who the media accept as authorities on the subject?" he wrote. "With their Squidgy tapes? Charles and Di as models of libido? With reporters who got aroused for 12 years in the mere presence of Margaret Thatcher, seeing in her a kind of national dominatrix? To each his own, of course, especially in this area . . . but each time you think the colonial mentality can sink no further. And then . . ."[11]

Judy Rebick, then the chair of the National Action Committee on the Status of Women, found this media adoration appalling. "They just fell in love with her," she says. "There was that first blush where suddenly everyone in media was touting Kim Campbell, and ignoring her record. I had more arguments with journalists in those few weeks when they were in love with Kim Campbell than I had in the three years I was president of NAC. They were ignoring her record—a very right-wing record—making her out to be progressive. Then they turned on her in a very specific way with all this incredible looking into her background, all the pop psychology."[12]

Within two months, the glow was off what the media had called Campbellmania. The second phase began when she was savaged for comments that appeared in an article by Peter C. Newman in *Vancouver* magazine. Campbell spoke freely about many things, from feminism to religion, and Newman was clearly quite taken with her. But several of her remarks—especially one about her being confirmed an Anglican "as a way of warding off the evil demons of the Papacy"—were ripped out of context and printed in news stories. Combined with her comment about being able to recite "all the books of the Bible off by heart," the stories made her look like a bigot and a braggart.[13] She also called herself a West Coast "wood nymph" and appeared to claim proficiency in several languages. But any fair reading of the full article shows that Campbell was often joking, sometimes at her own expense. Ever gallant, the *Gazette*'s William Johnson leapt to her defence, this time with eyes unclouded by V necks and pouting lips. "Sleazy, sleazy journalism," he thundered. "Much of Canada's media showed itself at its sensationalist, irresponsible worst."[14] So did politics: the stories about the *Vancouver* article were prompted by a tip from Jean Charest's camp.

Completely ignored by most in the media were far more important sections of the article, including Campbell's clear definition of her feminism. "I was raised to be a feminist," she told Newman, "but feminists are not necessarily people who walk in ideological lockstep. What unites us is our passion for equality of women and for making the reality of women a part of the consideration of institutions, government and society. But there are some feminists who seem to think that in order to be a feminist, you have to be left-wing, and it irritates them that there I was actually doing real things for women, and I wasn't in the NDP. Too bad for them. The Tory party is full of wonderful, independent, feminist women—and men, for that matter."[15] Whatever one thinks of her opinion, it is clearly and cogently stated.

Some of the media commentary, of course, was perceptive and sympathetic. Robert Mason Lee of *The Vancouver Sun,* in an insightful piece about the media's role in the episode, wrote that "Campbell no more meant the papacy was evil than John Lennon ever meant he was more popular than Jesus Christ." Ken MacQueen, Southam News national columnist, criticized Campbell's comments as unwise and perhaps arrogant, but wrote other understanding columns about women in federal politics. *The Toronto Star's* Richard Gwyn saw a bit of west coast flakiness as "exactly what this country needs." Reading these articles, one gets the feeling that the men were bending over backwards to show their new-age sensitivity. While they analyzed, another *Vancouver Sun* columnist, Lisa Fitterman, got to the heart of the matter when reviewing the various books about Campbell, all written by men. "It is doubtful that we will ever know her," Fitterman wrote. "In a sense, Campbell's quick-wittedness provides a nearly impenetrable barrier between her and the public, much like the comedian who leaves 'em laughing as he cries inside.

"Sure, Campbell is ambitious, but which politician isn't? Imagine, please, a potential leader who, faced with the reins of power, gently declines: 'No, no, really, I only came so far and spent practically my entire life in politics because I'm completely altruistic and have absolutely no interest in the job. Another cookie?'" Fitterman concluded: "Come on, guys, get a grip."[16]

As time went by, the grip was increasingly around Campbell's throat. She wasn't surprised. "I always expected to be left at the altar by the media," she told *The Globe and Mail* at one point, "and here I am, wilted flowers in hand." Her friend Senator Janis Johnson agrees: "That's exactly what happened. They rocket you to the moon and then, whoosh, right down again."[17] Former Liberal minister Iona Campagnolo, who sent Campbell a campaign contribution, predicted this even before it happened. "The scenario is to build her up, then knock her down," she said during the leadership contest. "Then see how she reacts to criticism, see if she makes some mistakes. If the mask doesn't slip, build her up again, *then* take her out. It's very much a man chasing a woman: all the excitement is in the hunt. The analogies are quite close in this case: she is fresh upon the scene, an unknown quantity."[18]

By the middle of the election campaign, Campbell began to crash in the Canadian media with headlines such as "Campbellmania Fizzles." But her friends the Brits soon made such limp Canadianisms seem charitable as their opinion of Campbell shifted from adoration to contempt, and she went from being "Canada's answer to Margaret Thatcher" to a "West Coast airhead." She was a blonde zombie, a know-nothing opportunist who "led her party to the scrap heap," according to wire service reports of the British assault. It was the end of what Quebec columnist Francine Pelletier, in an apt description of this strange interlude in our politics termed "Kim Campbell's Tinkerbell spell."

Worse was to come in the period between the October 25 election and December 13, 1993, when the party brutally terminated her brief reign as leader. Some senior Tories—including former Alberta premier Peter Lougheed and Jodi White, Campbell's former chief of staff—thought it was a mistake for Campbell to quit. She was still a media novelty and could help them rebuild, they insisted. At the very least, she could maintain a Tory profile while the party regrouped. But the old Conservative lust for vengeance was turned on Campbell with remarkable ferocity. (One unnamed Tory said, "Get real—this is the party that got rid of Joe Clark, and he won more than 100 seats."[19]) Allan Gregg, the flamboyant Tory pollster who crafted much of the disastrous campaign, added his own criticism. Campbell never had the political instinct to know when to speak and when to stay silent, he said. But it was not Campbell who created the anti-Chrétien TV ads that portrayed the Liberal leader as darkly menacing, and she was not shown them. Campbell was left first to defend, and then renounce, key campaign ads that she knew little about, although as leader they were ultimately her responsibility.

Any leader, female or male, would have faced retaliation after such an electoral rout. Joe Clark was savaged by his party after the 1980 electoral defeat, and lost the leadership to Brian Mulroney in 1983. The dispute over the Tory successor to John Diefenbaker was one of the nastiest episodes in Canada's political history. But there were some special delights in store for this female leader, including the strong suggestion that, after all, she was just a woman, and shouldn't she be getting back to her love life?

In an article about the Tories printed a week before Campbell quit, *Maclean's* carried a transcript of an interview with the former prime minister. First she gave standard answers to the following questions: "Are you going to stay as leader? Will you stay to fight the next election? Are you worried about being thought of as a loser? Has the magnitude of the defeat set in?" Campbell fought off all these blunt queries with considerable skill, but she had more trouble with the next one, the fastball reserved for the newly unemployed female politician: "Have you found love?"

Campbell replied, obviously exasperated, "I don't know why there is this prurient interest in my private life. When I spoke last year about the unspeakable loneliness of life in Ottawa, which is very true, I wasn't just talking about myself. I was talking about the life of politicians and I was talking about men as well. Yes, I have a social life . . . and one of the compensations of not being prime minister is to have both the time and privacy to pursue it. It's just such an invasion of privacy to be talking about that."[20]

Campbell might have added that she is the only prime minister ever to be asked such a question upon leaving or losing office. Behind the thoughtless query lies the assumption that if a woman has a career setback, there's only one thing left for her—the love of a good man. Iona Campagnolo was right about the sexual undertones of the media's pursuit of Campbell. She was captured and used, and she ended up discarded on the shelf, with everyone wishing her at least another chance at romance.

Campbell's experience was echoed when Barbara McDougall decided not to run for the Tory leadership. A rumour that she was leaving politics to get married went the rounds in Ottawa. "That's considered a legitimate reason for a woman to quit!" exclaims Audrey McLaughlin. "It's a legitimate reason why you would give up power! She was also giving up eighteen-hour days, travelling all over the world and probably absolutely killing herself. She looked very happy, actually."[21]

Following the election, Campbell was incensed by the media coverage even though she herself had invited much of it. She had been a true curiosity in this country of hidebound gender traditions—not just a female leader, but one with a personal past that could not be explained in one sentence or a quick news clip. Some attention to this was inevitable and perhaps even justified. Barbara McDougall noted after the election: "It is unusual to run for politics if you've lived in Russia and had two divorces. There aren't many of us like that. So of course people are going to write about it. . . . But I was struck by one thing on election night—both Audrey and Kim stood alone at the microphones, acknowledging defeat. And all of the men had their lovely brides at their sides. Really, that is the situation of women in federal politics."[22]

Many of Kim Campbell's problems were created the moment Brian Mulroney said he would resign, thus giving the Tory party, for the first time in its history, the chance to change leaders while still in power. Because the prize—the prime minister's office itself—was so rich, the infighting for the succession was every bit as ferocious among female Tories as it was among the men.

Senator Pat Carney and cabinet minister Barbara McDougall, close friends who had once roomed together while in Ottawa, were vigorously opposed to Kim Campbell. Mulroney aide Marjory LeBreton favoured her, as did Mary Collins, the junior minister for external relations who later became Campbell's health minister. Jodi White, another veteran Tory who had worked for Joe Clark, became Jean Charest's campaign manager (although Campbell later made her chief of staff).

Campbell's opponents, notably Carney and McDougall, didn't believe she had the personal qualities or the experience to take on the job. She had been elected in 1988, while McDougall came to Ottawa in 1984. "Barbara McDougall was my candidate of choice by far," Carney says. "One Quebec senator said, 'I don't like her hair, her voice is whiny.' But she's tough, she's fair, she has a good financial background, she's gorgeous, she's widely respected internationally. She's done it all and she can do it all."[23] LeBreton recalls that "I couldn't contain my delight at the idea of Kim Campbell as prime minister."[24]

Many Tory men also argued that Campbell wasn't experienced enough; from them, the complaint carried a whiff of sexism. In fact, she was far more experienced in terms of actual political service than Mulroney had been when he came to office. The man who won the Tory leadership in 1983 had never been a member of Parliament or held any other elected post. Indeed, he had not once run for public office. Mulroney became an MP by winning a safe by-election less than a year before the general election that swept him into the prime minister's chair. Although he had played politics in the Tory party for twenty-five years, Mulroney had little direct experience of government, except for his time as a junior assistant to John Diefenbaker and Alvin Hamilton. Remarkable as it now seems, Brian Mulroney began his tenure as the least experienced prime minister this century.[25]

Campbell, on the other hand, had been in Parliament for more than four years, serving as justice minister and then defence minister. Before coming to Ottawa, she was a Social Credit MLA in British Columbia and ran against Bill Vander Zalm for the leadership. Earlier, she did her time in local politics as a Vancouver school board trustee and chair. In theory, at least, she was far better equipped than Mulroney to take over the prime minister's office.[26]

The critics, one suspects, were not really complaining about Campbell's lack of experience in *government*. What they meant was that she was not truly a creature of the *party*. Mulroney spent years perfecting the musky male arts of massage and manipulation in the backrooms. Long before he won the party leadership, he knew everybody who counted and could reach them all by phone. His contacts—literally hundreds of them— helped him sweep the leadership from under Joe Clark in 1983. In the darkest moments of the GST debate and the Meech Lake crisis, he was astoundingly adept at holding the loyalty of his frightened caucus. Mulroney understood the core truth of Canadian politics: before a leader can win government, or anything else, he or she must win and hold the party.

Campbell saw this reality dimly, if at all. She had never used the telephone as Mulroney did, just to flatter and keep in touch, and she wasn't about to start. Platoons of influential Tories— Peter Lougheed, for instance—never once received a call from her. "Kim never phoned anybody," Mulroney says bluntly.[27] She also failed to develop a strong network of women and Westerners that was there for the asking. When she had to schmooze, Campbell preferred the personal touch to the touch phone. Perhaps this isn't too surprising, considering that the backroom party network was almost entirely male, with brave and persistent exceptions like Senators Marjory LeBreton and Janis Johnson. But the omission cost Campbell dearly.

During the leadership campaign, Campbell also became the target of a typically Tory attack from within her own party. As her support mounted, detractors from the Conservative right began to note publicly that she was childless and twice divorced. They questioned her "stability" and pointed to Jean Charest's "normal" status as a married father of three children. Terry Clifford, MP for London-Middlesex, announced his support for

Charest by saying, "Clearly, somebody who has a family—that they have to look after and bring up—has got a commitment to other people that have families. And I think it's part of why people can identify with Charest." Other Tories were more fair-minded: Al Johnson from Calgary North, a Charest backer who chaired the Tory family caucus, hardly a progressive group, rebutted Clifford sharply. "It's an absurd issue," he said. "If we're going to worry about marital status, we'd have to worry about John A. Macdonald and Pierre Trudeau and a whole bunch of people who had trouble in their personal lives."

The episode infuriated Tory women who supported Campbell. Janis Johnson, the Manitoba senator who was once married to former Newfoundland premier Frank Moores, says she "almost came to blows" with Clifford when they met by chance shortly afterward. "I found myself in the Parliament Buildings in the same elevator with him and I was ready to tear his face off. I said, 'Terry, I can't even talk to you today. Your remarks are so out of it. First you deserted our camp. Secondly, I just can't believe you would say those things.' It was just so outrageous."[28]

But the verbal assaults continued. Maureen McTeer, who, with her husband Joe Clark, was ardently backing Charest, took up the family values cry. "I think what the party's looking for is . . . a prime minister who we can count on, who gives not just an image but who represents stability, both personal and professional." It was a strange note from a feminist who had always insisted on her independence as the prime minister's wife. Jodi White, Charest's campaign manager, recalls that "when that word 'stable' was used by Maureen and Joe, I told them it was a code word and it would backfire—and it did."[29]

The wildest attack of all came from Bill McKnight, Campbell's predecessor as defence minister. "I can't believe the [Campbell] delegates are at Jonestown," he raved. "I guess they are, but I can't believe they're about to drink the Campbell Kool-Aid." He was referring to Jonestown leader Jim Jones, whose 900 cult followers committed suicide in 1978 by drinking Kool-Aid laced with cyanide.

Some of these volleys landed far across the razor-thin line that divides party infighting from blatant sexism. As always, social sins that would be forgiven in a male leader became a handicap for a woman. When Pierre Trudeau took office in 1968, he had the image of a playboy bachelor, and he won a later election after his marriage to Margaret Sinclair had collapsed in ignominy. Trudeau evoked sympathy and respect, not scorn, as the single parent of three boys whose mother had run off, even though the age and intellectual differences between him and his wife had always made a successful marriage unlikely.

Campbell's marriage also fell apart during her time in office—a fact that never won her any sympathy. When she was justice minister, Campbell came home from another long, exhausting day. Expecting to find her second husband, Howard Eddy, she discovered instead an empty closet and a farewell note.[30] Campbell, unlike Trudeau, received no points for marital martyrdom—only accusations that she was "unstable." Women politicians shake their heads in disgust at the profound double standard. "The fact of the matter is, she had two marriages," says Marjory LeBreton. "I'll tell you, there are many male politicians on Parliament Hill who've been married a second time, and the public doesn't even know who they are. And some of them have been sitting in cabinet."[31]

In the end, Campbell marched off to face a hostile electorate with many in the Tory party feeling as uncertain as the voters. Enjoying no margin for error with her own people, she was doomed as soon as she began to make campaign mistakes. When she seemed to suggest that no new jobs would be created until the turn of the century, when she insisted that social programs were too important to be discussed during an election, and when the disastrous anti-Chrétien television ads appeared, party workers fled like lemmings. Campbell was on her own, thrown to the wolves by her party and her own political misjudgment. The male party organizers were not entirely sorry that, if somebody had to lose, the victim was a woman. At least the Tories could attempt to rebuild with no more foolish illusions about gender experiments. After the election, the incensed party brass made the formal break with brutal haste, dumping their summer darling within two months. Today Brian Mulroney's judgment of Campbell is harsh, but typical of the current criticism: "Leadership is a series of unusual talents one finds in an individual," he says. "She didn't have them."[32]

In private, she often left people with the politically devastating impression that she was snooty. Judy Rebick of NAC found Campbell to be "one of the most elitist people I've ever met, and I've met quite a few. She is a very arrogant person. When she was a minister, I mean *she* was the *boss*. Not a team player. Her own personal style is very much the philosopher king style of politics."[33]

Reform Party MP Deborah Grey, from the other side of the political spectrum, noticed the same tendency in Campbell. "When I was first down there in Ottawa," she said, "Kim and I ended up in an elevator together. I said, 'Hi Kim, my name's Deborah Grey,' and she just said, 'I know that.' I said, 'We went to the same high school. My older sisters are Alexis, Alison, and Leslie, and we all went to Prince of Wales.' She said, 'Oh,' and then got off and just turned and walked away, and has never really said anything to me since then—except that I was part of the Reform Party and we were all snake-oil salesmen."[34] Another story best sums up this quality in Campbell: When the late columnist Charles Lynch was moving away from Ottawa in early 1994, says columnist Allan Fotheringham, "Kim Campbell sent a letter for his big party. Everyone was there and all the prime ministers and politicians sent Charlie friendly, informal letters. But she signed hers: 'the Right Honourable Kim Campbell.' That letter said everything."[35]

Campbell made the classic mistake of believing that rising polls would unite the party behind her and keep it on top. Mulroney always knew the truth: opinion-poll loyalty lasts only until the same polls begin to drop. To survive tough times, a leader must have a strong underlying base of party friendships, obligations, and accounts receivable. Campbell didn't have the stomach (or the time) to win over a party establishment whose attitudes toward women had changed only marginally since the days of Mulroney's hero, Sir John A. Macdonald.

Her fate recalled the warning that author Christina McCall had issued to Campbell in *The Globe and Mail* on the day she was sworn in as prime minister. "Watch out for the boys, *madame la première ministre*," McCall wrote. "They bond. And when they allow a woman into their circle, she's in danger of finding it's a trap."

But there was another, more hopeful side to Canada's brief fling with Kim Campbell. Her candidacy showed that women *had* advanced in Canadian political life. When Flora MacDonald made her brave and lonely run at the Tory leadership in 1976, she had only three MPs behind her. "There was no way I was going to be written up by the media as the front-runner," she laughs.[36] In Campbell's leadership race she was ahead from the start, with a majority of the mostly male caucus on her side.

Campbell also had the advantage of massive publicity. As a blonde baby boomer who made early magic with the media, she had been nudged toward the starting gate by the outgoing prime minister and blessed by many of the most powerful people in the party. Today, Mulroney denies that he favoured her over other candidates. "I put a half-dozen people in position to contend," he says. "Then the polls went berserk and Kim Campbell wound up as leader."[37] She defeated five men in the process.

Campbell did not fail because she was a woman: she lost because she was the wrong Conservative woman in a country that had come to hate the Tories. "It's terribly unfair to blame Kim Campbell alone," says Liberal activist Wanda O'Hagan, chair of the Committee for '94, a group that aims for equal representation of women in politics. "She had to drag the corpse of Brian Mulroney around with her."[38] Author and Canadian nationalist Maude Barlow believes Campbell was simply used by the Tory party. "The Conservatives thought that her gender, age, newness, and place in the country would act as a counterpoint to Brian Mulroney. The expectations were incredible, and being a woman only added to the judgment of her."[39]

There's little doubt, though, that many women felt terribly let down by Campbell. They remembered her effort to recriminalize abortion, and judged—correctly—that she did not want to be identified too closely with women's concerns. "Women gave her their confidence at first," says Glenda Simms, president of the Canadian Advisory Council on the Status of Women. "They were saying, 'Prove you deserve to be there.' Campbell didn't take that challenge. She ignored women's issues, even though strong women in her own party told her not to. Women leaders should embrace women's issues and if they are defeated for doing that, then let history record that's why the woman leader went down."[40] The ultra-conservative group REAL Women was just as angry at Campbell for all sorts of perceived failings, from communism to championing homosexuals.

Her tenure, brief as it was, pointed to a crucial weakness among women's advocacy groups. They want women elected only as long as those women espouse their ideology. This is an understandable position, but it's also a trap that will forever contain women in the limiting role of special interest group. There is only one way for women to infiltrate the male power structure and stay there: to elect large numbers of women of *all* parties. Men don't expect ideological loyalty from other men just because of gender. If women truly want to influence power on an equal footing, neither should they. NDP leader Audrey McLaughlin, for all her sincerity and hard work, is mistaken when she says that electing women just because of their gender does no good. "We have to elect women . . . who are feminists and who believe in social democracy," she argued at a labour conference in June 1993.[41] This is an excellent strategy for bringing the NDP to power, but the wrong one for leading all women to the centre of influence.

In a quieter way, and over a longer period, McLaughlin endured many of the same bitter experiences as Campbell. Canada's other female national party leader once said she would be branded "the slut of the world"[42] if she behaved as Pierre Trudeau had. She faced the same sort of early media treatment as Campbell, including questions about lesbianism and abortion. McLaughlin, however, handled all these pressures with considerably more grace and dignity, which finally led the media to conclude that she was merely bland and uninteresting. The neglect that resulted proved as lethal as all the frothy hype about Campbell.

McLaughlin could never overcome the stereotype invented for her—that she was a wonderful person in private but uninspiring in public. The first part of the image is correct—everyone who knows McLaughlin considers her to be warm, perceptive, and extremely funny—but the second half is grossly unfair. After she won the party leadership in 1990, McLaughlin was a wooden speaker, yet she quickly overcame this and became, in her quieter way, every bit as effective on a platform as Brian Mulroney or Jean Chrétien. When the stakes were high, as in televised campaign debates, reporters always noted with surprise that she did well. Time and again she exploded their stereotype, but rather than admit this, they wrote off each success as an exception. When she announced in April 1994 that she would step down as leader, *The Calgary Herald* again voiced the unfair image: "In person, she was witty, interesting and approachable. But in public, she just didn't have the royal jelly."

McLaughlin isn't surprised by this treatment, because she always refused, quite intentionally, to play by the men's rules. "In order to be successful in the system," she says, "you do have to become part of that culture. The other choice is to be part of bringing some balance to that culture. Of course, I chose the latter. It reminds me of people who go to work with Native groups—the beads and buckskin theory. If you put on the beads and buckskin, you can think you're one of them. But you're not and never will be. Similarly, I will never be a man."[43]

In the era after Kim Campbell and Audrey McLaughlin, women in Canadian politics stand on a balancing point of ambiguity, a fulcrum that could vault them higher or plunge them back into obscurity. McLaughlin expressed it best when she borrowed a quip from an American governor, Ann Richards of

Texas. "Being a woman in politics is kind of like being Ginger Rogers," she told a campaign breakfast meeting on October 8, 1993. "You have to do all the same dance steps as Fred Astaire, but you have to do them backwards and in high heels." Unfortunately for Canada's political women, the main ballroom is a nineteenth-century male institution called Parliament.

3

TESTOSTERONE
TABERNACLE

*"It was like throwing a cat out a ninth-storey window. . . .
You were not even told where the bathrooms were."*

Former Liberal minister Iona Campagnolo
on the treatment of female MPs in Parliament

As Audrey McLaughlin sat in the House of Commons, watching the men bellow at each other in their eternal quest for victory, she was often reminded of her favourite episode of the popular American TV show "Murphy Brown." "The men in the newsroom are having a huge fight that's all about their egos," McLaughlin laughs. "Murphy watches them in disgust for a while, and finally she bursts out, 'Oh, why don't you all just drop your pants and I'll get a ruler?'"[1]

In Canada's Parliament, male judgments and symbols are the only yardstick of victory. The Commons and the Senate were institutions created by men at a time when nobody ever imagined that women would intrude. The venerable symbols of parliamentary government were, and still are, drawn from the manly arts of war. The chief official in the Commons is the Sergeant-at-Arms, who carries a mace (a battle club dressed up to look regal) as the symbol of authority. His counterpart in the Senate is the Gentleman Usher of the Black Rod, named for the stick with which he thunders at the door of the Commons to gain occasional entry and command MPs to come down the hall.[2]

Tradition stresses hostility and division between the Senate and Commons; the chambers never refer to each other by name, only as "the Other Place," often pronounced in sarcastic tones. Upon election, a new Commons Speaker is surrounded by party leaders and dragged to the Throne in symbolic reluctance, a reminder that several Speakers were executed by monarchs in earlier times. (Even Jeanne Sauvé, the first female Speaker, was gently hauled to her ritual beheading in 1980.)

In the Commons, enemy MPs are stacked in rows on either side of a wide, carpeted aisle, a psychological moat across which they fire their modern versions of the flaming arrow—epithets like "liar," "jerk," "scumbag," "asshole"; and, to welcome the newcomers in their midst, "slut," "witch," "baby," and "bitch."[3] In their quest for deadly impact, the men prefer simple Anglo-Saxon words.

They are surrounded everywhere by images of male heroes— portraits and statues of prime ministers, Speakers of the Senate and Commons, opposition leaders, famous warriors, and even stone carvings of dead male journalists. The only prominent female images are of British Queens, especially Victoria, whose dominant statue was at first guarded by an Imperial lion in a state of too-obvious virility. In deference to shocked women and curious children, the beast's bronze penis was sawed off in 1908—the only emasculation known to have occurred on Parliament Hill.

Even today women have little impact on the masculine tone of Canada's governing structure. Since 1918, when women first earned the right to hold federal office, 3,656 male MPs have been elected, but only 120 women.[4] Nearly one-third of that number, thirty-nine, were voted in as new women MPs in the 1993 election.

It is no surprise that when Agnes Macphail, Canada's first woman MP, arrived for duty in 1921, a Commons employee tried to stop her at the door of the chamber. She entered anyway while he shouted, "You can't go in there, miss!" Once inside, Macphail was touched to find a bouquet of roses waiting on her desk, but humiliated later to learn that they were the penalty a male MP paid for betting she would lose the election in her Ontario riding.[5]

In 1987, when Audrey McLaughlin came to Ottawa, she learned how little had changed. The day she asked for her House of Commons identification, McLaughlin wrote later in her autobiography, *A Woman's Place*, "I was promptly ushered into an office where a woman was working at a desk. I smiled, told her my name, and stated my business. The woman searched through a typed list, studying it for a long time. Finally she looked up and said, 'I'm really sorry, but I can't find your name anywhere.' I replied, 'Oh well, it's probably because I've just been elected in a by-election.' 'Oh dear,' she said, 'I thought you were a spouse. I've been looking at the wrong list!' At the time, I thought the incident was funny, but it proved to be a portent that I had entered an alien world."

Dawn Black, a prominent New Democrat and former MP from Vancouver, recalls an equally bizarre personal reception to Ottawa: "The first invitation I received in the House of Commons came from the Speaker to attend a luncheon for new members. And it was a lovely invitation with gold tassels down the sides, all done in hand-lettered calligraphy. It was quite beautiful—but mine came addressed to 'Mr. Dawn Black.'" Black phoned the Speaker's office to say she would be delighted to attend, but only as a woman. "I thought that would be the end of it and at least I wouldn't get another invitation like that. I didn't know how seriously such *faux pas* are taken in this place. When I walked into the luncheon, there was somebody waiting for me from the Speaker's office with a new hand-lettered identical invitiation that was to 'Ms. Dawn Black.' So I took the two of them, and had them put in one frame and hung them in my office."[6]

Iona Campagnolo, the Liberal minister of the Trudeau years, still remembers how alone and at sea she felt in Parliament. "It wasn't made for us and in many ways it still isn't," she says. "If you start looking at the statuary, the gargoyles, and so on, there are very few women's faces. If you look at all the paintings, they're all men and war and swords and blood. But why should it be any different? It was a men's club.

"Once, we decided that the 'parliamentary wives' retiring lounge' had to go. It had those wonderful old chairs that were used for bustles. It also had the only bathroom. So we had the bronze plaque changed. But I was in there not long ago, and I see it had been changed back again to something about wives. So I guess in some areas we haven't made much progress."[7]

Even more daunting was the psychological atmosphere. The treatment of new women MPs, Campagnolo says, was like "throwing a cat out a ninth-storey window. No one told you anything. You were not even told where the bathrooms were. You were left totally on your own because they were watching to see who's got the stuff and who hasn't. And who's going to go to liquor or drugs, or who's going to go to too many women or men. Women were judged differently from men." When Judy LaMarsh was a cabinet minister in the 1960s, a male minister had to stand guard for her outside a men's room. Even today, locating a women's washroom in the vast Parliament Buildings can be a treasure hunt.

Before women began to be elected in numbers higher than two, it was a struggle just to have the men recognize their presence. "You had to make a tremendous effort just to indicate that both men and women were involved," says Senator Pat Carney, who was first elected in 1980. "When Flora MacDonald and I were the only women in a 101-person Conservative caucus, the Whip would always open the caucus by saying 'Gentlemen.' Flora and I would faithfully raise our arms and wave, which takes effort and makes you look stupid. To boos and derision from the men, we'd wave our hands and say, 'No, no, you don't use gentlemen.' It's tiring and enervating to have to constantly establish that it's not a room full of just men."[8]

If the reception was rough among "friends" of their own party, it was even worse on the floor of the Commons. In the 1970s, Flora MacDonald was regularly heckled in the House—sometimes by her own Tory colleagues—for raising women's concerns, such as the unfairness of laws that robbed women of pensions after their husbands died. Often she was the only person in the House fighting these lonely battles. Liberal Prime Minister Pierre Trudeau seemed to take a particular dislike to MacDonald and heckled her mercilessly. "He was always trying to put me down," MacDonald recalls. "It just would irritate me no end. We had an ongoing battle for years."[9] If any woman MP was "unspeakably lonely" in the Commons, as Kim Campbell claimed she had been in Ottawa, it was Flora MacDonald when the Tories were in opposition during the 1970s.

Sheila Copps, now deputy prime minister, captured the spirit of the history-blighted chamber when she wrote in her autobiography, *Nobody's Baby*: "From the moment you step inside, you sense that this place is foreign to women, alien to our spirit of co-operation, steeped in confrontation and simply not a place for traditional female virtues.

"The very composition of the chamber lends itself to confrontation. . . . The traditions of the House create an atmosphere which is combative, not conciliatory; aggressive, not consultative—a forum in which many women feel there is no place for them." Audrey McLaughlin agrees. "When a woman enters the House of Commons," she wrote, "she enters what in significant ways is an old-fashioned men's club. . . . I remember how amazed Marion (Dewar, former Ottawa mayor and NDP MP) and I were when we sat through our first Question Period. The posturing, the banging on desks, and the shouting made us think of school kids. And like children in the school yard, the men seemed to be constantly jockeying for territory and dominance."

All this would be far easier to take if the female MPs could have some special impact on policies that affect women, but historically, this has been incredibly hard for them to achieve. A burst of favourable legislation passed after Agnes Macphail was elected in 1921 had more to do with women getting the vote than with the efforts of one member of Parliament. Even with today's relatively high numbers of women in Parliament, party discipline hampers them within their own parties, and hinders co-operation with women of other parties. In the American system, women representatives are much freer to cross party lines to forge alliances on specific issues. But in Canada, as Jill Vickers and Janine Brodie note in *The Politics of the Second Electorate*, "legislators wishing to have their concerns included in the party's platform must first convince their fellow party members of their necessity. Unfortunately, Canadian parties have generally not placed much salience on the question of the status of women." This is classic academic understatement: many male MPs have shown a clear interest in the status of women, but only in lowering it.

The caucus system, where party solidarity is policed and enforced, also works effectively against women's interests. The whole purpose of caucus is to muster strength against the other parties. Women become part of a team made up mainly of men. They are isolated from other women in Parliament and are forbidden from co-operating with them on policy lest they be charged with disloyalty. Once in cabinet, any minister, female or male, is absolutely prohibited from talking about disagreements when outside the cabinet room. Some female ministers fight hard for women's concerns in cabinet, but once they lose, they are required to be silent. This is why Sheila Copps, who had an opinion on every women's issue while she was in opposition, has cooled down considerably as deputy prime minister.

With all these pressures working against them, recent efforts by women MPs to co-operate across party lines are little short of heroic. One powerful catalyst was the murder of fourteen women in Montreal by Marc Lepine in 1989. Women MPs were outraged, and angrier still to find that some of their male colleagues were not deeply touched by the horrible slaughter at the *École Polytechnique.*

New Democrat Dawn Black introduced a private member's bill to make December 6 an annual day of remembrance and action on violence against women. She sought support from Mary Collins, then the minister responsible for the status of women, and Mary Clancy, the Liberal women's affairs critic. They enlisted other women MPs and began lobbying the men, some of whom responded with astounding insensitivity. When the bill went to a subcommittee, MPs remarked that it was ridiculous, and wondered if women would soon want legislation to commemorate women who died in childbirth. They declared the bill unvotable. More lobbying by the women, with the firm backing of Minister Collins, overturned that ruling, and by 1991 the bill became law—an extremely rare outcome for a private member's bill. "There's no way I could have gotten that bill through without Mary's support," Black remarked later. "Even though voters don't see it, I feel that women transcend party lines on some issues because we experience life the same way."[10]

In 1990, women from all three major parties took the bold step of forming the Association of Women Parliamentarians (AWP). Again the players were New Democrat Dawn Black and Liberal Mary Clancy, and the chair was Tory Pierrette Venne, who later became a member of the Bloc Québécois. The main goal of the AWP was to combat sexism in the daily lives of women MPs. As Clancy told the House after the women met to discuss the slurs regularly aimed at them on the floor of the Commons, "Today marked a watershed because the women of all four parties met, discussed the issue, and there was such a sense of mutual support, such a sense of purpose, and such a sense that we as a group must come forward to the rest of you, our male colleagues, and say the time has come to make some changes."[11]

The women were inspired partly by American congresswomen, who in 1981 formed the Congressional Caucus on Women's Issues. But while the U.S. women have been able to tackle policy problems, party discipline has limited Canadian MPs mainly to problems of life on the Hill. As Lisa Young concludes in her analysis of inter-party co-operation, "Extensive AWP involvement on policy issues would be in flagrant opposition to the formal and informal rules of party discipline that structure parliamentary politics." There's no doubt, however, that the AWP has helped women MPs to recognize their bonds and make common arguments within their caucuses.

Another tool for women MPs was the Sub-Committee on the Status of Women. Formed without fanfare in 1989, it did not actually meet until December 1990, when the members decided to investigate violence against women. Once again, members included Black, Clancy and Venne, as well as Tory MP Louise Feltham and Barbara Greene, a tough-minded Conservative who acted as chair. Greene didn't want the job, but she finally accepted it because none of her colleagues on the main committee was interested. Like many women parliamentarians, she resented the constant offer of "women's issue" posts and preferred something "tougher," like finance.[12]

The subcommittee produced a unanimous report called *The War Against Women*, which instantly became controversial and showed how difficult it is for women to tackle policy together in a non-partisan spirit. Calgary Tory Bobbie Sparrow opposed the report mainly because of the title: she felt there was no war on women. Greene snapped that Sparrow was "trying to out-Reform the Reform Party. . . . She's running against Preston Manning [in Calgary Southwest] . . . and I understand the Reform Party is quite anti-woman."[13] The main committee took the highly unusual step of receiving the subcommittee's report without endorsing it. Vancouver Tory Stan Wilbee branded *The War Against Women* "feminist and confrontational." Nonetheless, the substance of the report proved to be very influential. Many of its recommendations became part of Bill C-17, the gun control bill that was later voted into law. The government also appointed a task force to study violence against women. Perhaps most important, the subcommittee called for a "no means no" rape law, and when Justice Minister Kim Campbell brought in new sexual assault legislation, it took this recommendation into account, as well as including guidelines for the inadmissibility of examining a woman's past sexual history in court testimony.

The subcommittee went on to study breast cancer on the suggestion of NDP member Dawn Black, who had two friends diagnosed with the disease. Once the group began studying the subject, said Barbara Greene, "we found it was so enormous." They were alarmed by pervasive ignorance about the disease, lack of knowledge about what was being done, and the failure to improve survival rates. More than 14,000 women a year discover that they have breast cancer, the subcommittee found, yet most women don't know how to do a simple self-examination properly. "I learned you were supposed to go under your arm," Greene said. "I didn't know that." Southam News columnist Ken MacQueen wrote: "The fact that it has taken this long for a serious parliamentary investigation of the disease is as eloquent an argument as you can find for a drastic increase in female representation in the Commons."

In its report, the subcommittee called for public education aimed at prevention, more sensitive treatment of women with the disease, and more funding for research. On December 15, 1993, the Tory health minister, Benoit Bouchard, allotted $25 million for a fund to assist in breast cancer screening, education, and developing national standards for treatment. At a time of spending restraint it was a tremendous achievement—even though, as Ken MacQueen wrote, action was "grossly overdue."

The subcommittee, in its four years of operation, was remarkably effective in pumping policy ideas into the political system. Cross-party co-operation among female members became routine (although they often disagreed, too). Observers have noted that the group would have been less successful in handling more divisive questions. "Had it been forced to deal with issues where there are clearly defined competing interests," writes Lisa Young, "it is much less likely that the subcommittee would have been able to have achieved unanimity in its reports." And the committee's power was at best indirect—as women's political influence has always been. Despite these limitations, however, the subcommittee showed that women's views had worked their way deep into the system, and were taken seriously at last. Unfortunately, when the Liberals took office in late 1993 all committees and subcommittees were automatically disbanded. This is normal when governments change, and there is a chance that the Liberals will replace the old subcommittee with something similar, perhaps as an adjunct of the new Canadian Heritage Committee. But this hitch in the system was a distressing reminder of how fragile gains for women can be.

Undeniably, some male MPs still resent the very presence of women in the Commons. And some women ignite these men like the fuses on locker-room stink bombs. The all-time champion is Deputy Prime Minister Sheila Copps, who can light the wicks just by walking down a Commons corridor. No woman in our parliamentary history has received so much public abuse or given so much back. Copps's explosive formula is so simple that it's a wonder the men didn't decipher it and discount it long ago. In political terms, she behaves just like many of them—she is aggressive, sometimes strident, and always highly partisan. She needles incessantly and calls them names: "liar" is one of her favourites. Once she caused a mini-scandal by leaping over a table in a committee meeting to get at a Tory debating opponent, Sinclair Stevens. But as a woman, she is earthy, sensual, and sexy, and she refuses to apologize for or hide these qualities. The combination drives conservative-minded men wild with indignation, if not something more. Once she posed in black leathers on her motorcycle, the perfect image of the uncontrollable woman.[14] Audrey McLaughlin says Copps inflames some men because she projects "the spit-in-your-face image, the bitch image. The other one available is the Madonna image. Because most people who write about this stuff are men, they like the Madonna image; they don't like the bitch image."[15]

Copps's awakening began when she was a twenty-nine-year-old MPP in the Ontario Liberal opposition caucus. "I was once serving on a travelling committee on child abuse," she wrote. "We had been hearing presentations all day and the all-party group dined together that evening. As I returned to my hotel room, I was followed by another member who invited me to his room for a drink. I refused politely, whereupon he grabbed me and started to kiss me passionately. I wanted to scream but couldn't, so I pushed him away and fled to my own room."[16]

Elected to the House of Commons in 1984, Copps promptly became a member of the Liberal "Rat Pack," the infamous group of MPs who devoted themselves to rooting out Tory scandal. The entire group was universally loathed by the Conservatives, but as a woman, Copps came in for a special brand of sexist insult. Over the years, she was called "baby," "slut," "witch," and "goddamn ignorant bitch." Tory minister Paul Dick once "apologized" to Copps by saying: "I said she was a stupid witch, and I do withdraw 'witch.'" John Crosbie, when he was transport minister, once told an audience waiting for Copps: "It appears that Sheila's broom is not working today. We hope she will be here shortly."[17] Copps policed these outbursts like an avenging feminist angel, constantly raising them in the Commons and demanding apologies. At the very time that former prime minister Brian Mulroney was promoting large numbers of women in government, and placing women in key cabinet posts, Copps hurt the Tories badly with women all over the country simply by showing that the attitudes of many Tory males were still mired in the 1950s.

For many years, Copps and Crosbie seemed to share some kind of fatal attraction. In 1990, when Copps was running for the federal Liberal leadership, Crosbie said her efforts reminded him of the song: "Pass me the tequila, Sheila, and lie down and love me again." (Mary Collins, who had been responsible for women's issues for just six days, told the happy Conservative crowd that "Crosbie was absolutely marvellous, as always."[18] Feminist loyalties often depend on feelings about the target.) In 1985, to quell Copps's heckling in the Commons, Crosbie shouted "Just quiet down, baby"—hence the title of her book, *Nobody's Baby*. Crosbie also offended Copps—and thousands of other Canadians—by saying, "We can't have women representing themselves or the next thing you know we'll have to have the crippleds and coloureds." He made that remark in a private exchange with Judy Rebick, then head of the National Action Committee on the Status of Women, who promptly told the media.

Not long before he retired in 1993, Crosbie outdid himself when he talked about sexual harassment. "Apparently, just about everybody who quits their job is being sexually harassed," he said. "We must have one hell of a lot of attractive people working. If this is the case I have to admit to you that I have never been sexually harassed. . . . If I were, I would certainly want to make it known that I had been so favoured." Crosbie said he was mocking frivolous Unemployment Insurance claims and also laughing at himself, but this time, even his Tory friends thought he had gone too far over the line.

Crosbie is one of those peculiar men who sounds like an outrageous sexist in public, but appears warm, friendly, and caring to his female friends. Many Tory women, including feminists, insist that anyone who knows him could never consider him biased against women. "John Crosbie plays to only one audience—Newfoundland," says his friend Jean Pigott. "The wit in Newfoundland is different than in any other place in Canada. Everyone there always thought he was hilariously funny. In downtown Toronto or Vancouver, they were appalled. It's just one of those funny things about being a Canadian.

"He is as 'managed' a man as I've ever seen. [His wife] Jane Crosbie tells him what socks to wear and she has tremendous influence. His daughter and his two daughters-in-law are strong feminists. He's got nine grandchildren and only one is a boy. Have you ever seen pictures of this flotilla of little girls from the age of ten down? He is managed by women, period.

"But John is an utter tease. He's always called me Queen Jean. He is a shy man and some of this show is to cover up. Sheila [Copps] ought to be so grateful he's given her so much ink."[19]

Tory senator Marjory LeBreton adds: "He's a victim of political correctness! There're a couple of things he's said over time that I thought were going a little too far. But when he was minister of justice he certainly supported women. I think political correctness has gone too far."

Nobody ever saw much wit in another Tory MP's attacks on Copps. Bill Kempling, formerly a veteran member for Burlington, once branded her "a goddamn ignorant bitch" in a committee meeting. On September 17, 1991, he sent the Commons into red alert by calling Copps "a slut." Kempling first tried to insist that he had said "a pain in the butt," but when he apologized in the House the next day he did not make that claim. This language was too much even for the dominant males in the musky old chamber. Speaker John Fraser termed the matter "grave and serious," and was pleased to receive Kempling's "abject apology." Kempling didn't reserve his attacks only for Copps. On one occasion he called New Democrat Dawn Black a "fishwife"; on another, he constantly shouted "bullshit" at Copps's Liberal colleague from Hamilton West, Stan Keyes.

Fraser convened a Special Advisory Committee, under Deputy Speaker Andrée Champagne, to look into the question of "unparliamentary language." With the backing of Mary Collins, the committee in its report called for tough measures against members who "use language, words, gestures or other behaviour which is racist, sexist or homophobic."[20] (NDP member Svend Robinson, the only declared gay in the House, had long been slurred as a "queen" or "fairy.")

Many politicians, including some Tory women, insist that Copps provoked these attacks for partisan gain. One of her few defenders in other political camps is former Tory prime minister Joe Clark, who admires her political skill. "She has the best raw talent in the House of Commons in terms of being a person who understands an issue quickly and whole," he says. "When I'd get a question and was being very careful in my responses, I'd sit down, and glance across to see if Sheila Copps had noticed. I didn't worry about anybody else over there."[21]

Whatever her feelings and motives, there's no doubt that her style drove the Commons bullmoose element wild, and frequently they fell into her traps. Her "aggression" seems to be the key, as she concedes in her autobiography. "Aggression in men is considered a positive quality. . . . If, however, you are female and you happen to be aggressive you're considered shrill, a snarler, insecure with your femininity. You don't enjoy your womanhood and are somehow bent on castrating all men so you can finally be their equal. There's no sense of the positive about the label 'aggressive' when it is applied to a woman."

Debating the definitions of "femininity" is a line that many male MPs retreat to when faced with a competent female. Women as able as Copps are often dismissed on the grounds of being old maids, ugly, or lesbian. Flora MacDonald and Judy LaMarsh were often brushed aside with the first two accusations, and sometimes with the third. NDP women are often assumed by male MPs to be homosexual. When former NDP member Margaret Mitchell once reminded the Commons that 10 per cent of Canadian women are beaten by their husbands, a male MP shouted to her: "I don't beat my wife. Do you beat yours?" Any successful woman politician is open to this assumption. After Catherine Callbeck became the Liberal premier of Prince Edward Island, a reporter called Halifax Liberal MP Mary Clancy and asked if Callbeck was gay. "I said give me a break," Clancy recalls. "I told him I don't know about the lifestyle choices and the sexual choices of a great number of my colleagues, male or female. And in the second place I don't give a darn. It isn't relevant. The reporter was a man."[22]

Copps was difficult to denigrate in these ways. She was still in her thirties, very attractive, with a young child. Clearly she was not a spinster, ugly, or gay. She presented the men not just with the thorny problem of gender, but with the unspoken spectre of sex. The only way for a woman MP with those qualities to gain acceptance is to be docile and adoring. The new generation of women MPs has little time for such coddling of male egos. Their attitude is best illustrated by Mary Clancy, who describes the first time she spoke in the Liberal caucus. "I got up and said, 'Now I want all you guys to know from square one that I'm a feminist.' There was this sort of groan from the audience, and then I said, 'The other thing I want you to know is that I'm very, very fond of men. Yes indeed, I think every woman should have one as a pet.' There was a ten-second time lag and then they all cracked up."

If women MPs often feel surrounded by and subjected to bias, their experiences pale beside those of thousands of female civil servants who work for the government. Members of Parliament at least have the power to protest and publicize; female employees, on the other hand, have long been a powerless and voiceless underclass.

Their problems begin with the House of Commons itself, where hundreds of women work for MPs. Barbara Greene told the House in 1991 that "systematic sexual discrimination and harassment are rampant." Greene might have been feeling especially bitter because a while before, she had been physically assaulted in a dark Commons parking lot. Women MPs and staff had long pressed for better lighting in this parking area, where *Toronto Star* columnist Carol Goar was also mugged. New Democrat Dawn Black says Parliament Hill "is not a woman-friendly place. In the Association of Women Parliamentarians we've dealt with these safety issues. A lot of us women, MPs and staffers, work very late at night. The lighting was very bad here. So we went collectively to the Speaker and asked about getting the lighting improved. We also got a little tuck shop here carrying things women need, like pantyhose, sanitary napkins—just ensuring that supplies women require are available on the Hill."[23] Within the bustling community of Parliament Hill, with its myriad services aimed at males, women were given less consideration than they would receive in any rural Canadian town with a drug store.

Some MPs have taken up the cause of Commons workers who are abused and discriminated against. Svend Robinson has threatened to expose abusive MPs and civil servants. The presence of growing numbers of female MPs and senators has also encouraged women to come forward. "There's a lot of relief among secretaries and others on the Hill who know that there are people like us and others they can go to," says Tory senator Janis Johnson. "They know they don't have to put up with this any more. That's great, and it also keeps the guys on their toes, where in the past they just had *carte blanche*. If the secretary was being harassed and said one word about it, they just fired her—that was it, end of movie.

"Now they can't do that," Johnson continues. "They themselves end up on the carpet if the charges are proved to be correct. The only thing is, sometimes it builds up resentment among the males because they've been so used to having it their own way." Another problem is that even if an MP or senator is "on the carpet," there is extreme reluctance to make his name public, because this kind of publicity tends to have a serious impact upon an MP's chances for re-election—as it should. Some still take their chances; only a few years ago, a male MP engaged in an office dalliance accidentally locked himself out of his office dressed only in a House of Commons towel.[24]

Long ago, the traditional maleness of the Commons seeped down into every corner of the bureaucracy, reaching into departments far from Parliament Hill and creating a rigid patriarchy that coloured every attitude and decision. Women were welcome only in the menial clerical jobs, and when they aspired to more they were marginalized in ways both subtle and devastating. Until the 1950s, for instance, women who managed to reach any senior level in the External Affairs Department were required to quit when they married.

In the mid-1980s, the Conservatives embarked on the most exhaustive study of women in the public service that any nation has ever conducted. Still a model to other countries, this mammoth enterprise was begun by Pat Carney, who saw the problem through a woman's eyes but used a man's power to get results. As the first female president of the Treasury Board, she was responsible for the whole civil service, but she still had to ram the project through against a chilly, resistant bureaucracy. As she wrote in the foreword to the four-volume report *Beneath the Veneer*, "In a period of downsizing, reduced promotion opportunities and possible male backlash to employment equity initiatives by the government, few people wanted to tackle the issue of women in the public service."[25]

But the study went ahead, with the backing of Brian Mulroney, and in 1990 the task force presented four volumes to Robert de Cotret, who succeeded Carney in the Treasury Board. They provide depressingly detailed proof that women in Canada's most crucial institution are fearfully discriminated against. The numbers alone are revealing: In 1990, 93,000 women worked for the public service, and fully 40,000 of those were in clerical jobs. Of 13,743 secretaries, stenographers and clerks, only 154 were men. There were 1,985 male air traffic controllers but only 69 women. In the top management categories, there were 4,283 men and only 502 women. Seventy-three per cent of employees earning less than $20,000 were women, while 93 per cent of those earning $80,000 to $100,000 were men.[26]

The report is liberally sprinkled with quotes from many of the thousands of women interviewed. The women are unnamed, for very good reason. One employee said bitterly, "I was harassed by one gentleman so much that I had to go see his manager (who is also mine) and tell him that unless he did something about the situation, I would have to file a grievance. They talked to him, made him apologize to me, but I am the one who received a poor evaluation and was told I don't interact well with others and have a bad attitude. The gentleman in question received a glowing evaluation."

Another woman reported: "My superior would ask me out at least once a week. As my tolerance level became thin, I made my position clearer. . . . His affection soon turned to personal harassment, although he stated that I knew exactly how things could get better. After several years I was no longer alone, so several of us put in a complaint to the Public Service Commission. It is two years later and our complaint is still not settled. The harasser is doing quite well—supervising and acting in his manager's position. I moved to another town. Others involved have resigned, transferred or remained there in frustration. All of us are considered as problems, not the harasser." One woman said, "When I was in the process of divorcing my husband and very unsure of my future, my boss used to remark that if he were my husband 'he would beat me black and blue.'" A woman who worked as a carpenter complained, "Every single time you have to prove yourself. You go on new jobs all the time . . . so every time somebody is going to ask, "What is she doing here? Am I going to have to carry her boards? Am I going to have to do her work?' Or, 'What is she after anyways? Sex?' . . ."

The litany goes on: complaints of serious harassment—sexual, emotional, and even physical—but little pressure on the men to change. Indeed, the pattern is for men to be forgiven their boyish pranks while the women are branded as trouble-makers. These realities are all too common in the private workplace, but women have a right to expect better of their federal government.

Even more pervasive is the quiet prejudice against the promotion of women. The report contains one plea after another from women who are experts in their fields but are passed over by less qualified men. One woman says, "Many bosses do not want to lose a good secretary and will deliberately hold her back from training . . . and may even rate her lower than deserved on her performance appraisal or give her a lukewarm reference to prevent her being successful in competition."

A female worker in management information processing found herself a victim of such systematic discrimination. "I had been doing a lot of work back and forth in Washington. I had a lot of experience and really knew more about it than anyone. The director of the division called me and said they wanted a hotshot to go down to Washington for six weeks and learn all about it. Neither one of the men he was considering knew as much about it as I did. They did not even consider me although I was doing it all."

Women are frequently overlooked because of the casual assumption that their only legitimate role is to raise a family. One woman, passed over for promotion, was told that she should spend more time with her child. A woman who sat on a promotion panel once turned this attitude back on the men, to their intense embarrassment. "The other members (all male) were asking dumb questions such as 'What are your intentions about family?' and so on. One candidate was a man so I asked him, 'What about your family? How many children have you got? What are your intentions about enlarging it? Is it going to interfere with your work?' . . . He was so discomforted and so were the others on the board. . . . But how else do you make the point?"

This little tale of psychological retribution also makes a larger point about prejudice against women in Canadian politics. It is many men's deeply rooted belief that women's role in government is essentially behind-the-scenes, and should stay that way so that men can strut the public stage and do what the great pioneer Judy LaMarsh called "the big shiny jobs."[27] Until we understand that powerful idea and change it, women will not break through the glass ceiling to true political equality.

4

HOLLOW CHIVALRY

An MP once asked Agnes Macphail, Canada's first
female member of Parliament, "Doesn't the honourable
member wish she were a man?"
Macphail snapped, "Doesn't the honourable gentleman
wish he was?"

In 1972, just two years after the groundbreaking *Report of the Royal Commission on the Status of Women* was published, *Chatelaine* magazine sent a questionnaire by registered mail to 262 federal MPs, hoping to determine how they would represent women. Only 108 completed and returned the forms, and two of the replies were anonymous. Doris Anderson, the magazine's distinguished editor, reported in her May column one response from the office of a man elected to serve Canada and his constituents. "Signing himself 'Joe Blow' from 'Scratch-Ass-Tickle,' he thought we needed officers in Manpower centres to 'counsel women on sex'; that there are already too many women in the Senate; that we don't need more day care centres but 'bigger and better whore-houses.' If working mothers need more cash, says this wit, they should earn it in the whorehouses."[1]

The same *Chatelaine* issue reported the remarks of John Lundrigan, Tory MP for Gander-Twillingate, Nfld., who said, "I have no time for women's liberation. It's a lost and misguided cause led by people who don't know what they're talking about. That kind of woman turns me off—you know, the leather jacket type who wants to play a male role."

Such verbal assaults, although startling and discouraging, are mild compared to the trials that women faced when the battle for equality in Canada began in the last century. "It is almost impossible for a young woman of today to realize what life would have been like for her then," Doris Anderson wrote in 1991. "A little more than one hundred years ago, she would have been completely dependent on either her father, a husband or a male relative. She could not have voted, attended university, trained for a profession, or, except in rare circumstances, stood for election, even for her own town council. She had no control over the money she earned herself or received from an inheritance. Her children could be taken away from her and she could be denied access to them. She could be beaten and raped, yet she could not even have turned to the legal system for help."[2]

By then, the international struggle to change such conditions was already more than a hundred years old. The towering pioneer in the modern movement for women's equality was Mary Wollstonecraft, who wrote *A Vindication of the Rights of Woman* in 1792. It was to become a manifesto of the feminist movement in England, America, and Canada. A teacher and writer in London's radical literary circles, Wollstonecraft was heavily influenced by the egalitarian ideas of the French Revolution, and reasoned, unlike most men, that these noble notions should apply equally to women. In 1790, a pioneer French feminist, Olympe de Gouges, was prompted by the Revolution to draft a powerful declaration of women's rights, *"L'admission des femmes au droit de cité."*

Wollstonecraft "optimistically assumed [that] human beings—including women—were capable of perfecting society themselves and that equality would be the basis of new relations among people."[3] Her aspirations were personal as well as ideological; she was one of six children born to a vulnerable mother and a tyrannical father. As a young woman, Wollstonecraft made her own way in a harsh world, and became a single mother after bearing a child to an American, Gilbert Imlay. In *A Vindication,* she wondered how men could deny women the capacity to reason and then use this peculiar logic to bar them from public life. She later married the radical philospher William Godwin, but died while giving birth to their daughter, Mary, in 1797. Mary Godwin married the poet Percy Bysshe Shelley in 1816, and later wrote the horror classic *Frankenstein*—a fact often noted with irony, given her mother's long struggle against male power.

Though Mary Wollstonecraft's writing was trapped in the conventions of its time, her ideas were radical. They were also brave, because the British monarchy and establishment, terrified by the French overthrow of the aristocracy, viewed any sympathy with revolutionary ideas as treason. (The French abolished the monarchy the year her work was published and guillotined King Louis XVI early in 1793.) Undaunted, Wollstonecraft declared that women should be admitted freely to business, law, and politics on a basis of absolute equality. "[A woman] must not be dependent on her husband's bounty for her subsistence during life, or support after his death—for how can a being be generous if it has nothing of its own? Or, virtuous, who is not free?" With passionate language and crisp logic, Wollstonecraft revealed to thousands of women the weakness of arguments for continued male domination. But her faith in French radicalism proved a deep disappointment. Although all French citizens were given the right to elect representatives, women were still not considered citizens. French women would have to wait another 150 years, until 1944, when they were given the vote in recognition of their war effort, after the Germans were expelled from France.

During the last half of the nineteenth century, agitation for women's rights grew steadily in Britain, the United States, and Canada. Women reformers sought many changes, including better education and health care, unemployment relief, anti-smoking laws, and the prohibition of alcohol. They considered liquor and beer to be the root of many women's problems, as drunken husbands led to abandonment, poverty, and abuse. Without legal, political, or financial rights, women were virtually help-less to improve their lot. And many women began to see that the only way to change these conditions was to influence gov-ernments through the vote. Thus the movement for woman suffrage was born.

The idea that women should be able to vote on an equal footing with men was radical and highly emotional. For more than a half-century, it provoked hot debate and even violence in Britain and America. Men who opposed it (for a long while, almost all of them) branded the activists as dangerous and even criminal, while at the same time arguing that the majority of women were too pure and noble for politics. At first most women agreed—Queen Victoria was only the most notable female oppo-nent of woman suffrage. As a result, the British "suffragettes," in particular, began to fight with increasing militancy, finally taking their struggle to the British Parliament.

In 1866, a petition signed by 1,499 women demanding the vote was presented to the House of Commons by John Stuart Mill, then a Liberal member of Parliament. Three years later Mill published *The Subjection of Women,* one of the great feminist doc-uments of history. This manifesto was composed in collaboration with his wife, Harriet Taylor Mill, who also wrote widely on the women's movement. *The Subjection of Women* compared women to slaves while exploding the hypocrisy that they had to be kept on a pedestal as morally superior. "They are declared to be better than men; an empty compliment, which must provoke a bitter smile from every woman of spirit, since there is no other situation in life in which it is the established order and considered quite natural and suitable, that the better should obey the worse."

By 1903, the British suffrage movement took a more radical turn with the formation of the Women's Social and Political Union, led by Emmeline Pankhurst and her daughters, Christobel, Sylvia and Adela. Growing more violent over the years, the suffragettes began to disrupt public meetings, destroy mail, and set fire to houses. When arrested, they started hunger strikes, prompting jailers to force-feed them. This caused such public revulsion that Winston Churchill, then Home Secretary, once arranged to be force-fed himself to determine if the practice was humane.[4] His opinion isn't recorded, but there's no doubt that force-feeding bordered on barbarism. A tube was driven through a woman's nose and into her stomach by one doctor, while another poured in liquid. In one year, Sylvia Pankhurst staged ten successive hunger and thirst strikes, and was fed by this method twice a day. A poignant prison photo of her and her mother, standing arm in arm, shows the young woman dishevelled and exhausted, staring defiantly ahead.

Suffragette demonstrations often ended with hundreds of arrests. On one occasion a woman chained herself to the railings in Downing Street while a cabinet meeting was going on inside. The police came with a hacksaw to cut her loose, but she continued to shout "Votes for Women" while an accomplice, one of the Pankhursts' trusted lieutenants, was able to slip into 10 Downing Street and shout "Votes for Women" inside the prime minister's own house. In 1912, two hundred women with bags of rocks broke most of the windows in the smart shopping area of Picadilly Circus, Regent Street, and Oxford Street. Feelings against the militants ran so high that during a 1912 march in Wales, suffragettes were beaten by a mob of men.

Violence and arson escalated until, in 1913, a Suffragette named Emily Davidson threw herself under the galloping race horses at the Derby. She could not have known which one would trample her, but, in a ghastly example of appropriate symbolism, she was hit by King George V's horse, Anmer. The thrown jockey recovered but the suffragette died of her injuries four days later. A huge procession of women accompanied the coffin from Victoria to King's Cross; for once, the divisions between moderate "Suffragists" and radical "Suffragettes" were forgotten.

The popular press responded for many years by slurring the suffragettes as failed women who couldn't attract men. "Women who wanted women's votes also wanted women's charms," said *Punch* magazine. Only the gauche and the ugly needed the artificial support of votes; for true women, beauty was enough. The Pankhursts didn't quite fit the description; they were beauties who drove the establishment wild. Mrs. Pankhurst was "a woman of immense determination, considerable skill in speaking and in propaganda and . . . no regard for her health, her safety, or her life itself, if that had to be sacrificed for the cause."[5]

Ultimately, their radicalism did less for female suffrage in Britain than did women's service in the First World War. When fighting began in late 1914, feminist agitation was swept aside by a wave of patriotic enthusiasm. Women volunteered in droves to work on farms, in offices, and in war industries. When men saw women doing war work, they realized that life had changed and were ready to do a certain amount to recognize that change. At first, their concession did not amount to much: a bill allowing women aged thirty and over to vote, but only if they were married, or householders, or university graduates. By contrast, all men had the vote at age twenty-one. Not for another ten years, with the "Flapper Bill" of 1928, did British women win the same voting rights as men—and they were not allowed to sit in the House of Lords until 1963.

The American suffrage movement was never marked by the same violence and raw fury as its British counterpart, but it was nonetheless a long and difficult struggle. As early as 1848, women met in a Wesleyan church at a women's rights conference in Seneca Falls, New York—the first recorded assembly held anywhere on the rights of women. In a feminist paraphrase of the U.S. Declaration of Rights, the women demanded equality in education, divorce, property, and inheritance.[6]

After this meeting, one historian writes, "it was possible for women who rebelled against the circumstances of their lives, to know that they were not alone—although often the news reached them only through a vitriolic sermon or an abusive newspaper editorial."[7]

American women, however, had help from many prominent men, including Ralph Waldo Emerson, who spoke at another women's rights conference held in Boston on September 20, 1855. "Let the laws be purged of every barbarous remainder, every barbarous impediment to women," Emerson said. "Let the public donations for education be equally shared by them, let them enter a school as freely as a church, let them have and hold and give their property as men do theirs;—and in a few years it will easily appear whether they wish a voice in making the laws that are to govern them. If you do refuse them a vote, you will also refuse to tax them,—according to our Teutonic principle, No representation, no tax."

Before and during the American Civil War, from 1860 to 1865, northern women worked for the abolition of slavery, for temperance, and for other social causes. Many of them became convinced that they would never make a real impact until they won the vote. The war effort raised their hopes. When it was over, however, Congress extended the vote to black men but not to women, whatever their colour. This disappointment led to increasing militancy over the next half-century, and by the early 1900s there were frequent demonstrations and heated rhetoric. Rose Schneiderman, a union organizer for female hat makers, launched this response to a senator's statement that women would lose their "feminine qualities" if they got the vote: "We have women working in the foundaries, stripped to the waist, if you please, because of the heat. Yet the senator says nothing about these women losing their charms . . . the reason they are working in the foundaries is that they are cheaper and work longer hours than men. . . . Surely these women won't lose any more of their beauty and charm by placing a ballot in a ballot box once a year. . . ."[8]

Emmeline Pankhurst's American visit in 1911 caused a huge stir and prompted more suffragette parades. Women chained themselves to the White House fence, and in 1913, an orderly march that coincided with President Woodrow Wilson's inauguration turned into a riot when the women were attacked by a male mob. But the main reform organization, the National American Woman Suffrage Association, never believed in violence or the destruction of property. Two young leaders, Alice Paul and Lucy Burns, preached militancy only after they returned from England, where they had worked in the Pankhurst movement. They rose briefly to high positions in NAWSA, but were soon pushed out by the moderates. Paul and Burns went on to organize the Women's Party, whose members took radical action and picketed the White House. They had financial backing from William Vanderbilt's former wife, Mrs. O.H.P. Belmont, one of the wealthiest women in America. She knew that her ex-husband was adamantly opposed to suffrage, and used a portion of her millions to torment him.

The American movement was tamer largely because of geography, which tended to spread the struggle across the entire vast country, and the U.S. federal system. As in Canada, the vote had to be won not just at the federal level, but in local jurisdictions as well. Progress came early in some states, especially in the West. When Wyoming became a territory in 1869, women were given full voting rights—and, more important, they kept those rights, after a battle with Congress, when the territory was granted full statehood in 1890. This meant that Wyoming women, alone in the Western world, could vote not just for their local legislators but in national elections as well.

Internationally, they were closely followed by New Zealand women, who received full voting rights in 1893. Soon after, suffrage was won in the American states of Utah, Colorado, and Idaho. Granting women the vote, however, did not bring equality. Much later, a group of women newly elected to the Idaho legislature were warned not to carry a pocketbook or bag, or wear flapper earrings or "skirts so short that colleagues might look at their ankles instead of listening to what was being said."[9] Liquor and beer interests in the U.S. were vehemently opposed to female suffrage; in Michigan, they successfully stuffed the ballot boxes in many precincts during a suffrage referendum, robbing women of their right to vote.

Once again, the real impetus for change was war. American women were vital to the U.S. effort in the First World War, and in 1919 the Congress adopted a constitutional amendment that gave women the right to vote in federal and state elections. The required three-quarters of the forty-eight states agreed, and the amendment became law in 1920. But resistance remained fierce throughout. Even with prohibition imminent in 1918, the angry brewers' lobby in Washington continued its fight against the vote for women.

The Canadian struggle for women's suffrage, although heavily influenced by ideas from Britain, America, and France, was always quieter, less radical, more co-operative: that is, it was thoroughly Canadian. Although the fight was much shorter, in the end it was arguably more successful. Certainly there was plenty of hostility toward Canada's suffragists, but they did not endure the lengthy public battles that plagued the United States' suffrage movement. This isn't to suggest that the women who led the movement were dull or docile. Often highly educated, with quick intelligence forged in a frontier country, they tended to be fair and good-humoured, but very determined. Militants like Emily Stowe, her daughter Augusta Stowe-Gullen, Nellie McClung, and Emily Murphy were more than a match for the men of their day. The conclusion that "first-wave feminism was a weak and disjointed movement in Canada"[10] may be true for the organizations, but such epithets do not apply to the individuals.

From the beginning, thoughtful Canadian women turned to the goal they considered crucial, the right to vote. Firmly locked into abject legal inferiority in the years before and after Confederation, these women perceived that political power was critical to changing their status. Early legislation ruled the husband the head of the family, with absolute power to decide the fate of his wife and children. "Even guardianship rights were invested in the father by the terms of the 1867 British North America Act . . . the general practice was for the father to have absolute authority over his children," political scientist Sandra Burt has noted.[11] Women were expected to focus firmly on the private sphere, where they were pressured to procreate and care for the family.

To cement this duty into social reality, an 1892 amendment to the Criminal Code prohibited the sale, display, or advertisement of birth-control devices. This law remained intact until 1969. Even early divorce decrees demanded different conduct from women than from men: in Nova Scotia, a man could divorce his wife by proving adultery, yet a woman had to show not only adultery, but cruelty, incest, or some other crime. Society was organized around a series of double standards designed to keep women ignorant, inferior, impregnated, and immobile.

Even when the laws began to change in the late nineteenth century, allowing women some control over property and family, there was no intention of making them equal. "It was assumed that men would support their families financially in return for their right to rule as masters in the home," writes Sandra Burt. But men were often remiss in this, so "both levels of government decided to intervene to protect women from the consequences of this failure but without disturbing the distribution of power or roles in the family . . . the new laws protecting women did nothing to alter women's status. Legislators adhered firmly to the principle that the wife owed allegiance to her husband, and provided some financial relief only to women with children who had been left without a husband, through death or desertion."[12]

These beliefs, universal in Western culture, grew out of a feudal doctrine called coverture. Derived from the Christian ideal of woman's place in society, coverture clearly established the wife's subordination to her husband. The eighteenth-century British legal authority Sir William Blackstone confirmed this relationship in his *Commentaries on the Laws of England*: "By marriage, the husband and wife are one person in law; that is, the very being or legal existence of the wife is suspended during marriage, or at least is incorporated and consolidated into that of the husband; under whose wing, protection, and *cover*, she performs every thing."[13] There was some tinkering with this doctrine to address certain social realities, but the core of it remained intact, to the growing disgust of many women.

Between 1852 and 1857, three groups of women brought petitions to the legislature of Canada West requesting passage of a property act that would give them some degree of independence from their husbands. Prairie farm women were especially vulnerable if their husbands died, because they were left with no authority to maintain farm business. These are the earliest known cases of women going to the legislature on behalf of their own rights, and they had some effect. In 1859, an Upper Canadian law was passed that finally allowed a married woman to own property. Although she could not sell the property, her permission was required if her husband wanted to dispose of the land.

Despite this token progress, many women began to realize that they could not change these basic inequalities without some influence in the political structure. At that stage they had none— indeed, some provinces actually repealed women's voting rights in the years before Confederation. In Quebec between 1809 and 1834, women with property who were assumed to be eligible voters exercised their vote until the Quebec legislature rescinded this right. Thus, the first Canadian women to enjoy suffrage were the last to regain it: Quebec women were not allowed to cast ballots in provincial elections again until 1940, more than twenty years after most provinces had relented.[14] Pressure from the Catholic Church was largely responsible for this long delay. Women in pre-Confederation New Brunswick and Nova Scotia had the technical right to vote, although there is no record that any of them did. However, in case they tried, male legislators in those provinces expressly denied them the franchise, in 1848 and 1854, respectively.

Not until much later in the century did women begin to organize and agitate for the vote. In 1872, a bill calling for woman suffrage was introduced into the British Columbia legislature.

Only two members supported it, but the next year female property holders in B.C. were allowed to vote in municipal elections.
The first formal pressure group aimed at winning the franchise
was formed in 1876, when Dr. Emily Howard Stowe helped create the Toronto Women's Literary Club. In 1882, after some
Ontario women won the municipal vote, the Club "threw off its
disguise" to become the Canadian Woman Suffrage Association.

Stowe was a role model for many women: when her husband,
John Stowe, fell ill with tuberculosis, she was inspired to pursue a
career in medicine. Because no Canadian school would accept her,
she attended the New York Medical College for Women, and after
graduating set up a practice in Toronto in 1867. Her daughter
Augusta Stowe-Gullen, who was equally active in the suffrage
movement, became the first woman to earn a medical degree in
Canada. She graduated in 1883, three years after the profession
had finally granted her mother a licence. The Stowes were
Canada's version of the British Pankhurst clan—determined to
make changes for women, but within the system.[15]

As various women's groups sprang up to battle social ills like
poverty, alcoholism, abuse, and abandonment, they usually
developed an interest in the franchise as well. Much early activity
centred on the Woman's Christian Temperance Union (WCTU),
which was founded in Ontario in 1875 and quickly spread from
coast to coast.[16] Because the suffrage-seeking WCTU saw drink
as the root of family breakdown and societal decay, the beer and
liquor interests quickly copied the tactics of their American
booze buddies. To stop women from winning the vote, they lob-
bied and rallied the politicians of the day, many of whom enjoyed
a drink.

But the WCTU, with its added religious focus, soon came
into conflict with the non-denominational National Council of
Women of Canada. Founded in 1893 under the sponsorship of
the patrician Lady Aberdeen, wife of the Governor-General, the
National Council had little use for the WCTU, whose leaders
and members tended to come from lower social ranks. "They
train their younger women to be so painfully aggressive and self-

asserting on all matters & on all occasions," Lady Aberdeen wrote. "They are essentially *American*." The National Council, with a middle-class focus, was more interested in women's education. This was the first major split between Canada's formal women's movements, and one of many to follow. But these divisions were always polite compared to similar schisms in the United States and Britain.[17]

By 1897, another important vehicle for women's concerns—the Women's Institute—was formed in Ontario, and soon began to grow with remarkable vigour across rural Canada, especially in the West. Spurred by Adelaide Hoodless of Hamilton, whose youngest son had died after drinking impure milk, the Institute focused on nutrition, sanitation, and "domestic science."

All these organizations, whatever their degree of militancy, brought women together in living rooms, kitchens and meeting halls to discuss persistent problems. The result was a growing consensus that women needed and deserved more power in society.

In the 1890s, Manitoba became a hotbed of agitation for the vote, partly because women from the province's Icelandic community couldn't understand why they were not allowed full rights. They had been treated as equal in Iceland and in their new Canadian communities; only in the wider world of Canada were they considered inferior. These women formed suffrage groups and petitioned the legislature. Margret Benedictsson, with her husband Sigfus, published a magazine called *Freyja*, or *Woman*. The Icelandic agitators were a bit too radical for their Anglo-Saxon sisters and the groups tended not to co-operate closely. But the Manitoba WCTU group, one of the liveliest in the country, was propelled by skilled strategists, including Dr. Amelia Yeomans, journalist E. Cora Hind, and Mrs. J.A. McClung, who would become the mother-in-law of Nellie McClung. In 1893 they staged a mock Parliament with women wittily debating the pros and cons of suffrage; it was a huge hit with the press.

Such agitation steadily increased toward the turn of the century. Between 1895 and 1898, an Acadian woman living in Nova Scotia, Emilie Cartier LeBlanc, sent a series of thirteen letters to the newspaper *L'Evangeline* under the pseudonym "Marichette." Powerful, clever, and sardonic, the letters provoked such an outcry that the newspaper formally announced its opposition to female suffrage and vowed not to publish any more supportive stories. *L'Evangeline* was compelled to continue "Marichette," however, because her letters were so popular. In one, Marichette mocked men through a retelling of the creation of Eve: "When He was making woman, He found Adam, 'le boss' of all men, dozing with the sun shining on his belly, too lazy to work in his garden. He ripped out Adam's brain and took the best stuff out of it and made woman, who has saved man from disaster." In a society that was not only patriarchal but deeply religious, these words were more than provocative; they bordered on sacrilege.

In the early years of the twentieth century, women broke into the paternalistic pools of medicine, teaching, and law. Their progress was severely hampered by professional prejudice and intolerance, but these experiences served only to bolster their resolve for political recognition. The suffrage associations extended invitations to American and British activists, including Emmeline Pankhurst. In 1909, the year of her visit, women's groups co-operated to stage a huge rally at the Ontario legislature. Supporters now included the wives of many of the city's leading businessmen. Clearly, the movement was building a powerful momentum that politicians could no longer ignore. And some of the leaders were becoming increasingly militant—another troubling trend to the male power structure.

One such woman was Flora MacDonald Denison, an influential Toronto suffragette who insisted that women did not simply *deserve* equal treatment but had a natural right that was being denied by the forces of capitalism and religion. Denison asked: "Why should women, who represent half the human family, not have equal rights and privileges . . . or all the *natural* conditions of their brothers, or civil conditions made by the laws of their country . . . for the benefit of the human family in general?"[18] Initially, Denison rejected the tactics of the British suffragettes, but she changed her mind after attending a 1906 conference of the International Woman Suffrage

Alliance in Denmark. "I am inclined to think that the press has woefully exaggerated the behaviour of the women who are not lunatics or fanatics," she said, "but earnest women anxious and willing to sacrifice themselves that the race may be benefitted. . . ."

By 1913, when the campaign in England was growing more violent, Denison had become one of the few Canadian women to identify herself publicly with the British radicals, and her gesture caused dissension. Some colleagues also seemed troubled by her working-class background and connections: she grew up poor with a drunken father, became a journalist, wife, and mother, took jobs in the needle trade, and later wrote about her experiences for *Saturday Night* magazine.

Of all the talented gallery of Canadian suffragists, none was more remarkable than Nellie Letitia Mooney McClung. Born in Ontario in 1873, she travelled to Manitoba with her family when she was seven and grew up on a farm. Charming, yet unconventional, Mooney became a teacher and moved to Manitou, where she met Mrs. J.A. McClung. "She is the only woman I have ever seen whom I should like to have for a mother-in-law," said the captivated Nellie.[19] Luckily, McClung's son Wesley harboured both a devotion to Nellie and a deep regard for women's rights. Wes McClung, a druggist, believed that wife and husband should be equal partners, and supported Nellie after she became nationally famous and highly controversial. They had five children and enjoyed a strong and harmonious home life, although they would always wonder how they were seen by outsiders. Nellie would begin her speeches by assuring audiences that the children were happy, well fed, and in bed. One of her sons once hurried his dirty, dishevelled younger brother home with the words: "It's a good thing I got you before the *Telegram* got a picture of you—Nellie McClung's neglected child!"

McClung brought a sense of humour to everything she did, and often the joke was on herself. She told her audiences that once she staged a standard temperance demonstration—dropping a worm into a glass of water and then into a glass of whiskey—for a group of schoolchildren. When the worm played its part by perishing in the whiskey, she asked the children what they had learned. One boy said: "We learn that if we drink lots of whiskey we'll never have worms." At a rally in 1915, a heckler yelled at McClung: "The prime minister would quit politics if a woman were ever elected," to which she replied, "This proves what a purifying effect women would have on politics."

McClung's devotion to temperance, equality, and woman suffrage breathed passion into her career as a writer. Her first book, a romantic comedy about life on the early frontier, *Sowing Seeds in Danny*, sold an astounding 100,000 copies in Canada and the U.S. and earned her $25,000, a huge sum in 1908. She published sixteen books and hundreds of articles and newspaper columns. One of her stories in verse, the true tale of a farm wife who died of exhaustion at age thirty-three, won international acclaim in 1914. Much of her work was frankly political and feminist. "Women have cleaned up things since time began," she once wrote, "and if women ever get into politics there will be a cleaning-out of pigeon holes and forgotten corners, on which the dust of years has fallen, and the sound of the political carpet-beater will be heard in the land."[20] It was an inspiring summary of the suffragists' view that women would have a cleansing influence on politics.

McClung found the perfect foil in Sir Rodmond Roblin, the pompous, patronizing pre-war premier of Manitoba. Governing in Colonel Blimp fashion, Roblin said that, unlike Nellie McClung, "nice" women stayed away from factories and polling booths. McClung responded: "By nice women you probably mean selfish women who have no more thought for the under-paid, overworked woman than a pussycat in a sunny window has for the starving kitten in the street. Now, in that sense, I am not a nice woman, for I do care . . . I'm talking for a great many women, of whom you will hear more as the days go on."

He did indeed, in an episode that showed the humour and intelligence so typical of Canada's early women's movement. In 1914, Roblin characterized suffrage as the concern of "short-haired women and long-haired men." Women petitioned to appear before the legislature, and when the day came, Roblin spouted the standard line: he praised his mother, stated that the women before him were proof that society was good enough, and declared that he could not permit such virtue to be sullied by politics. McClung soaked up every word, for she was to appear the next night in the role of Sir Rodmond at Winnipeg's Walker Theatre.[21]

At this "Woman's Parliament," a burlesque of the legislature proceedings, the women were in power and received men pleading for the vote. McClung, playing the premier, took rhetorical flight to hilarious effect. Congratulating the men on their "splendid appearance," she told them that "man is made for something higher and better than voting. . . . Men were made to support families . . . Shall I call man away from the useful plow and harrow to talk loud on street corners about things which do not concern him? Politics unsettle men, and unsettled men mean unsettled bills—broken furniture, and broken vows—and divorce. . . . When you ask for the vote you are asking me to break up peaceful, happy homes—to wreck innocent lives."[22] The crowd of sympathetic women and men roared, the press reported the affair with delight, and Roblin was on his way out. His government was defeated the following May, and the year after that, in 1916, woman suffrage was enacted for provincial elections in Manitoba.

With the floodgates opened, women won the provincial vote that year in two other western provinces, Alberta and Saskatchewan. British Columbia followed early in 1917. By now the suffrage movement was strongest in the West, partly because Westerners felt ignored by Ottawa and believed that more electors would mean more power. And many men recognized that farm women were just as important as men in settling the huge new land. On some homesteads, a rough equality had been imposed by relentless work.[23] The farms themselves, Nellie McClung wrote, had "a demanding look, a clamorous imperative voice." Those demands compelled every able creature within barking distance to perform whatever task was immediate and necessary. Any strict divide between women's and men's work lay in the mind of the dreamer or the well-heeled remittance man.

As in England and the United States, the First World War blasted away the final barriers to the vote. Canadian women were heavily involved as volunteers, nurses, and workers on the home front. Almost invariably, MLAs' speeches introducing suffrage bills mentioned their efforts. But governments considered a less noble factor as well: they judged, often correctly, that grateful women would support the government that gave them the vote. Two Liberal governments, in Manitoba and B.C., were elected on promises of suffrage and quickly kept their pledges.

The sweep of suffrage victories continued. Ontario granted the vote in 1917, Nova Scotia followed in 1918, and New Brunswick in 1919. Prince Edward Island women won provincial voting rights in 1922, while Newfoundland followed in 1925 (although women had to be twenty-five, while men could vote at twenty-one.) The provinces also allowed women to hold office from the day they won the vote—except in New Brunswick, where women had to wait until 1934, another fifteen years.[24]

Winning the crucial federal vote was just as tied to politics, but the war effort also had a powerful effect. In 1917, the Military Voters Act gave the franchise to nurses serving in the war. Later the same year, the Wartime Elections Act extended the vote to widows, mothers, sisters, and daughters of servicemen. This was clearly designed to help Robert Borden's Union government win re-election, and it did not please all feminists. But, after being returned in 1918, the government kept its campaign promise by passing the Women's Franchise Act, which gave women of twenty-one the same voting rights as men. Wartime events made this a popular move: in the same month the bill passed, German bombardments seriously damaged two Canadian field hospitals in France. Four Canadian nursing sisters died, and others acted heroically to save the wounded. Some were awarded the Military Medal for bravery. In 1920, Ottawa dismantled the final franchise barriers by affirming the right of women to be elected to Parliament. They created a separate federal voters list that freed women from remaining provincial limitations. Still, after seventy years of struggle, suffragists could not celebrate a total victory—women in Quebec would have to wait another twenty years before they could vote in provincial elections.

Women activists also had another lingering grudge against the federal system. Although women could now run and serve in nearly every part of Canada, the government refused to appoint them to the Senate because of a technicality. The British North America Act stated that any qualified person could be a senator, but there was legal ambiguity about women's status as full "persons." This was bizarre indeed, given how recently women had been encouraged to risk their lives overseas. Many saw in the provision another insulting reminder of the old, rigidly patriarchal system.

The issue had been simmering since 1916, when Edmonton judge Emily Murphy, the first female magistrate in the British Empire, one day sentenced a bootlegger to serve serious time in jail. The man's lawyer jumped to his feet and challenged Murphy's ruling on the grounds that as a woman, she was not a "person," and therefore was occupying her office illegally. Another woman jurist, Magistrate Alice Jamieson of Calgary, was challenged in the same way a year later. Judge Murphy began to work for change, and various women's groups demanded that the government open the doors of the Senate, but nothing was done despite the promises of prime ministers.

In 1927, Murphy discovered that any five persons could ask the Supreme Court for an interpretation of any part of the BNA Act. She banded together with Nellie McClung, who by then was living in Alberta, and three other Alberta women: Irene Parlby, Louise McKinney, and Henrietta Edwards, a journalist and artist who was seventy-eight when the petition was forwarded to Ottawa.[25] McClung had already served as an Alberta MLA for five years, and Parlby was in the middle of a fourteen-year term as an Alberta minister without portfolio—the second woman in the British Empire to become a cabinet minister. McKinney, a teacher and temperance worker, had won an Alberta

riding in 1917, thus becoming the first woman elected to a legislature anywhere in the British Empire. A more distinguished
group of applicants is hard to imagine—but the Supreme Court
ruled that they were not "persons," and thus were unfit to serve
in the Senate.[26]

The case was immediately appealed to the British Privy
Council, and on October 18, 1929, common sense finally prevailed. The court ruled that the word *persons* "includes members
both of the male and female sex . . . and that women are eligible
to be summoned to and become members of the Senate of
Canada." Nellie McClung, with her usual wit, noted that
Canadian women had not known they were not persons until
they heard that they were. By 1930, the first female senator,
Ontario's Cairine Wilson, took her place in the Red Chamber.

The Persons Case was a great symbolic victory, but also a
reminder that the forces of reaction in Canada remained very
powerful. (It's significant that over the next twenty-two years, a
string of federal governments found the opportunity to appoint
only one more female senator, Ontario's Iva Campbell Fallis.)
The victory left one important piece of unfinished business:
women in Quebec were still denied the right to vote in provincial
elections. Besides the usual male objections to woman suffrage,
Quebec women also faced the implacable opposition of the
Catholic Church, which was enthusiastically supported by
Quebec governments. Political scientist Manon Tremblay writes:
"The Church's resistance to allowing Quebec women to vote
rested largely on tradition; the survival of French-Canadian cul-
ture depended on maintaining the status quo."[27]

La Fédération Nationale Saint-Jean-Baptiste supported
woman suffrage for a time during the height of the ferment, but
the Church forced it to recant in 1920. The president of the
Fédération, Marie Gérin-Lajoie, then prompted the formation of
a Provincial Franchise Committee; she headed the French section
and Anna Lyman led the English chapter. Gérin-Lajoie took her
case to Rome in 1922, hoping for papal support. Instead, the
decision was turned back to the Churches in each country.

Quebec's Cardinal Bégin wrote: "The entry of women into politics, even by merely voting, would be a misfortune for our society. Nothing justifies it, neither the natural law nor the good of
society." So powerful was this male voice that the *Saint-Jean-
Baptiste* federation withdrew its support from the Provincial
Franchise Committee, and Gérin-Lajoie was compelled to resign
its presidency. For the next eighteen years, Quebec women who
could vote in federal elections were forced to stay home when
the province went to the polls.

The Provincial Franchise Committee languished until 1928,
when the remarkable Thérèse Casgrain took up the presidency
and began her relentless drive for the vote. Born to a wealthy
family, she married Pierre-François Casgrain, a lawyer who
became Speaker of the House of Commons and secretary of state
in Mackenzie King's federal Liberal government. With her powerful social and political connections, Casgrain campaigned
relentlessly, both in private and through her lectures, writing,
and radio broadcasts. Every year, she and her allies took a delega-
tion to the premier, and in 1936 they petitioned King George—
an embarrassing tactic for Quebecers to use against their own
provincial government. After the Union Nationale regime of
Maurice Duplessis was defeated in 1939, the new Liberal government finally passed a suffrage bill that also allowed women to
hold office.

Casgrain went on to lead the Quebec wing of the Co-operative
Commonwealth Federation and to mobilize women against
nuclear weapons. She fought many battles, including a famous
public campaign to humiliate the re-elected Duplessis, who in
1945 directed the federal government to send the new family
allowance cheques only to fathers. Noting that other Canadian
mothers received the benefit directly, Casgrain urged mothers to
protest and phoned her friend Louis St. Laurent, then the federal
justice minister. She argued that Duplessis would "demean the
mothers of Québec in the eyes of all Canada by letting it be seen
that they were legally incapable."[28] In 1970, in recognition of
Casgrain's many achievements, Pierre Trudeau made her a senator.

But such distinctions for women remained rare. After the legal barriers were battered down, Canadian feminists quickly discovered that equality in law had little impact on the real world. In 1970, *The Report of the Royal Commission on the Status of Women* revealed figures that startled even women who suspected the worst: between 1918 and 1970, 6,845 legislators were chosen in a total of 134 provincial and federal elections held across Canada. Only 67 of those were women. In that half-century, 18 women sat in the House of Commons, and another 11 made it to the Senate. The first female MP, Agnes Macphail, served alone from 1921 until 1935 before another woman, Martha Black, joined her. For the next five years they could at least see each other, alien invaders in a strange land, although they could hardly rise to vote in solidarity during a political battle: Macphail was a CCFer and Black was a Conservative.

Agnes Macphail was one of those outstanding and gifted individuals who are born to blaze lonely trails for others to tread. Socialist, feminist, and single, she hardly seemed the kind of candidate to win and then hold a rural Ontario riding for nearly twenty years. But Macphail was also a born politician, with warmth, unshakable humour, and integrity. Only those qualities allowed the "spinster schoolteacher" to defeat ten male candidates for her first nomination in South-East Grey. Before the election, there were protests from the public and her own constituency organization because of her gender. "It took strenuous campaigning for two months just to stop people from saying 'We can't have a woman,'" Macphail recalled later. "I won that election in spite of being a woman."[29]

Nonetheless, Macphail went to Ottawa with bright hopes. On December 7, 1921, she told *The Toronto Star:* "I shall never forget that what I do in a measure represents all the women of Canada, and what I do will strengthen or weaken their cause. . . . It is my hope that I can be the listening ear of all such women's bodies and assist them in presenting their case to the House." Macphail managed to be popular in spite of social resentment, partly because a good many of the male MPs found her at once formidable and attractive. When one of them heckled her by say-ing "Aw, get a husband," she asked him to stand, fixed her gaze long and hard, then said scornfully, "How could I be sure that someone I married might not turn out like this?"[30]

Yet, over the years, Macphail found her time in Ottawa deeply alienating, an early foreshadowing of Kim Campbell's "unspeakable loneliness." "The misery of being under observa-tion and being unduly criticized is what I remember most," she wrote years later. "Visitors in the gallery couldn't help seeing one woman among so many men, but they made no effort to dis-guise the fact that I was a curiosity and stared at me whenever I could be seen." Macphail felt the hostility of a harshly impenetra-ble system. "I couldn't open my mouth to say the simplest thing without appearing in the papers. I was a curiosity, a freak. And you know the way the world treats freaks."[31] Treatment by male MPs was little better. "I was intensely unhappy," she wrote. "Some members resented my intrusion, others jeered at me, while a very few were genuinely glad to see a woman in the House. Most of the members made me painfully conscious of my sex."[32] When the men covered up their hostility with gallantry, she snapped, "I'm not a lady, I'm an MP. This old-fashioned chivalry is all hollow. It means nothing except that men think women inferior."

That would be the rule in the House of Commons for many years, as Macphail's successors struggled and searched for true equality. All of them would discover that the law was a weak weapon against implacable patriarchal tradition.

5

WIDOWS TO
WARRIORS

*"Columnists asked me about anything and every-
thing—except my job. . . . And always the whispers and
speculation about my sex life—how much, and with
whom?"*

Judy LaMarsh, 1960s Liberal cabinet minister

Martha Black, an American who had separated from her
first husband, walked across the border into Canada in
1898 while pregnant with her third child. On her own,
she became a successful sawmill owner near Dawson City, and in
1904 she married George Black, who became the territory's
commissioner and later its MP. In 1935, she was sixty-nine years
old, but as vigorous as ever, when her husband fell ill and she ran
to replace him in the Yukon riding. Later she wrote: "There were
the younger women who said: 'What can this damned old

woman do for us in Ottawa?' That was hard to take, yet I hurled back, 'You'll be lucky when you reach my age if you have my sturdy legs, my good stomach, my strong heart, and what I like to call my headpiece.'"[1]

Black was one of a curious breed of female politicians—the inheritors—who followed Agnes Macphail to Ottawa as members of Parliament. For over half a century, well into the era of Pierre Trudeau, it remained nearly impossible for women of independent mind and lifestyle to be elected in Canada; it was even more daunting for a married woman, as Macphail realized very well. "Agnes remained single by choice; marriage would have cost her her job," observes Heather Robertson. "The idea of married women working outside the home was anathema to the majority of Canadians, and Agnes would have been expected to parrot her husband's opinions."[2]

A married woman might be elected, however, if her husband had been an MP who was either too ill to serve or newly dead. His wife could then become his surrogate, ever ready to voice the views of her dearly departed, without fear of contradiction. In the four decades from 1921 to 1964, only seventeen women were elected to Parliament; seven of them succeeded to the ridings of their dead husbands. (This happened as recently as 1982, when Tory Jennifer Cossitt won the Leeds-Grenville riding in Ontario after the death of her husband, Tom Cossitt.) The usual practice was for the men in the party riding association to take pity on the widow and secure for her the party's nomination. Altruism, however, was not necessarily their main motive. If the husband had been popular enough, and dismay at his departure was deep, the widow would often win a by-election for the party, and perhaps an election beyond.

It's hardly surprising that when these women arrived in Ottawa, they were not revered by their male colleagues. But they were certainly easier for the men to understand than an Agnes Macphail or, later, a Judy LaMarsh. With her clear eye, the dynamic Liberal minister of the 1960s described her trials as a woman. "I was lonely, of course," LaMarsh wrote, "but thought my colleagues would be friendlier when my newness wore off. They never really were friendlier—they just got used to me and accepted that I was one of the rare breed to get elected, and re-elected, exactly as they did, not because I was someone's widow who needed the salary." She noted that other female MPs, "[f]rom Cora Casselman to Grace MacInnis . . . were mostly elected as widows or daughters of parliamentarians." (MacInnis came into federal politics in 1965 with a powerful family credential: she was the daughter of J.S. Woodsworth, first leader of the Co-operative Commonwealth Federation.)

Once in Ottawa, however, female MPs with family ties often proved to be surprisingly adept as politicians. Cora Taylor Casselman, elected in 1941 in an Alberta riding after her Liberal husband died, was an excellent parliamentarian. Perhaps the most remarkable of all was Martha Black, who served for five years in place of her husband, focusing much of her attention on pensions and unemployment. By 1940, George Black had recovered, Martha retired, and he won again in the Yukon riding.

Tory Jean Casselman Wadds, the daughter of parliamentarian Earl Rowe, replaced her dead husband in Grenville-Dundas in 1958; later, appointed by Joe Clark, she became High Commissioner to Great Britain, the first woman to assume such a lofty diplomatic posting. In 1961, Conservative Margaret May Macdonald inherited the Kings riding in Prince Edward Island. In the 1962 general election, after her husband died in office, Isabel Hardie won his Mackenzie River riding for the Liberals. Margaret Rideout, a Liberal, won a 1964 by-election precipitated by the death of her husband in Westmorland, a New Brunswick riding. Jennifer Cossitt's victory in 1982 seems to have ended this dubious tradition, more than sixty years after women won the legal right to vote and to hold office on their own merit.

Even when women reached the House of Commons, through whatever route they could carve, they failed to penetrate the executive branch of government: the cabinet, where all the important decisions are made. It simply would not have occurred to prime ministers like R.B. Bennett, Mackenzie King, or Louis

St. Laurent to bring women into the inner circle. That would be an unthinkable breach of the public–private barrier; and besides, there were so few women to choose from. Bennett had none in his caucus from 1930 to 1935; nor did King during his long administrations, which stretched from the 1920s to the late 1940s. The sole woman in St. Laurent's caucuses from 1948 to 1957, Marie Shipley from Timiskaming, Ont., was allowed no higher honour than being the first woman to move the Address-in-Reply to the Speech from the Throne.

It was left to Conservative Prime Minister John Diefenbaker, never a defender of the feminist cause, to name the first woman to cabinet. She was Ellen Louks Fairclough, a chartered accountant from Hamilton who captured a Commons seat for the Conservatives in 1950. When Diefenbaker won a minority government in 1957 he recognized, very reluctantly, that it might be wise to name a woman to his ministry. But the Prairie warrior resisted Fairclough, one of only two women in his caucus, because she had voted against him for party leader.[3] She might not have been considered at all but for the death of a Diefenbaker friend, Bill Blair.

When Diefenbaker finally swallowed enough pride to summon Fairclough to his office, he said, "It looks as though I'll have to form my cabinet from amongst my enemies. You can be secretary of state." Fairclough fumed at his backhanded blessing. "I'll let you know," she snapped. It took George Drew, the former Ontario premier, to convince Fairclough to accept the job. Known for her hard work and attention to detail, Fairclough later served as minister of citizenship and immigration and as Postmaster-General. "People recognized that administration was my strong point, and I imagine this robbed me of some color," she said years later.[4]

Although Fairclough didn't define herself as a feminist—a word hardly known at the time—she was never reluctant to advance the cause of women. While she was opposition labour critic, she introduced a bill calling for equal pay for equal work, and advocated a Women's Bureau in the Labor Department. With the support of the Organization for Business and Professional Women, of which Fairclough was a member, the second initiative was adopted. Later, in 1956, the Liberals embraced the cause of equal pay for women working under federal jurisdiction.

Within the Tory caucus, many men respected Fairclough's business expertise, even if they weren't enthusiastic about her concern for women. For all her hard work, though, Fairclough found herself judged on irrelevancies—her hats, for instance. In 1962, a reporter for Montreal's *La Presse* wrote: "Since becoming a federal cabinet minister in 1957, Mrs. Fairclough has travelled some 240,000 miles, mostly in Canada, and worn out more than three dozen hats. The functions she has attended over the last four years have permitted her to wear several styles of headgear that are not specifically feminine. While flying, she wore a helmet used by pilots. . . ."[5]

Fairclough slogged through such nonsense determined to keep her dignity and achieve what she could. "She's the woman I admire most, an incredible woman," says Tory veteran Jean Pigott. "There's one word to describe her—she's got spunk. She's earthy, she drinks straight Scotch. She's kept herself up-to-date on the issues that concern the country. I've never felt she's taken on women's causes specifically—she's taken on humanity's causes. She has always lifted the whole role of women."[6]

Plenty of that spunk remained in 1993, when Fairclough was eighty-eight years old. She drove her husband and herself to Ottawa from Hamilton for the Tory leadership convention in June and gave the introductory speech for Kim Campbell. One observer said it was the most effective moment in Campbell's presentation. Then Fairclough spent time working the convention while her husband, who was too frail, watched on TV from their room in the Chateau Laurier.[7]

When Liberal prime minister Lester (Mike) Pearson named Judy LaMarsh his minister of national health and welfare in 1963, she became Canada's second female cabinet minister. LaMarsh inherited the Fairclough tradition of tenacity and spunk and added a good measure of charisma. Her whole career as a

Liberal MP, from the time she came into Parliament in 1960 until the moment she left in 1968, was a blaze of colour and controversy. The lawyer from Niagara Falls did not take slights lightly, and tended to see them everywhere, as often as not from within her own party. Usually she was justified: Pearson, first Opposition leader and by 1963 prime minister, would treat her with disdain. The gentle public manner that helped win him the Nobel Peace Prize did not extend to his only female caucus member and minister. (Pauline Jewett, elected in 1963, was a Liberal MP from Ontario for only two years.)

Most male ministers could phone Pearson directly, but he insisted that all calls from LaMarsh go through an appointments secretary. "Pearson treated Judy like shit," recalls Nancy Morrison, her former law partner. "She used to come back in tears after speaking with him."[8] Morrison felt that LaMarsh was "big and tough and strong and swore too much" for the liking of men in the Liberal caucus. A male colleague dealt LaMarsh the deadliest insult: "Well, can you imagine going to bed with *that?*"[9] LaMarsh, ever the battler, returned Pearson's contempt in full measure. "Mike's office was hopelessly badly organized and no one ever knew what anyone else was doing," she wrote in her autobiography, *Memoirs of a Bird in a Gilded Cage.* "Mike could not organize or communicate, so that what could have been welded into an effective small group . . . was a shambles."

After Pearson brought LaMarsh into cabinet, he wasn't about to take any chances with yet another troublesome female. When Pauline Jewett asked for a cabinet position, he replied with astonishment, "But we already have a woman minister!" Jewett snapped, "Mr. Prime Minister, why don't you be really, really radical and have two?" Such episodes prompted Jewett's later decision to switch from the Liberals to the NDP.[10]

More than any woman in our history, Judy LaMarsh embodied the contradictions women face in political life. She was born a generation too soon for the political role she deserved, and became a prisoner trapped in time. She could be as aggressive and combative as any of her male colleagues, but could switch to coy and coquettish behavior if she felt the situation required feminine froth. Always ferociously frank, she called Pierre Trudeau a "bastard" on national television during the 1968 leadership convention at which he replaced Pearson as party leader and then prime minister. She detested Trudeau partly for his sexual politics. "The present government is oriented to one man," she wrote, "and that man has little understanding of women as people. He talks about civil rights, but it would not even occur to him that inequality because of sex alone haunts half his people. Nor does he see women as other than ornaments to a man's life; someone or something to enjoy himself with after the business of the day is over." Those were brave words to write in her memoirs, which were published in 1968, just as her party adversary swept into office on a national wave of Trudeaumania.[11]

Yet LaMarsh, a single woman, was pulled all her life toward a traditional family that she never had. In a revealing interview with CBC television on December 13, 1964, she said, "In a moment I would exchange politics for the right husband—certainly." After four years as an MP in Mike Pearson's Liberal caucus she looked overworked, overweight, and overwrought. "I don't have very many dates," she said morosely to the whole nation. "The next worst thing about being single is that horrible thought that one is old and alone—a pitiful creature and nobody cares. I'd hate to wind up an old lady with a budgie bird or a canary." LaMarsh brightened briefly to say "I don't think I will,'" then added bleakly, "I'll go out and jump off a bridge or something, or take in strays." As the cameras showed her playing with nieces and nephews, she continued, "I often thought about adopting a child. I'd like to have done that." Then, with sad finality, "But while you're in politics you can't do it."

Another film clip exposed with aching poignancy the deep conflicts LaMarsh felt between her life as a public figure and her desire to be a private woman. In her book she called herself a "Bird in a Gilded Cage"; for television, she was willing to play the role too literally. The results, on scratchy black and white film, are painful and pathetic to watch.

It is June 11, 1971, and welcome to "The Tommy Hunter Show," with Tommy's special guest, Judy LaMarsh. There she is, dressed in a fluffy white gown trimmed with feathers and standing in a huge bird cage. She looks enormous, like a giant fallen flamingo. When Hunter turns to her, she steps out of the gilded cage and walks to the front of the stage, where they sit and begin to exchange excruciating banter. "You've been a very naughty boy this evening," she says coyly. "You don't know how to treat a lady." All these beautiful girls are running around backstage and nobody pays any attention to them, LaMarsh complains. "You wouldn't even think of doing a show like that with a lot of men, would you?" Hunter replies: "As a matter of fact, we're thinking about doing a show just like that right here next week." With that LaMarsh utters the ultimate putdown of herself, the inevitable stereotype of a single, desperate woman. "Really?" she says eagerly. "Do you suppose there's a room backstage where I could hide a little bit?" The audience seems to feel embarrassed for her; the laughter is nervous and tentative. LaMarsh and Hunter then sing a strained version of "I remember it well." ("We met at nine," he croons, and she replies, "No, we met at eight.") Three years after leaving politics, LaMarsh was still struggling to cope with her sense of failing to live up to society's demands on her as a woman. More than anything she ever said or wrote, these film clips reveal how despairing her time in politics had been.[12]

Like Flora MacDonald after her, LaMarsh was plagued by the extra burden of all the government's "women's work," as well as being expected to perform the regular job of a man. Just to read her list of extra duties is to see the desperate sweat pouring from her brow. "I grew tired of being the woman's watchdog," she wrote bitterly. "I grew tired of having the role thrust upon me simply because I was a woman. I was paid exactly what my male colleagues were paid, although many of them did not perform one-fifth of the work I did for the Government and the Liberal Party."

Her clothes and wigs were a matter of constant public discussion, as were her weight, age, home, cooking, hobbies, friends, and tastes. Reporters followed her into the hairdressing salon. Women tagged after her into washrooms and mobbed her at airports. Children and teachers wrote to request cooking tips and advice on how to succeed as a woman. "Columnists asked me about anything and everything—except my job. . . . And always the whispers and speculation about my sex life—how much, and with whom?"

The sexual innuendo hurt her more than any of the other indignities. Articles were written about the alleged jealousy of her colleagues' wives, about how she travelled with several young male staff members (although, as she said, she was always careful not to travel with just one man). "I am no more a saint than anyone else," she said, "but I cannot say I have heard the same rampant speculation about my male colleagues and their friends. Scandal is the first weapon, the most continuous one, and the last weapon used against a woman anywhere, and particularly one of political prominence. I have had repeated to me by friends, families and foes the most horrendous stories of my personal life. I have been accused of the full spectrum of sensual impropriety—funny had it not been so malicious."[13]

Like many women in Ottawa, LaMarsh fought a long battle with her politically induced obesity. Photographs published in her book show her as a slender young woman when she ran for office in 1960. By 1963, she was expanding rapidly, and in 1967 she looked fat and unhealthy. Her weight was fair game for cartoonists, who regularly portrayed her as an absurd befeathered behemoth. When a newspaper reported her as saying, "My personal hope for 1967 is to retire from politics," someone sent her the clipping with the scribbled words: "That's everybody's hope, you cute little ton of fun."

Of all the idiocies perpetrated against LaMarsh, one stood out from the rest: a columnist for her local newspaper asked her, shortly after she was first elected, "Are you a politician or a woman?" (In 1987, U.S. presidential aspirant Patricia Schroeder was asked: "Are you running as a woman?" to which she replied, "Do I have an option?") Comparing her own complaints with those of Agnes Macphail, LaMarsh said: "After forty-five years, that soul-destroying public avidity is unchanged. The public still devours its own . . . . Where there are twenty-five men, the public's interest is split; when there is one woman, she becomes a focus for criticism and for curiosity."

LaMarsh could seem sad or joyous, aggressive or compliant, but rarely did she appear to be truly happy and secure. Even her fine record of accomplishment in government did not reward her with serenity. As minister of national health and welfare, she was instrumental in establishing medicare and the Canada Pension Plan. She was "hostess" of the hugely successful 1967 Centennial celebration (a woman's job, after all), and in those more innocent times spent too much of her own money travelling the country. The list of achievements should have made LaMarsh proud, and she did it all while sending those recipes and attending Women's Institute teas. But she would not appear tranquil, free of conflict and bitterness, until twelve years after her political career had ended, when she knew she was dying of cancer in 1980.

In a final interview with the CBC's "Take Thirty" TV program, LaMarsh looked gaunt rather than stout. Her sickness had carved deep lines into her thin face. But despite being mortally ill, she exuded confidence and inner well-being. "I always thought I'd die young, at around forty," she told Harry Brown. "I've just turned fifty-five—that's a good enough life. I've had many good breaks in my life. You can't really squawk if the last one is a bad break." Gone was all trace of the struggles that defined her public life: between male and female, public and private, her single status and her desire for family. She was simply herself, Judy LaMarsh, peaceful and strong, her powerful intelligence completely unclouded at last. Watching the tape, one can't help but wonder what she would have achieved had she been born a generation later.

But for all her intellect, LaMarsh was a victim of her time. She saw the symptoms of her existential malaise, and felt them passionately, without really naming the disease. She didn't use words like "sexism," "paternalism," or "patriarchal." Like most political women of her day, LaMarsh believed her difficulties could be addressed by solving a string of individual inequities. But the real problem was the system itself—not an evil system, just one that was alien to women, profoundly male, built by another culture for its own power. LaMarsh's greatest contribution, perhaps, was to help begin the process that led to Canada's first full description and understanding of that culture.

As the only woman in the Liberal caucus, she urged Prime Minister Pearson to create a Royal Commission on the Status of Women. LaMarsh was responding, a bit reluctantly, to a great popular movement among Canadian women's groups. "No matter how little a suffragette by temperament," she wrote later, "circumstances gradually forced me into the role of acting as spokesman and watchdog for women. If there had been a dozen women in the cabinet, that wouldn't have been necessary, but I had to carry out this dual, unasked for, entirely unofficial and unpaid role."[14]

In some ways, the drive for a royal commission was like the Persons Case forty years earlier: it tended to unite women of all ideological stripes around one narrow and well-defined objective. Hundreds of women were involved, but the prime mover was Laura Sabia, president of the Canadian Federation of University Women. Educated in a Montreal convent school, Sabia was appalled by the condition of the nuns' lives. Later, as a Conservative, she remained active in women's issues while raising four children in St. Catharines, Ont. "We did more crossing of political lines in those days than we've ever done since," Sabia said. "We never even thought of our political affiliations. We were all working for women."[15]

In 1966, Sabia called together the heads of some thirty national women's organizations. They created the Committee on Equality for Women and in a brief to Prime Minister Pearson asked for a royal commission to deal with women's status. *Chatelaine* editor Doris Anderson, who was at the meeting, wrote a powerful and reasonable editorial in support. "What we don't need in a Commission," she said, "is an all-woman witch hunt. We do need a forward-looking Commission composed equally of impartial men and women prepared to take a cool twentieth-century approach to our problems."

Sabia was more inclined to the plane of gut politics. In 1986, her son, Michael Sabia, described her tactics in an article for *Chatelaine:* "Picture, if you will, a typical scene from our household in the '60s. Mother is preparing dinner. Father, a surgeon, and his 10-year-old son are waiting to be fed. The phone rings, and a brief discussion ensues, mother calmly saying: 'Tell the prime minister that I will lead an uprising of Canadian women'".[16] Sabia's recollection of the episode was slightly different. A reporter pried a quote about a possible demonstration out of her, she said, and it led to a sensational story in *The Globe and Mail:* "Two Million Women may . . . march on Ottawa."[17]

After the paper hit the street, Judy LaMarsh called Sabia to relate a conversation she had just had with Prime Minister Pearson. "Who the hell is Laura Sabia?" he asked. Sabia conceded later that she couldn't have raised nearly that many women for such a march, but the tough talk had an impact on the minority Liberal government. On February 16, 1967, Pearson announced the creation of the Royal Commission on the Status of Women with a mandate "to recommend what steps might be taken by the federal government to ensure for women equal opportunities with men in all aspects of Canadian society. . . ."[18] One touch showed that the old order was far from dead: the married women commissioners, including chairman Florence Bird, were listed in the Order-in-Council by their husband's names—Mrs. John Bird, Mrs. Ottomar Lange, and Mrs. Robert Ogilvie.

The commission helped launch the high-profile careers of at least two very able politicians. Quebec lawyer Marc Lalonde, then a special policy advisor to Pearson, quietly co-ordinated much of the preliminary work.[19] The executive secretary of the commission was Monique Bégin, a twenty-nine-year-old Quebec sociologist and founding member of *La Fédération des Femmes du Québec.* Bégin took it upon herself to write much of the historic 487-page report. Lalonde and Bégin, after winning election as Liberals in 1972, would become prominent ministers in the government of Pierre Trudeau, Lalonde as the first minister responsible for the status of women.

When the report finally appeared on September 28, 1970, it was instantly controversial. *Toronto Star* columnist Anthony Westell called it "a bomb already primed and ticking . . . packed with more explosive potential than any device manufactured by terrorists . . . a call to revolution." The rhetoric was overblown, given the report's moderate tone, but others reacted just as sharply. Men who opposed "women's liberation" on principle discredited the report (although many of them had never read it). John Lundrigan, a Newfoundland Tory MP, said in *Chatelaine* in May 1972, "Any good sociologist or two or three women together could have put that report together."

Hardly. The commissioners considered 468 briefs and 1,000 letters, toured 14 cities in 10 provinces and both Territories, heard 890 witnesses, and commissioned 40 separate studies. Monique Bégin's writing is brilliant in its organization, grasp of detail, and clarity of language. Seamlessly weaving the history of women in Canada with their modern reality, the report is a true rarity among government documents, a page-turner that engages the reader even today. In 1970, thousands of women avidly read each of the 167 recommendations, and the insights they gained prepared them for every battle to come.

Finally there was proof, laid out in cold type, that women were systematically discriminated against in every area of Canadian life. The report chronicled women's poverty, discrimination in education and the workplace, disadvantages in family life, and the barriers against women in the political world. The conclusions about politics were a unifying call to action: "The last 50 years, since woman suffrage was introduced, have seen no appreciable change in the political activities of women beyond the exercise of the right to vote. In the decision-making positions, and most conspicuously in the government and Parliament of Canada, the presence of a mere handful of women is no more than a token acknowledgement of their right to be there. The voice of government is still a man's voice. The formulation of policies affecting the lives of all Canadians is still the prerogative of men. The absurdity of this situation was illustrated when debate in the House of Commons on a change in abortion law was conducted by 263 men and one woman."[20]

The royal commission report generated a new solidarity and political will among a generation of women. It led to the creation in 1972 of the National Action Committee on the Status of Women, a lobbying federation of 289 women's groups. The government appointed a women's minister, Lalonde, and set up the Canadian Advisory Council on the Status of Women, a quasi-government body that reported to the minister (but not to Parliament, as the report recommended). Women could now point not only to officially documented proof of discrimination, but to sensible suggestions for righting the inequities.

The barriers to political power were beginning to crumble, pebble by pebble, stone by stone. But as women stoically picked away, they found a government too entombed in tradition to take full notice. And they would need more than one report to dull the smoking-club din of these patriarchal chambers.

6

REGIMENTAL MASCOTS

*"We were aliens—real aliens. If we'd come from another
planet we could not have been more alien."*

Iona Campagnolo, former Trudeau cabinet minister,
on the differences between female and male politicians

Monique Bégin could never understand why she always
felt the worst when she won the most. As a member of
Pierre Trudeau's cabinet from 1976 to 1979, and
again from 1980 to 1984, the accomplished *Québécoise* had
major battles to fight, especially for medicare funding as minister
of national health and welfare. On cabinet days, Bégin would
arm herself with facts and figures, draw a deep breath, and take
on tough characters like Marc Lalonde and Trudeau himself. As
often as not, through solid preparation and sheer passion for her
cause, Bégin would win. But whenever she did, another minister,

usually a man, would lose. And Bégin would leave the meeting feeling sick inside.

For a long time, she says today, she thought it was just her—some inadequacy, some unexplained sadness deep within. She told no one of her feelings, not even female colleagues and friends like Iona Campagnolo and Judy Erola. After all, winning battles was supposed to make a cabinet minister happy; she always saw male ministers transported with joy when *they* won. Why couldn't she enjoy it too?

Bégin already considered herself a feminist. She had come up through the women's networks in Quebec, notably as a founding member of *La Fédération des Femmes du Québec*. Before being elected as MP for the Saint-Michel riding in Montreal, she had been executive secretary of the Royal Commission on the Status of Women. The years spent in that enterprise made her as familiar as anyone in Canada with our long and discouraging history of political discrimination against women. Bégin knew her federal politics too; before stepping into the cabinet room, she had been a backbench Liberal MP for nearly four years. But none of her vast experience prepared her for the realities of cabinet: for the bickering and games-playing, the intellectual jousting so dear to Trudeau, the high formality of discussion, the sly put-downs of women ministers, and the win-or-lose stakes that rode on every point of debate. Like Judy LaMarsh before her, she began to gain weight. It was the only public sign that the confident woman who argued her causes so eloquently was living in misery.

After she left politics in 1984, Bégin had time to reflect on the root of her constant feelings of alienation, depression, and inadequacy. In a sense, she had been a stranger in a foreign culture, but one who is expected to perform her duties without being told about the local customs. All of her training as a woman—her belief in conciliation, compromise, and helping an opponent to save face—was useless for her political survival. These qualities merely ensured that she could never enjoy what was defined by the men as a "victory"; in her mind, the very word meant something completely different. Psychologically, she was as vulnerable as a pacifist facing armed border guards on an alien planet.

"What I lived as minister was really a feeling all the time of being different and marginal," Bégin recalls. "I kept thinking it was me personally who was inadequate. I was smart enough to shut up and never say it, never even share it with another woman because you wouldn't even think of that. I reacted according to the way I had been socialized as a girl, which meant I have never felt comfortable with competition. So when I won big victories in cabinet, I would feel guilty as hell. When I won money or other battles against other ministers, I would feel extremely bad."

Through the insights of women's studies, Bégin says, she began to understand what she had lived through. She has since discussed her feelings with two female cabinet colleagues of the day, Judy Erola and Iona Campagnolo. "Judy is very balanced. She's not a dogmatic person at all, she's very pragmatic and realistic. And she felt the same things. I discussed it with Iona and she feels the same way too. But at that time, the only concepts I was equipped with were concepts of discrimination *against*. This had nothing to do with discrimination *against* in the usual sense. It had to do with me coming from a socialization and a set of values and a universe of women's roles in society—and the guys were from another universe entirely."[1]

Bégin and her female cabinet colleagues, with their background in activism and interest in the royal commission, were better prepared for Canada's political universe than any women before them. But psychologically, they were still lost and alone, because their male colleagues were only dimly aware of how to deal with politicians who were also women. Indeed, the women themselves often had little idea of how to cope. It's startling to learn that Bégin, the astute feminist who had spent half her life studying women's role in society, had felt so adrift when confronted with the reality of everyday life in politics. Part of the reason was Pierre Elliott Trudeau himself, and what he represented.

Trudeau came to office in 1968, a Jesuit-trained intellectual who had been repressed and shy as a young man, but in middle age developed a taste for beautiful young women. With his sensual looks, physical prowess, and intellectual wizardry, he proved irresistible to many women in the hippie era of free love and the mini-skirt. "Every girl in Montreal is sitting at home tonight in case Pierre will call," good friend Alexandrine Pelletier said in 1968.[2] At the height of the strange national obsession the press called Trudeaumania, groupies flocked to him as if he were a rock star. In those burgeoning days of feminism, liberation sometimes meant freedom for women to do what men enjoyed most, and Trudeau was a happy beneficiary. He squired Barbra Streisand, pirouetted at Buckingham Palace, dressed like a bohemian aesthete, and eventually married Margaret Sinclair, a West Coast beauty less than half his age. Judy LaMarsh had some reason to suspect him of seeing women only as "ornaments to a man's life." He fostered the impression in public, and obviously enjoyed the resulting admiration.

Yet Trudeau also had another set of women friends, intellectual equals of his own age whom he respected, including cabinet minister Jeanne Sauvé. Partly through them, the prime minister was aware of the swelling tide of the women's movement and certainly felt no urge to swim against it. After the Royal Commission on the Status of Women Report was released in 1970, Trudeau made groundbreaking appointments of women. In 1972, Muriel Fergusson from New Brunswick became the first female Speaker of the Senate, and in 1974 Trudeau designated another woman, Renaude Lapointe, to succeed her. Then, in 1980, he named Sauvé the first woman Speaker of the House of Commons, and in 1984 ensured that she was appointed Governor-General. Trudeau always tried to manoeuvre women into cabinet posts where they would be highly visible, politically profitable, and, if possible, elegantly alluring. He had a shrewd knack for political display, and like a card sharp shuffling his marked deck, Trudeau publicly invited women to join the game, but privately dealt them a weak hand.

When the Royal Commission on the Status of Women urged the parties to nominate more female candidates, Trudeau agreed and ordered his party to find them. In Quebec, his close friend Jean Marchand enlisted eight female candidates from the ranks of "moderate" feminists such as Bégin. But the "anglophone" party—meaning the Liberals in the rest of Canada—ignored the directive. As a result, three strong Liberal women from Quebec were elected in 1972: Bégin, Sauvé, and Albanie Morin (who died in 1976). Only two women were elected in the rest of Canada, neither of them Liberals. (They were New Democrat Grace MacInnis from Vancouver, and Tory Flora MacDonald from Kingston.[3]) It wasn't until the 1974 election that the Liberal Party outside Quebec, shamed by the 1972 results, made an effort to find candidates to run in winnable ridings in English Canada. Five Liberal women were elected: Iona Campagnolo and Simma Holt from B.C.; Ursula Appolloni and Aideen Nicholson from Ontario; and Coline Campbell, the first female MP from Nova Scotia. This was progress of a sort, but nowhere near the "critical mass" of one-third women members that many academics feel is necessary to make a real difference.

Of all his female colleagues, Trudeau seemed most comfortable with Sauvé, who was born in Saskatchewan but spent her adult life in Ottawa and Montreal, and identified most strongly with Quebec. Her husband, Maurice, had been an MP in Lester Pearson's time but fell out of favour when he supported Paul Martin over Trudeau for the Liberal leadership in 1968. This didn't stop Trudeau from naming Mme. Sauvé to cabinet as soon as she won election in 1972, thus making her the first woman from Quebec to serve as a federal minister. With her aristocratic bearing, silvery hair, and healthy self-confidence, the former CBC broadcaster quickly made it known that she wasn't to be trifled with in cabinet. Reflecting her thoughts, an aide to Sauvé once said, "There are many ways to win, are there not? You can kill your opponent and win. You can maim him and win. You can also charm him and win." Charm was Sauvé's preference, but she also knew what to do when that failed.

At first Sauvé emphasized her hopes for Quebec over her role as a woman in power, but at times the feminist mantle was thrust upon her. After Trudeau made her Speaker of the House of Commons in 1980, she was instantly in the front lines of the pitched battles of the sexes when they erupted in the Chamber. When she asked Tory MP Mike Forrestall if he had a question, and he replied, "I certainly do, my dear," she snapped, "Don't call me 'my dear.' Call me 'Madam Speaker.'" She was infuriated by the men-only membership policy of the prestigious Rideau Club, and used her position to deny Commons business to the club. Finally the Rideau yanked itself into the twentieth century and named Tory Jean Pigott as its first female member. (Not long afterward, the club burned down, prompting Pigott to quip, "When you deal with 'hot broads,' things start to sizzle.")

Sauvé, who had interrupted her career at age thirty-seven to care for her newborn son, Jean-François, understood the demands of a young family. But when she set up the House of Commons day-care centre in 1980 she was "viciously attacked by the press" for what they termed "extravagance," according to Senator Marcel Prud'homme, who fumed at the media's "lack of sensitivity." Added Sheila Copps, "That's probably something that wouldn't be attacked now. What Mrs. Sauvé did in 1980 is very important."[4]

When Trudeau secured Sauvé's appointment in 1980 as Canada's first female Governor-General, she deemed it "a terrific breakthrough for women." In this role she was often considered haughty and aloof, but in truth she was frequently ill. In Ottawa she is best remembered, and still disliked, for closing the grounds of Rideau Hall to the public, a decision that was not necessarily her own. To the rest of Canada, she became a symbol that the old ways were starting to waver. Sauvé died on January 26, 1993, after a long illness that she was determined to battle in private.

"She was a very warm and friendly person, always interested in everyone. And she loved children," says Sharon Orr, who worked with Sauvé on her Governor-General's staff for several years. "After she died, people would say to me that it must have been hard working for Jeanne Sauvé. I told them, 'No, it was absolutely wonderful.' She was a mentor of mine."[5]

Despite such public gestures as the elevation of Sauvé, the inner chambers of Trudeau's governments remained entirely male in tradition and attitude. Cabinet meetings, heavily influenced by Trudeau's Jesuit training, were formal exercises in logic and subtle one-upmanship. There were some influential women in Trudeau's inner circle, including his legislative assistant, Joyce Fairbairn (now Jean Chrétien's government leader in the Senate). But in general, as Christina McCall-Newman wrote, "the women didn't have the men's entrée to the [prime minister's office] or their expectations of advancement."[6] And those who reached the charmed inner circle of cabinet found themselves without the cultural training they needed to thrive. This changed little through Trudeau's four governments, which lasted, with one short break for Joe Clark in 1979, from 1968 to 1984.

Marcel Prud'homme, a veteran former Liberal backbencher from Quebec who is now a senator, expressed perfectly the ambivalence and even fear that Trudeau's male MPs felt when the women began to win positions of power. Speaking to the Royal Commission on Electoral Reform in 1993, Prud'homme said: "Right from the start I witnessed the incredible arguing that went on in order for them to get a seat. We knew that, once they were elected, they would surpass almost all of the other members around them. I was one of them. They surrounded me.

"They became ministers and all that and I was happy for them. It's not easy for men to absorb the shock, but it's a worthwhile war. It's only normal. We need women, and if we need women, they have to be treated equally and given the same positions as men. . . . For some men, it is not easy to accept the fact that they are going to be replaced by women, but that's life. We must accept this with a glad heart."[7]

With all these mixed emotions at work even within a man of goodwill, it's hardly surprising that men found many ways to let the women know who was still boss. For Monique Bégin, the most puzzling and frustrating cabinet episode was the debate over Bertha Wilson's appointment as the first female Justice of the Supreme Court in 1982. "It was not the result of a women's crusade across the country," she recalls. "It was more low key than that. But her name had the support of enough women's organizations for Judy [Erola], as minister for the status of women, to push the name forward and fight for that candidate. It came to full cabinet and we were the only women in cabinet, Judy and I, by that time."

Bégin and Erola threw their support behind Wilson's candidacy and expressed their view clearly in cabinet. They thought they had won, but then it became obvious that Trudeau wanted the position to go to the famous Quebec judge Gérard LeDain. He became the official nominee, Bégin says, despite the women's support for Wilson. "It was very extraordinary, and it came through the person of Trudeau himself. It was somehow the very essence of maleness, of chauvinistic stuff, very subtle and very damaging. . . . They [the male ministers] just spoke of how intellectually Wilson had never produced, and how she was not known in the circles, the intellectual elite of jurisprudence.

"We kept speaking of her set of values and the kind of judgments she had already contributed, and we were totally dismissed, Judy and I. It was really like two planets bumping against each other. The whole thing got to a solution when Jean Chrétien, who was then minister of justice, suddenly said to Trudeau, 'Well boss, the girls are right, I think it's time for a woman, otherwise we'll have problems." And that was it! That's the way she was appointed! That shocked me. We had glimpsed how they despise women's intellect."[8]

Bégin had won—again—but it's little wonder that the victories caused such conflict and pain. In this case, a woman rose to the nation's highest court only because the men decided to open the door a crack to avoid "problems." Chrétien, when he described Wilson's appointment more than ten years later, did not mention the struggles of Bégin and Erola on Wilson's behalf.

"When I was minister of justice, I named a lot of women as judges," he said. "I named the first woman justice of the Supreme Court. But it was difficult because there are so few of them. When I named Bertha Wilson, it was because I really searched. A lot of people were opposed because she was not known. And she turned out to be a fantastic judge."

Chrétien said he started with the premise that naming the first woman to the Supreme Court would be a major step forward. He asked for a list of all likely women, with the proviso that the judge come from Ontario. "So we looked, and there was this judge," Chrétien recalls. "She was a good judge, but if you asked people in the bar to rate them one, two, three, four, she was not at the top at all. But the more I studied the case, the more convinced I got. After that I had to persuade people, but it was difficult because a lot of people thought she was being named just because she was a woman. And I didn't want that. It was very important to have great success. If you name a very bad woman, it's a disservice. Now, if you ask anyone in the community, they will all say she was a great judge. But the opposition I had to face! Not only from the ministry, but from the judges. Someday I will write about it."[9]

Bégin, it appears, was absolutely right—"the girls" had little to do with the decision. Chrétien guaranteed Bertha Wilson's elevation by pushing the correct male buttons that day in the private confines of cabinet. After his shrewd intervention, the men could leave feeling that they had done something worthwhile while relinquishing none of their power.

Political women react in many ways to this constant feeling that they are cast adrift in foreign waters. A common defence is to project an unconscious shield of some sort, often by gaining vast amounts of weight. When Bégin became an MP she was a slender woman; so she remained for several years, until she was invited into cabinet. "I created around myself a physical protection," she says. "I know that now, because it happens to a lot of women. I would arrive home at midnight and eat chocolate bars. I misused food, I know that, but I did not do it consciously. I put on sixty pounds in six months, as soon as I became a minister. I suffered for it enormously and was laughed at by the reporters. They would ask me at the door of the House: 'When is it due? Who's the father?' It was very unpleasant."[10]

Male reporters weren't the only offenders. Brian Mulroney, when he was new in the Commons and still uneducated by Flora MacDonald, Marjory LeBreton, and the Tory troupe of gender-sensitizers, made exactly the same kind of comment to Bégin. On his second day in the House, reports John Sawatsky, Bégin "heckled him with the word *'Accouchez!'*—meaning literally 'Give birth' but idiomatically 'Get to the point.' Without a pause Mulroney shouted back: *'Ça s'en vient, Monique. En parlant d'accouchement, Monique, ça s'en vient?'* ('It's coming, Monique. Speaking of childbirth, Monique, is it on the way?')" Mulroney later apologized, and changed the official version of the exchange in *Hansard* to: "I can assure the Honorable Minister of Health and Welfare that I will get there in due time."

Bégin's expanding girth coincided with growing hostility from Liberal colleagues. "I was really treated very nicely for the first year or year and a half," she says. "I was, as we say in French, *le mascot du régiment*—the favourite of the caucus. The guys were very patronizing and wanted to teach me everything. But between my first year and the fourth year as a backbencher, things started to deteriorate a lot. And I heard some very, very nasty remarks—either that I was sleeping with Trudeau—which was totally untrue, period—or that I was this or that because I was a woman. There were very nasty remarks about me.

"When I thought about all this after leaving politics, I realized that this deterioration coincided with me being elected vice-president of national caucus, being appointed by Trudeau for a month in New York as the delegate to the United Nations, and being appointed co-chair of the national party convention of 1974—the crucial one, the first vote of confidence on Trudeau's leadership." Bégin learned, like many women before and after her, that she was tolerated and even welcomed as long as she appeared to be a humble student (or mascot). But as soon as she began to rise and gain power on her own, the reaction against her was vicious. Her gender, which had secured her favoured treatment as long as she seemed subordinate, suddenly became a target. Yet Bégin still was expected to face the world as the serenely confident voice of Liberal policy on health care, even during ferocious battles with male ministers in the provinces.

Almost all women MPs, as they walk within the alien culture, adopt some form of protective cloak, whether through weight gain, a clothing style, or a masculine manner. Iona Campagnolo says, "I used to wear bows and ribbons and scarves. It was some months after I was out [of politics] that I began to notice that I was finally taking off the armour with which I had surrounded myself."[11] Some of her armouring was quite intentional: at times she acted tougher than the men, as she once did during a ferocious run-in with an African official during negotiations for the 1978 Commonwealth Games in Edmonton. "This guy was the head of the African Sport Congress," Campagnolo recalls. "I had to take him aside, after being treated dreadfully by him in my own country, and say, 'Listen here, you're a black and I'm a woman and we're both equally being put against, and I won't have you do this to me in public—so back off!' "

At other times, Campagnolo consciously tried to make herself seem bigger than she was. "I would wear very high heels when I was going into battle. I always wanted to have the highest heels possible so I could fight eye to eye with the men. I had some of those heels in which I could barely stand." Author and political activist Maude Barlow notes that only two U.S. presidents have been shorter than the men they defeated; women, she adds, are always looking up to their opponents and the cameras. "It's a very physical reality that many women in politics have to overcome."[12] Campagnolo fought the problem with spiked heels.

Campagnolo's beauty and femininity were impossible to disguise, so the alien culture had to find other ways to demean her. Despite her obvious intelligence and refinement, she was often portrayed by other ministers as some kind of West Coast barbarian on the loose in Ottawa. (She represented the Prince Rupert area riding of Skeena.) "The lady with the hobnailed boots, that's what they called me. Or dragon lady. They would act as if I went home on weekends and shot grizzly bears. There was always sort of an audible sigh when I chose the correct silver, as if I was unfinished."

Trudeau surprised the country in 1976 by naming her minister of fitness and amateur sport. The job seemed so bizarre for this unathletic female that today it's hard to resist the conclusion that Trudeau was having a little joke with her. "I recall the day very well," she says. "I went in and he said I was getting Fitness and Amateur Sport. I laughed out loud and said, 'I'm a hothouse flower. What on earth would you want me to do that for?' And he said, 'Sport is totally dominated by men, and if you can go in there and set an example, you can probably begin the process of changing the dynamic within.' He was always so logical, you know."

On the way to her swearing-in, Campagnolo heard a male radio announcer ask slyly, "But is she fit for sport?" It was the first of many trials in a post where the odour of the locker room was more familiar than the scent of perfume. But Campagnolo made the best of the peculiar assignment. "It was a tiny little portfolio, but I went back to the old actor's guide, which says there are no small parts, only small actors." Within a year, largely because of her energy and ability, she was one of the most famous ministers in Trudeau's cabinet. The prime minister's little joke had a handsome political payoff; he could boast of a high-profile female minister, but she had very little real power in the government. "Intellectually, Mr. Trudeau was committed to feminist ideals," Campagnolo says. "But the part about him that's never really concentrated upon enough is his Roman Catholicism, which is extremely deep. Had he not been what he was, he might more successfully have been a Jesuit. That's the style of man he was, and of course that colours a large part of his responses."

Years later, in 1984, Trudeau coaxed Céline Hervieux-Payette into taking an equally junior job, the Youth portfolio, with the original argument that she was saving him from rapacious men. "When we created that department I refused it the first time," says Hervieux-Payette. "And Trudeau phoned me back and said, 'Please, Céline, I have seven men who would like to have the job, and you would do me a favour by accepting it. The fact that you are a woman and you have children—this is going to really be very helpful to me. We'll stop the war with all these males who see themselves in cabinet.'"[13] Hervieux-Payette accepted and moved into Youth from Campagnolo's old post, Fitness and Amateur Sport. Trudeau was showing his puckish side again, but his belated attempt to woo the youth vote came to nothing; less than nine months later Mulroney's Tories crushed the Liberals, newly led by John Turner, in the 1984 election.

Today, Campagnolo is a committed feminist who admits to feeling angry at the way she was treated both within the government and sometimes by her own party. Like Bégin, she finds that her conviction grows deeper as the years go by. And she wishes she had fully understood back then that her problems were cultural, not political.

"In my time, women were always incredibly underestimated as to our abilities, training, background, our talent for devising strategy or tactics. Because we were aliens—real aliens, if we'd come from another planet we couldn't have been more alien—our culture, our lifestyle, our life history, which is totally different, causes us to act in a different way. For men, used to the ways of the boardroom and the backrooms of politics, we seem to be utterly uncontrollable."[14]

During much of this time, the only female in the national Conservative caucus was the redoubtable Flora MacDonald, a woman so convinced of conservative principles that she simply soldiered on, either ignoring the walls of party prejudice or smashing through them. Before she was elected for the riding of Kingston and the Islands in 1972, MacDonald was executive secretary of the Progressive Conservative Party for five years and national secretary of the PC Association for three years. She lost the first post when John Diefenbaker fired her for organizing a review of his leadership, and gained the second after Robert Stanfield, with MacDonald running his campaign, replaced Diefenbaker.

Despite all that evidence of skill, many Tories saw MacDonald as a good sport, but basically a party worker—until she actually won a riding. MacDonald recalls, "In a sense I came to be taken for granted. People forgot that I was a woman."[15] A male Conservative put it even more bluntly: "Flora was well liked. She was a drinking buddy, but she was, well, a secretary. We didn't think of her as a politician."

Very soon, they did. A slim, commanding woman who knew how to make her voice carry, MacDonald was an adept critic of Liberal policy in the Commons, as she hounded Jean Chrétien, then the minister of Indian and Northern Affairs. But Native leaders needed plenty of convincing before they would accept a female advocate. "Stanfield never had any hangups about women, one way or another," MacDonald remembers. "But if there was a no-no department for women, it was Indian and Northern Affairs. . . . One or two heads of aboriginal organizations went to see Stanfield and said, 'You have insulted us tremendously: you have appointed a woman to this portfolio. We're going to hold a press conference to denounce it.' Stanfield was taken aback. He asked them not to hold the press conference but to wait for three months and if I hadn't performed well he'd move me someplace else. It totally went against their traditions. The reason I heard this story at all was that [native leader] George Manuel told it a year later, saying, 'She's the best critic we've ever had.' By putting me in there, Stanfield broke the tradition of where women could go."

When Stanfield decided to quit after losing two elections, MacDonald made a run for the Tory leadership. She had many hundreds of friends in the party and imagined that she had a chance to win. Looking back now, she realizes that the times weren't yet right for a woman leader. For one thing, talented B.C. politician Rosemary Brown had failed to capture the NDP leadership in 1975 after mounting a strong challenge to Ed Broadbent.[16] According to MacDonald, "The idea that a woman would even try for the leadership was shock enough. That alone was a real breakthrough. But the idea that I would come into it and suddenly have headlines saying it's going to be a coronation couldn't have been contemplated by the farthest stretch of the imagination."

Canada was seventeen years away from Kim Campbell, yet the gap in perception seemed like a century. "Recently I was looking at some copies of speeches I was making at that time, in 1975," MacDonald adds. "I was speaking to the Toronto Women's Real Estate Board about the difficulties of women in politics. I said, 'The day we will move toward equality will be when I see a woman read the national news on the CBC.' The time was as far away as that. There were no women prominent in the media, no women university presidents, no women in key commercial and financial positions. There were no prominent women even in cabinet."

Many Tories promised to support MacDonald at the convention in 1976, but when voting day came, she received only 214 of more than 2,000 votes cast. Then she took her support to Joe Clark, who beat out Brian Mulroney. MacDonald's weak performance was blamed on "the Flora Syndrome"—people promising to support a woman in public, but casting their ballots for a male favourite in private. Without doubt, MacDonald did very poorly, especially among Tory women. "The difficult part was to get women to support me," she says. "Up until that time women had never seen another woman in a key position. There weren't that many women who had persevered and won in politics. Since women hadn't had the opportunity of seeing other women there . . . they couldn't relate a positive to some other woman. So I had less women supporting me than I had men. This has changed tremendously. Kim Campbell was the beneficiary of a lot of women having tried and made it at the provincial level or federal level and shown that they can handle it."

Joe Clark still isn't sure if Tories voted against MacDonald simply because she was a woman, or if their reasons were more complex. "Every candidate has people wearing their colours who aren't voting for them," Clark said. "People back away from frankness. I think that for some people who wanted to be considered ahead of their time, Flora's campaign was considered the place to be. Yet they were not prepared at the end of the day for whatever reason, maybe gender, maybe something else, to vote for Flora."[17]

Award-winning filmmaker Peter Raymont, who documented MacDonald's leadership run, was hoping to do the same with Kim Campbell's until her organizers balked. "The last thing we want is the filmmaker who did the Flora Syndrome," they told him nervously. Raymont feels that "Flora would have been a much stronger candidate in 1993 than Kim Campbell. She would have run a better campaign, and would have done a better job. Flora advanced the women's movement, while Kim set it back. Kim had a certain arrogance while Flora had a slight vulnerability. Kim didn't lose because she was a woman, but Flora did. And it's amazing how many women voted against her."[18]

MacDonald's campaign had one lasting effect on Canadian politics: it made people aware that women could aspire seriously to party leadership. Flora MacDonald broke the trail that Kim Campbell would follow to the leadership in 1993.

In 1979, Joe Clark's Conservatives won a minority government that lasted only 259 days before the Liberals, with Pierre Trudeau hoisted out of retirement, beat them again.[19] It was a time of intense regional rivalry over rising oil prices and a looming independence referendum in Quebec. Women's issues were very low on the public's agenda, but Clark, to his credit, considered them important anyway, although he had only two women MPs to work with: MacDonald and Diane Stratas from Toronto. (Jean Pigott, who had won an Ottawa riding in a 1976 by-election, was defeated in the 1979 general election.)

Clark's most striking gesture was to appoint MacDonald his secretary of state for external affairs. She became the first woman to run a "hard" portfolio dealing with conflicts that are usually handled (or mishandled) by men. In the brief period women had been in cabinet—just twenty-two years—only five had served, always in "soft" roles such as health, communications, or sport. In international terms, Clark's move was even more striking: MacDonald was the only female foreign relations minister in the world. The choice felt natural to him, he recalls. "In 1979, Flora just seemed, of the people who were available for that position, the best there was." He caught some flak from John Diefenbaker but feels the animosity "had more to do with personality than with gender." Together, MacDonald and Clark quickly sent Jean Casselman Wadds to London as High Commisioner, making her Canada's first female ambassador.

As Canada's top diplomat, MacDonald soon realized that she was loose in a man's world. She turned down an invitation to visit Saudi Arabia because "I refused to go there as an honorary man. Not on your life! They wouldn't accept me as a woman, so I wouldn't go as *not* a woman." Only three weeks after being sworn in, MacDonald learned how cultural differences between men and women can cause problems abroad. During a trip to Japan, she recalls, "I was royally treated. At the end, the foreign minister accompanied us to the airport. There was a picture showing Joe Clark very properly shaking his hand. I had thrown my arms around the foreign minister and kissed him. In Japan you don't do that. So this ran on their TV." While she was visiting Cameroon in West Africa, a Canadian diplomat made a career-threatening mistake by asking MacDonald, his boss, to wait in a room with the women. MacDonald froze for a moment and then said, "That plane turns around and goes back to Canada—and you're on it."[20]

Many women who have worked with Joe Clark describe him as highly supportive and unthreatened by their presence in powerful positions. In his many years in political office he simply assumed that female colleagues were equal, and treated them with dignity and respect. The former prime minister credits his mother, and his childhood in rural Alberta. "I grew up in High River during the war," he said, "and while the men were off fighting, the women ran the town, the businesses, everything. I think that is the case in agricultural communities; there has been a sharing of labour, if not always of the rewards. So I was used to seeing women in these roles." As prime minister, he was startled by the absence of women in high positions. "When I first convened my deputy ministers in 1979," he remembers, "Sylvia Ostry was out of town, so there was not a woman in the room. She was the only female deputy. She was regarded as an exception, as 'Sylvia' more than anything else."

Clark's casual acceptance of women as equals led him into one of the most damaging controversies of his career. Many conservative Canadians were offended because his wife, Maureen McTeer, continued to use her family name. "Both Maureen and I were surprised by the outcry," Clark recalls. "She had done it not particularly for feminist reasons—she was just proud of her father. *The Globe and Mail* did a three-week investigative study to see whether she had ever used my name. They thought it was a calculated thing, that maybe we'd done a poll or something." The fuss might seem ridiculous today, but some observers felt that because of it, Clark was forever branded a wimp by many Canadian voters, including women.[21]

In a subtle way, McTeer had breached the public–private barrier by refusing to subordinate herself meekly to her husband. "It was ludicrous," says Audrey McLaughlin. "The image was that he didn't have control. You have to give him credit. He swallowed it with very good grace. I don't recall him ever making a comment that wasn't supportive."[22]

Clark didn't have time as prime minister to do very much for women, but the reborn government of Pierre Trudeau, elected in 1980, reluctantly produced the greatest breakthrough in modern times. In a few short months of fierce lobbying, Canadian women achieved what their American sisters have failed to do despite sixty years of effort: force an equal rights amendment into the national constitution. The chance came when Trudeau pledged to bring the constitution home from Great Britain after Quebec voted "No" to independence in the 1980 referendum. Trudeau saw the exercise as a way to make Quebec feel at home in Canada; women viewed it as their one opportunity to make *themselves* feel comfortable in their country. They seized the moment.

The old Bill of Rights, enshrined by John Diefenbaker's Tory government in 1960, had proved virtually useless in protecting women from discrimination. When Trudeau promised a Charter of Rights and Freedoms as part of his package, many women were eager to correct that mistake. In 1980, the National Action Committee on the Status of Women, and many of its member groups, made concrete suggestions in committee hearings. (The chairman, Liberal Senator Harry Hayes, infuriated them by asking who would look after the children while "you girls were out running the country.")

In response to this pressure, Justice Minister Jean Chrétien offered to amend Section 15 of the constitution to say: "Every individual is equal before and under the law and has the right to equal protection of the law and equal benefit of the law." But women activists, still uneasy, wanted more explicit guarantees, and their suspicions seemed justified when the government cancelled a crucial meeting of the Canadian Advisory Council on the Status of Women. Most women on the Council complied with the demand (they were Liberal appointees, after all), but president Doris Anderson surprised everyone by quitting. Very quickly, furious women formed the Ad Hoc Committee of Canadian Women on the Constitution, and pledged to hold the meeting as planned. It went ahead on the date originally set— Valentine's Day—but was no love letter to Trudeau and his government. The anger and determination of delegates drove home the message that women would not be shoved aside.[23]

In April 1981, after continuing uproar and national publicity, the government produced Section 28, which stated: "Notwithstanding anything in this Charter, the rights and freedoms referred to in it are guaranteed equally to male and female persons."[24] It was a satisfying moment, considering that little more than sixty years earlier women had not been considered persons at all.

But the women hadn't counted on the provincial premiers, all male, who were more concerned about their local powers than anybody's individual rights. At a federal–provincial meeting that excluded Quebec, the premiers worked on a deal that would allow them to override the Charter guarantees with short-term legislation. The hard-won Section 28 was deemed so trivial that it wasn't even discussed. This casual insult led to what Sheila Copps, then an Ontario MPP, called "an explosion of all-party activity, the likes of which I have never seen before or since. . . . Etched in my mind was a meeting (in Toronto) organized on very short notice. . . . The room was packed. The stage was peopled by more than a dozen representatives from across the political spectrum. Liberals, Conservatives, New Democrats and non-party women were there, seeking consensus on the most important political debate that would face our generation. Were we going to sit back and allow a couple of male premiers to railroad through a constitution which denied basic equality to the majority of people in our country? A resounding 'No.'"[25] The nationwide campaign of phone calls and petitions was so overwhelming that the premiers relented: when the constitution was finally patriated, it included a guarantee of equality that could not be overturned. Women had the added pleasure of seeing Sterling Lyon, the Tory premier of Manitoba who was the Charter's most adamant critic, defeated at the polls while the talks were still going on. The revised constitution was proclaimed on April 17, 1982.

For Canadian women, this change was every bit as important as the winning of the vote in the early years of the century. The new Charter brought almost immediate changes in law and practice that affected women. The Indian Act was modified to put Native women on the same footing as men. The Canadian Forces allowed women to join, and the Supreme Court invalidated the old abortion law in 1988. For the first time, provinces and the federal Parliament had to ask whether there was anti-female bias in the laws they proposed. American women still have no such specific protections, which leads political scientist Manon Tremblay to conclude that "in many ways, the situation of Canadian women can be compared quite favorably to that of American women."[26] Gloria Steinem, the celebrated American feminist, enthusiastically agrees. "You've pioneered so many things," she said during an appearance in Toronto. "There is a greater degree of justice for women on this side of the border than on my side of the border."

The major benefits of the Charter battle were both political and psychological. "It politicized and mobilized many women who had not been associated with the women's movement," says political scientist Janine Brodie. "For them, it seemed incredible that Canadian politicians were at first unwilling to endorse an equal-rights clause; and then, after endorsing it, were willing to barter it away to achieve a constitutional agreement." The leadership of the women's movement, Brodie continues, learned how to play hardball—to draw on personal networks, to pressure unwilling politicians, and to mobilize its constituency.[27]

Most important, women knew that there were now no reasons to deny them equality, only excuses. Over the next decade, as they continued to storm the gates of Canadian politics, they would make more progress than they had in the previous half-century. Finally, there would be enough women in political life to begin changing the alien culture that Monique Bégin and her female colleagues had found so crushing.

7

BORN-AGAIN BRIAN

"I became a one-man affirmative action course."
Brian Mulroney
on appointing women to his government

I n his younger days, Brian Mulroney was a creature of the male-dominated backrooms and boardrooms, as sexist as the next cigar-smoking Scotch-drinker. Mulroney admits this. "I wasn't a great feminist when I was young," the former prime minister laughs. "I was as obtuse as ninety-nine per cent of Canadian males."[1] He allowed his lively libido free rein among the co-eds at university, and when he first spotted Mila Pivnicki in a bikini by a swimming pool, he said, "That's for me," set down his cool summer drink, and began the pursuit. Mila was just eighteen, and Brian was a fast-talking thirty-three-year-old lawyer with unlimited ambition and the world on a string.[2]

Yet this standard-issue Canadian male, when he became prime minister years later, did more to advance women politically than any other leader in our history. His motives were pragmatic in part, for he saw the growing influence—and anger—of 51 per cent of the population. But they were also tempered with genuine friendship and goodwill toward female MPs, ministers, and bureaucrats. The truth is that Brian Mulroney did what thousands of Canadian women wish the men in their lives would do: he became aware of a problem with his attitude, and he changed it.

Mulroney did not undergo this conversion spontaneously; he was led to it by various female friends and colleagues. Both before and after his first election victory in 1984, they sat him down and educated him in the realities of women in modern society and politics. Mulroney was a willing student, but, by all accounts, he had plenty to learn. Recalls Pat Carney, the veteran Mulroney minister and now a senator, "This was not something that was natural to Brian Mulroney. I admire him for that. This was something he took on, even though the leader we elected really was a chauvinist. He didn't have any feeling for these issues. And yet he learned them; he learned the issues.

"When he started, Flora [MacDonald] was the one who had to coach him in the debates on women's issues. She had to try to sensitize him to what women's concerns were. And he had a hard time with it. It was foreign to him. It wasn't in his nurturing or background." MacDonald echoes this thought: "Mulroney was brought to the recognition, and I'll give him full marks for that. With Joe Clark it was natural. He didn't need to be told. That was part of Joe's make-up, his upbringing, his own home environment."

But Mulroney was always eager to be liked and admired, and various women convinced him that one way to do it (and perhaps to do the right thing as well) was by taking up the cause of women. He was heavily influenced in this by his wife, Mila; by veteran Tory MP and worker Jean Pigott; by Flora MacDonald; by his daughter, Caroline; by Senator Marjory LeBreton, then his assistant; by LeBreton's sister, Kay Stanley; by Janis Johnson, national director of the party and later a senator;

and by Jocelyn Côté-O'Hara, his advisor on women's policy during the 1984 campaign.

Stanley and Côté-O'Hara created a two-hour teaching package on women's issues, which was used at the PC Party's campaign school for candidates. In June 1984, Mulroney asked Côté-O'Hara and MacDonald to give "training sessions" to the full caucus. Côté-O'Hara recalled later: "We covered women's organizations, language to use around women, the meaning of the gender gap, and major issues. And the Whip took attendance. I think the MPs were better equipped afterwards. Some were already in the 20th century, and some were still in the Dark Ages."[3]

Mulroney, to give him credit, relished his unexpected role as the champion of women. But he had another motive that Flora MacDonald spotted when she was "tutoring" him. "I remember going with Brian Mulroney to a number of meetings sponsored by women," she recalls. "And he began to see the tremendous power that these groups were acquiring. They may have had numbers before but they hadn't tried to exercise power. By 1984, they certainly did. Coming out of the constitutional fight [to recognize equality for women], women had achieved a sense of power that they could change things."

Mulroney always had a shrewd sense of where power resided, and how to court it. Even before the election campaign began, he moved quickly to improve the status of women within his own party. In 1983, soon after he became Conservative leader, he named Westerner Janis Johnson to be the first woman to serve as national director of the PC Party. "It was quite a thing for him to do to pluck me out of western Canada and put me in as national director," Johnson says. "It pretty well shocked the caucus and the backroom boys. It was a very strong message that his intentions with regard to women were going to remain firm. One of the first things he had me do was set up an advisory council of women across Canada who could help him in the process that later appointed women to boards, agencies, commissions, the Senate—and any other appointments he could make of qualified women. He followed through on that promise to an incredible extent. In some cases against tremendous pressure from men."[4]

During the 1984 election campaign, the National Action Committee on the Status of Women and their president, Chaviva Hosek, staged a tremendous coup by convincing the major party leaders to debate women's issues on national television. The choices did not seem very appealing: women could cast their lot with Mulroney, NDP leader Ed Broadbent, or Liberal leader and prime minister John Turner, the locker-room hero who would pat Iona Campagnolo's bottom during a campaign rally. During the debate, the three leaders bent over backwards to portray themselves as loyal soldiers in the feminist cause. They may as well have been part of a Monty Python skit extolling the virtues of Spam. The most memorable line of the evening went to panelist Kay Sigurjonsson, who asked, "With your dismal records, why should we trust you now?"

The debate showed that male leaders felt it necessary to court the "women's vote," but it also illustrated, in the most graphic way possible, that women still had to ask them for help. Yet the debate was undoubtedly a breakthrough. In the fifty-eight years since women had won the vote, this was the first time the party leaders—still all male—seriously attempted to understand what women were talking about.

At an auditorium in Ottawa, 400 women watched the debate on TV and then graded the men: they awarded a B+ to Broadbent and a "gentleman's C" to Turner and Mulroney.[5] These results reflected the NDP's more progressive policy on women, but Broadbent's performance produced relatively few votes for his party on election day, when the Tories won 211 seats and the largest majority to that point in Canadian history. Whatever else might be said of Brian Mulroney, he kept his promise to begin raising women toward numerical equality in federal politics. Mulroney feels that he became, in his own words, "a one-man affirmative action course."

Mulroney was "prepared to take risks," recalls Barbara McDougall, whom he named minister of state for finance in

1984. "He didn't know me if I crawled out from under his desk. He knew I was active in the party at the riding level, that's all. I think it was the same with a great many of the other women he put in the cabinet. He took risks with his new members. Sometimes it cost him, not just in the case of Suzanne Blais-Grenier,[6] but with some of the men as well."[7]

Usually Mulroney had some firm basis for his decisions; McDougall, for instance, came to Parliament from a successful career in the financial industry. Mulroney wasn't put off by her image as a salty talker who smoked slender cigars. (At a huge roast for John Crosbie, attended by Mulroney, Chrétien, and even René Lévesque, McDougall leaned forward and said seductively into the microphone: "John Crosbie . . . What can I say about John? I mean, what a body."[8])

Mulroney began with the most visible institution of all—his own cabinet. In 1984, when only 9 per cent of all federal MPs were women, six of his twenty-nine cabinet ministers (21 per cent) were female. After the 1988 election, seven of thirty-four ministers were women—again 21 per cent of the cabinet, at a time when only 13 per cent of all MPs in the House of Commons were women. In both 1984 and 1988, Mulroney appointed one-third or more of all the women elected as Tories to his cabinet. (Nineteen elected in 1984 and twenty-one in 1988.)

He also shattered the dubious tradition, established by Pierre Trudeau, of naming women only to "soft" cabinet portfolios such as Health or Sport. Mulroney gave Pat Carney first the Energy portfolio, then International Trade at a crucial time in negotiations with the United States on free trade. He also made her the first female president of the Treasury Board, the powerful department that controls internal spending. McDougall, after serving as minister of state responsible for financial institutions, took on Privatization and, later, External Affairs. (Flora MacDonald, appointed by Joe Clark, had been the first woman in that prestigious post.) Monique Vézina was minister for external relations. Kim Campbell became Canada's first female justice minister, later the first woman in Defence, and she appeared at one time to be

Mulroney's choice to succeed him, although he strongly denies it today.

"Kim Campbell was an excellent minister, and that's why I promoted her as quickly as I did," says Mulroney. "I did *not* put just her in for the leadership. I put a whole flock there: Michael Wilson; Barbara McDougall; Kim Campbell whom I moved out of Justice because it's not a leadership portfolio, it's kind of a huggy, feely, one, and into Defence; and Jean Charest." Mulroney still placed some women in the "soft" positions; Andrée Champagne was Mulroney's first secretary of state for youth. But in the main, he gave women jobs that really counted.

He also began a determined push to increase the number of women in government. Although he could not bring in more women than were elected to the House of Commons, he had immense power to change the hundreds of appointments made at the discretion of cabinet or his office. Mulroney resolved to raise the level of women's participation in all areas controlled directly by government—including boards, commissions, and agencies—to 30 per cent. "All of these appointments would come in," he recalls. "On a given day you might get one hundred. We'd look at the list in cabinet, and sometimes there would only be three women. I would say 'I'm not going to approve only three women on this list.' I'd tell cabinet to find women or I would find cabinet ministers who *can* do that. Guess what? They started to find talented women everywhere."

In little more than a year, the percentage of women appointed to these federal bodies more than doubled from 15 per cent to 32 per cent. There was progress in several crucial areas of the civil service, including that male bastion, External Affairs. In 1984, there were only two women among 118 foreign ambassadors and consuls-general. By 1993, the figure had risen to 18 out of 120. This may not seem impressive, but in the patriarchal world of the foreign service, where some countries still refuse to acknowledge women in official positions, the advance was substantial.

"We needed somebody for the United Nations," Mulroney recalls. "That was then the top appointment. They gave me a list of five people—every old boy in the network. I said, 'What about Louise Frechette? What's wrong with her?' I said, 'Either you call her or I will.' It was Sunday evening and I was just driving back from Harrington Lake. I was in my car and I called her and asked if she'd like a new assignment. And she said that would be nice. 'How about the UN?' I asked. 'Holy Jesus,' she replied, and just about fell over."

In the same period, the number of women serving as deputy ministers or equivalents rose from seven to twenty-two. The total number of female judges appointed by Ottawa jumped from 37 to 118, and many were named to Courts previously cool to women jurists: provincial Appeal Courts, the Tax Court of Canada, and the Federal Court. And Mulroney named more women than any previous prime minister to the Supreme Court. "I appointed women in every kind of position in Ottawa in non-traditional appointments. Today we would have had three or possibly four women on the Supreme Court. I was turned down by one because her husband was sick. . . .

"The system in Ottawa discriminates against women, which is why I discriminated in *favour* of women," he says. "How could I go out and make speeches about fairness and justice when 50 per cent are treated unfairly by government—as an employer and in the House of Commons and in the Courts? So I made appointments and decisions to try to change that. Not because I expected thanks or applause but because I thought it was right."

Some of his appointments, of course, were pure patronage: for example, Margaret McGrath, wife of former Tory MP Jim McGrath, became deputy commissioner of the Canada Pension Plan Review Tribunal. Other appointments were temporary: after boasting of Judith Maxwell's appointment to chair the Economic Council of Canada, the Tories abolished the Council along with her job. Yet it's abundantly clear that under Mulroney's Tory regime, the number of women in government grew at an unprecedented rate.[9]

Flora MacDonald knows how important a female presence can be when the government confronts problems that relate to women. "If you're trying to get a decision through in cabinet and caucus—cabinet, in particular—you know that unless you've got the bureaucracy with you, your efforts will be defeated. It was always very important to have a number of key women in other departments to whom I could explain what we were trying to do and how it would impact on Transport or on Finance or whatever." When MacDonald was a minister in Joe Clark's government, she had precious few female bureaucrats to call upon (and as Clark pointed out, only one deputy minister, Sylvia Ostry).

Another influential figure in Mulroney's drive to promote women was Marjory LeBreton. She worked closely with Mulroney through this period, first as a campaign toiler, then as the person responsible for government appointments, finally as his deputy chief of staff. Before leaving office in 1993, he made her a senator. It's hardly surprising that LeBreton is one of Mulroney's most ardent boosters; but as a Tory feminist, she has some good reasons.

"When the prime minister won the leadership in 1983 and then the government in 1984," LeBreton says, "he made some very definite commitments to women in the party. There were positive signs right after he won the leadership. For instance, he was very conscious of the national campaign organization and he was upset that women weren't in as major a role as he would have liked. . . . Then, when he formed the government and named women to the cabinet and started working with them, he became even more comfortable. Because of his business and legal background in Quebec, this was a new experience for him. But he was never uncomfortable with it and became more aware of the importance of the appointments process to get more women in government."[10]

LeBreton says that when he put her in charge of appointments in 1986, with a special mandate to advance women, "I could not have done it if he had not at cabinet literally made me count the number of women and the percentages. Often times at cabinet, people would be putting forth names and he'd say 'unless you come back with women, forget about your list.'" Pat Carney adds: "What Brian Mulroney did was set specific goals—it had to be 30 per cent women. Nothing could come to the cabinet table without a 30 per cent limit. . . . One of the crucial things we learned in the task was that you have to have a critical mass before you get gender neutrality in decision-making. If there's only one woman, she is expected to be the spokesperson for day care, women's rights, and employment equity regardless of her background. That was the role that Flora was put into." (And Judy LaMarsh and Ellen Fairclough before her.)

Mulroney supported Carney's plan, when she was president of the Treasury Board, to conduct the first detailed study of women in the federal civil service. The result was the four-volume task force report called *Beneath the Veneer*, which outlined the staggering problems still faced by women who want to be promoted.[11] Carney says she got the idea through her own experience in various departments. "Often there were no women in the room, and when I would ask my deputy minister where the women were, they were not even at the entry level. And I looked into that. I asked, 'Where are the women?' We wrote a whole report on the answers we got. So we made a major attempt to advance women in the public service. And it's finally happening. We're starting to get the critical mass that's necessary." (Many academic experts agree that when 15 per cent of a group is female, they are taken seriously; when the number reaches 30 per cent, they can have a major impact.)

LeBreton found Mulroney endlessly sympathetic to these ambitions. "I'd talk to him as easily as I talked to my sister [Kay Stanley]," she says. "During hot debates such as the abortion debate, I would sit and tell him the incidents that happened when I was a teen-ager going to high school with friends of mine. He was like most men. He just wished it would go away. But he came to understand the issue. . . . I felt totally comfortable telling him how I felt about it. I've worked with four party leaders and I've never been as comfortable as a woman working with a political organization as I have been with him. He gave me a confidence in myself that I didn't even know that I possessed."

LeBreton credits Mila Mulroney for much of his positive attitude toward women in politics, a perception at odds with her image as a world-class shopper without much interest in women's concerns. "Mila has a very big influence on him. She has some definite views and they are certainly not subservient, even though the left always tried to portray her that way." LeBreton says Mulroney also respects the views of his daughter, Caroline. "She's very bright, and being his only daughter and his oldest child, she'll make her feelings known. He has a lot of time for her opinions."

But Mulroney's cabinet and government, although they were huge improvements over anything before them, were still far from the promised land. Women had more influence and more ability to "network," but they were still vulnerable to the old prejudices, although these were expressed in more subtle forms. Joe Clark tells a fascinating story of how, when the slugging got tough in the Mulroney cabinet, stereotypes would be pinned on the women: "There was still a very powerful double standard around the cabinet table," he says. "You notice prejudice in extreme times. We had some really intense debates about the free trade agreement in cabinet. There was one time when a meeting started in the afternoon and went on to midnight until somebody had the good sense to adjourn it.

"During a long, intense meeting like that, everybody says something a little silly. That night, Flora, Pat, and Barbara were among the ministers who said something a little silly. A number of other ministers who were not female said even sillier things. But there was a dismissiveness of the silly statements made by the three women that did not attach to the others. I think the fact that we have women holding senior portfolios does not mean they are yet equals."[12] Barbara McDougall saw the double standard from an even more bizarre angle. "We had more phone calls to my constituency office about my hair during the free frade debate than we did on free trade itself," she recalls.

Yet from time to time, just because there were more women in cabinet, they found themselves in charge of the battlements with no men scaling the heights. Mary Collins, who was associate defence minister and minister responsible for the status of women, recalls the forbidden thrill. "The Foreign Affairs and Defense Committee was chaired by Barbara McDougall as secretary of state for external affairs. I was there as associate defence minister, and often Marcel Masse (the defence minister) would not be there. So I would carry that portfolio, and Monique Landry would be there as minister responsible for CIDA (the Canadian International Development Agency). Often it would just be three of us at those meetings. That was real change, for women to be dealing with foreign affairs and defence issues."[13] Later in Mulroney's government, the same roles would be filled by McDougall, Kim Campbell (as full defence minister), and Monique Vézina. For brief moments, women had the access and influence necessary to make major decisions in a critical area.

In the Mulroney years, foreigners suddenly began to notice Canadian women in these high-profile international roles. Many times, however, their reactions showed little change from the days when Flora MacDonald met with blank incomprehension on her foreign trips. In January 1991, Mary Collins, unlike MacDonald before her, went to Saudi Arabia, as well as to Bahrain, Qatar, and Dubai, as associate defence minister. With the Gulf War looming and Canada a firm ally, the Saudis tripped over themselves to provide exotic courtesies, but they were still deeply confused.

"I was wondering, how would they cope with a woman defence minister?" Collins laughs. "Actually, I think they did it by pretending I was a man. But I was on TV, I was in the newspapers—they gave me the full treatment. Of course they were so thankful for our military involvement. My gift was this fantastic automatic machine gun. The question is, what was I going to do with it? You can't say; 'Sorry, I'm not into machine guns.' . . . So I gave it to the RCMP and they had it for quite a while."

Collins once found herself trapped on a U.S. aircraft carrier, the only woman among 5,000 men. (Completely unimpressed by military jargon, she calls it "a ship for planes.") "We flew out from Shearwater and we were just going to be there for two hours," Collins says. "So I took nothing with me. I didn't bring my coat, my purse—nothing at all. We went up and saw the exercises and it was great fun. But a huge storm came up, a mammoth North Atlantic storm, actually quite scary because they were trying to get all the planes back down. There was a tanker in front of us that turned the wrong way, and the aircraft carrier —it was the USS *Saratoga*—almost rammed it. The weather just kept getting worse and worse, so we ended up having to stay aboard. Here was I, the one woman among 5,000 men. . . . The captain gave me his cabin, and he had armed marines at the door. I wasn't too sure whether it was to keep them from coming in or to keep me from going out. I learned my lesson. That's the last time I go anywhere without my lipstick, or my toothbrush or anything else."

As the second female external affairs minister, after Flora MacDonald, Barbara McDougall constantly worked in completely male environments. "I went to a NATO meeting of foreign ministers shortly after I was sworn in," McDougall recalls. "They'd never seen a woman at a NATO meeting before and they were elaborately courteous. They have a photo session before lunch, so I darted into the washroom right beforehand to comb my hair. By the time I got back the picture-taking was practically over. I said to the secretary-general, 'Now listen, you're going to have to make allowances. We always like to straighten ourselves up before we appear before cameras.' The next time there was a decent interlude before the pictures were taken."

Russian leader Boris Yeltsin, McDougall says, "was just outrageous. I always enjoyed him—you have to be ready to have a sense of humour about this stuff. He treated me with a lot of respect; he would always see me if I was in Moscow. We had very substantive conversations. But he loved to flirt, so I'd have to be ready for that."

McDougall recalls that when U.S. president Bill Clinton met Yeltsin for the first time, at a summit in Vancouver arranged by Mulroney, both leaders were a bit uneasy. McDougall was the only woman at a private luncheon for the heads of government and their foreign ministers, when Yeltsin began to tell mildly off-colour jokes. "All his jokes had to be laboriously translated from Russian," she says. "President Clinton didn't know what to make of this. He's very smooth, but even his face was bewildered. And it went on for a few minutes while Yeltsin made his little jokes. . . . He has a good sense of humour, he likes women and he likes to flirt. . . . President Clinton relaxed a bit when he realized that we were all able to deal with it. I don't know what he told his wife when he got home, though."

In the afterglow of their time in Mulroney's government, these women ministers don't talk much about their experiences of sexism in the Tory cabinet and caucus. It had not been many years, after all, since Pat Carney and Flora MacDonald were forced to raise their hands and object when the caucus chairman called everyone "gentlemen." McDougall insists that she "never felt like a second-class minister, not for one moment." One incident, however, suggests she was sometimes treated that way. In 1987, she flew to Edmonton in her capacity as minister of state for privatization to announce a plan to sell off part of Air Canada. When she landed and was just about to meet reporters, she learned that senior ministers had scrapped the plan without telling her.[14] Male ministers sometimes suffer similar embarrassments (including Jean Chrétien when he was a junior member of Pierre Trudeau's cabinet), but women often suspect, with some reason, that their gender makes them especially susceptible.

Pat Carney would use her famous temper to let male colleagues know she wasn't to be trifled with, and today she still has problems with men whose attitudes are frozen in earlier generations. "I sit in the Senate, where women are tolerated at best, and mostly ignored," she says. "Being in the Senate is like being in 1956. Those of us who have been in an unelected Senate would prefer an elected Senate by far—but how do we get there?"

Yet to Carney and McDougall, such episodes seem trivial compared to the political advances women made during the Mulroney years. "I think it is now an advantage to be a woman in politics," McDougall insists. "I think we should all accept that as good. For forty-seven years of my life it was a disadvantage. For nine years it was an advantage. I'll take it, thank you."

Carney feels that women ministers were finally judged only on performance, especially by Mulroney. "The prime minister and I, we developed quite a comfortable working relationship because he quickly understood that we were a team, and I, having run my own business and being a pretty hard-nosed negotiator, knew what he needed to do. I did not come to him as some ministers do and say, 'Well, you know, I've got this problem, and I need $60 million. What do you think?' I would go to him and say, 'This is the situation, these are the three options that I've considered. Do you agree or not agree?' That made it easy for him to say, 'You should look at option four.' I gave him a standard of decision-making, which he utilized. That was important to him. It was often the men who sat at his table and cry-babied and dithered with indecision."

At the quieter committee level, Tory MPs like Toronto member Barbara Greene worked steadily to advance women's causes. As academic Lisa Young has noted, "Women within the Conservative caucus have pushed the government in the direction of gun control legislation, action on violence against women, 'no means no' rape legislation, and increased funding for breast cancer research."[15] But Mulroney was not amused or impressed when some of his MPs, including women, made their internal debates and disagreements on such measures public. Once he told his caucus that "he didn't spend all this time improving the status of women in government to have this kind of difficult press."

Despite these gains for women in senior political positions, however, there's no doubt that the lot of women in Canadian society actually deteriorated during the Mulroney years. Poverty and joblessness increased along with violence against women. (The 1989 massacre of fourteen women in Montreal was only the most horrendous example.) Many women's groups believe that free trade has hurt women more than men by eliminating thousands of the low-paying industrial jobs they occupied. The Tories drastically cut funding for women's groups, battered women's shelters, and Charter of Rights court challenges, many of which involved women's concerns.

Their vaunted plan for a national day-care program, which helped them win the 1988 election, soon drowned in a sea of government red ink and Tory caucus hostility. When Mulroney introduced the bill on August 11, 1988, he pledged, "Child care will be regarded by all Canadians as a fundamental right." After the government was re-elected on November 21, the plan was allowed to slip slowly from public view. As *Toronto Star* columnist Carol Goar wrote later, "It was no secret that many Tory MPs were glad it died. As far as they were concerned, subsidized day care was an unwelcome concession to the feminist lobby."[16] To many critics, it seemed that the Conservative agenda was inherently hostile to women, no matter how many female politicians were able to have a private chat with Brian Mulroney.

Some academics, such as Lise Gottell and Janine Brodie, argue that, paradoxically, the election of more women actually means that less attention is paid to women's problems. The parties tend to recruit highly visible and loyal women who are more interested in the party agenda than in women's issues, and can then point to these trophy politicians as proof of progress while ignoring the real problems. The only solution, Gotell and Brodie claim, is to keep the pressure on by "strengthening a distinct women's constituency in the federal electorate."[17] Judy Rebick, former president of the National Action Committee, states the case more bluntly: "The political system is such a male culture. What happens to women is either they get sidelined within it or they get co-opted into it. It's very difficult not to do one or the other. And there are very few opportunities where women can work together to change things."[18]

Some of the toughest critics of the Tories have been Liberal women such as Chaviva Hosek and Lorna Marsden, both former presidents of NAC. During Mulroney's first term, Hosek blasted the Conservatives for failing to keep their promises to create economic equality for women, and Lorna Marsden, then a Liberal senator, said they were willing to promote women into management while pursuing policies that eliminated jobs for ordinary women. (She cited jobs cuts in the environment department that affected female field staff, but not managers.[19]) Sheila Copps regularly flayed the Tories for their record on women's issues. "It is the Tories who have cut funding for housing for battered women," she charged just before the 1993 election. "It is the Tories who have made a fiasco out of the Royal Commission on Reproductive Technologies . . . and the Conservative cabinet brought in proposals which would make it next to impossible for a sexually harassed woman to quit her job."[20] (She was referring to Unemployment Insurance changes, applying to both women and men, that made it difficult for employees to get benefits unless they had just cause for quitting.)

All those women, and many more, are now influential in the new Liberal government—Copps as deputy prime minister, Hosek as a key policy aide to Prime Minister Chrétien, Marsden as president of Wilfrid Laurier University. These replacements for such Mulroney followers as Barbara McDougall, Marjory LeBreton, and Janis Johnson at the seat of power now have the opportunity to do better for women.

Brian Mulroney, however, is proud of his record and suggests, rather bitterly, that it will be harder than they think. He resents what he perceives to be their double standard. "Pierre Elliott Trudeau, for all those years, didn't do very much at all," he says. "Yet for all this sustained period, he was very fairly treated by women. Then, when I'm prime minister, NAC is all over me. The assumption was that you couldn't have any moral fibre if you weren't socialist or Liberal."[21]

In the end, Mulroney was a conservative politician who believed in numerical equality, and even in "discriminating" to achieve it, but he was never enthusiastic about implementing social policies that bettered the lot of disadvantaged groups, including women. Mulroney also faced a good deal of quiet opposition from Tory men in his caucus even to his goal of increasing the number of women in government. His chief contribution, perhaps, was to begin changing historical assumptions about the role of women in politics and in government. Because of Brian Mulroney (and all the women who pushed him), Canadians grew accustomed to seeing women in top cabinet jobs. He helped create an image that every new prime minister, including Jean Chrétien, will have to live with—and live up to.

8

TRADITIONAL MAN

"I was just sixteen when I met him, and I was already going to listen to his speeches."
                    Aline Chrétien on her husband

"They tend to be more emotional."
                    Jean Chrétien on female politicians

When Iona Campagnolo was a junior minister in the tough world of Pierre Trudeau's caucus and cabinet, she found a good-humoured friend in Jean Chrétien. "If I was speaking in caucus," she recalls, "Jean would sometimes write a note, fold it in tiny little pieces, and then ping it at me. It would say something like: 'You've made your point. Now stop.' Jean Chrétien was my mentor." Campagnolo remembers another Chrétien quality, too: when he is angry, he turns as quiet and chilly as a passing iceberg. "He doesn't shout, he just goes very cold," she says. "He never raises the temperature of the room when he's angry; he lowers it."[1]

By nature and experience, Chrétien is a cautious politician who measures every word, action, and response. Nearly thirty years in Ottawa have taught him that victory goes to politicians who make the fewest mistakes, not to those who score the most spectacular successes. Brian Mulroney, new on the Ottawa scene, tried to be a race horse; Jean Chrétien is content to be a work-horse, slogging his way by slow steps toward a distant goal. "He is a listener," says Alberta senator Joyce Fairbairn, Chrétien's government leader in the Senate. "He encourages debate and argument, but when the time comes, he's ready to make the decisions."[2] Another woman who has worked closely with the prime minister states, "Jean Chrétien is extremely shrewd about people. He can come into a room and make everyone at ease, and yet somehow focus all the attention on himself. As a woman, you're always aware of the fact that he's aware of you. He's very secure with women, because he's very secure with his wife, Aline."[3]

Chrétien's relationships with the women in his life have always been comfortably traditional. The second youngest of Marie and Wellie Chrétien's nineteen children, only nine of whom survived childhood, Chrétien was always determined to excel. Aline Chaine, when she began seeing him at age sixteen, was struck at once by the feeling that this young man was going somewhere. After they married, she encouraged his political ambitions, and he responded with intense loyalty and support for her private role. "He got me involved in what he was doing," she says. "Jean has always made me feel good about it. He said that what I did was very important, even when he was living in Ottawa, and I was in Shawinigan looking after the kids. He would tell people in his office: 'Phone my wife about this, she's going to look after it.' I always felt that I was a part of things."[4]

Today, people who know the Chrétiens insist that he always considers her advice before making major political decisions. It was Aline, for instance, who convinced him to abandon highly scripted speeches and the use of Teleprompters—methods that made him seem stilted and wooden. "I told everybody, 'When he can express himself, he will pass along the right message,'" she says. "I knew, because Jean is a great communicator." A friend of the Chrétiens says they are "like two fingers on the same hand."[5]

"I was just sixteen when I met him," Aline Chrétien laughs, "and I was already going to listen to his speeches. . . . I've always really felt that even if I was not in the limelight, I was part of the team. This is the big thing—to get involved and to be close together. We do the same things and we're ambitious and we want to do things for people."

Jean Chrétien says that he knew very soon, from observing the wreckage of so many parliamentary marriages, how much work was needed to keep one healthy. "I saw some of my colleagues who didn't want to put in the effort to keep their family and they lost it," he says. "It's really easy to do. If your family is back home and you're on the Hill having a drink with the boys and so on, eventually your marriage breaks down. . . . All the families are away and you're a bunch of guys having fun, and eventually you do some crazy things."

"All my career as minister, I would not sleep in Toronto. I would take the last plane to come to sleep at home. I will never sleep in Montreal. I will leave Montreal at one o'clock in the morning and drive to be home at three o'clock, even if I didn't see anybody. If I arrive at five and I don't wake up at seven, the kids will at least know, because the door is closed, that dad is there. I've always done that. Some of my colleagues won't do it. . . . If I'd been Mackenzie King, I would not have had to worry about it. But that's what you do when you have a family."[6]

Chrétien has always kept his family life as far from public view as possible, refusing to use it for political advantage. In his 1985 autobiography, *Straight from the Heart* (re-issued in 1994), two of the Chrétiens' three children are not even mentioned. When he was minister of Indian and Northern Affairs in 1972, the couple quietly adopted a Gwich'in Native, whom they named Michel Chrétien. This was not publicized at the time, and was virtually unknown to the public until 1992, when Michel, after a troubled youth and problems with alcohol, was convicted of sexual assault in Montreal and sentenced to three years in prison. Chrétien was at the trial every day—another fact he did not care to publicize.

All these family and personal experiences combine to form Chrétien's view of women in politics. It is not a feminist view. Chrétien believes that women, like men, should earn their own way without special favours or anything resembling affirmative action. "Most women don't want to succeed because they are women," he says. "They want to succeed because they are good. That is the right attitude." He feels that women in politics work harder than men, but they also "tend to be more emotional."

In an interview, Chrétien bluntly stated his belief that women face no special barriers in politics. From a politician who has confronted just about every hardship except sexism during his thirty-year climb to the top, including humiliation and ridicule in his home province, this comes as no surprise. Chrétien believes women should prove themselves by enduring the tests faced by men. Asked if a woman with several children would have more difficulty running for office than a man, he said, "A very good woman with three kids could run. . . . The problem is how. But if a man had no wife and three kids at home it might be difficult." Reminded that Pierre Trudeau did exactly that, Chrétien continued, "Yeah, but a woman could do the same thing. Trudeau did it. Why couldn't a woman do it? You'd think that the people would say Trudeau had three boys and no wife. Nobody ever referred to that. . . .

"The problem, though, is that sometimes a woman with three kids feels she cannot run. It's the way you look at your family. If the woman thinks she has to be with her kids every day at lunch and dinner, better not to be in politics. But it's the same thing for a man too. A man should not choose politics if he wants to be with his family every weekend and every night of the week. Some put family objectives ahead of their career. . . . But it's good to have a family, I have to tell you. You need an anchor in politics . . . you need other interests than politics. Politics is extremely demanding; and for your brain, it's better to have fresh air into it once in a while than to be in the pressure cooker twenty-four hours a day."

Chrétien's views are apparent in the composition of his government. He will never be what Brian Mulroney proudly called himself: "a one-man affirmative action course." Chrétien is willing to help women to the starting gate in order to increase their numbers so they will achieve the so-called "critical mass" necessary for real influence. But after being elected to his caucus, a woman MP becomes just one of the gang who can expect no special favours because of gender. He is certainly not unfriendly to women in politics; but if they have not yet shown their merit, he isn't about to advance them simply because they are women. When he became prime minister in 1993, with the economy still shaky and special interests in deep disfavour, this was exactly what the majority of Canadians seemed to expect.

Chrétien's first cabinet appointments showed that "gender balance" wasn't high on his priority list. He named only three of the thirty-six female Liberal MPs to his twenty-three-member cabinet. Two were newcomers—Energy Minister Anne McLellan from Alberta, and Health Minister Diane Marleau of Ontario. Marleau was elected in 1988 and impressed as a critic, but Professor McLellan, the acting dean of law at the University of Alberta, had no background in elected politics. (Ironically, it was Marleau who got into deep trouble first, over her quick decision to cut tobacco taxes in order to curb smuggling. Health advocates predicted that over time the measure would cause 250,000 extra deaths.)

Chrétien made history with his other two senior female appointments. Sheila Copps assumed the role of deputy prime minister—the first woman to be appointed to the job. (Women have sometimes been appointed acting prime minister for brief periods; in 1958, Ellen Fairclough held the top post for two days.) Senator Joyce Fairbairn of Alberta, a thirty-four-year veteran of the Ottawa scene, became the first female government leader in the Senate. Chrétien passed over some Commons veterans, including Montreal's Sheila Finestone, Mary Clancy of Halifax, and Western Arctic's Ethel Blondin-Andrew. The omissions caused some controversy: women seemed most concerned that Chrétien had overlooked the able Blondin-Andrew, whose abuse at the hands of her estranged husband hit the headlines in 1993. In the end, the percentage of women in cabinet (just over 17) was almost exactly that of women in the House of Commons (slightly below 18). The numbers are a striking reflection of Chrétien's reluctance to tinker with the views of the voters. Clearly, Chrétien wanted to assemble a cabinet that consisted mostly of seasoned veterans whom he could trust not to make naive mistakes in the first crucial months. After the Kim Campbell misadventure, Chrétien probably judged that the right gender mix in cabinet was a low public priority. In this he was absolutely right; after a few days of relatively mild editorial comment, the issue dropped from sight.

This attitude might look like a retreat from the days when Mulroney aggressively promoted women, but to Joyce Fairbairn, it was a decided improvement over her early days in Ottawa politics. In the 1960s, the Lethbridge native was the *Ottawa Journal*'s "only female newsman"—the first woman to cover politics full-time on Parliament Hill. The sight of a female reporter was so novel that during the 1963 election campaign, tour organizers wondered aloud if they'd have to carry her luggage. The Liberal "wagonmaster" told her to show up for a bus a half-hour ahead of time, then made sure it pulled out thirty minutes before that—just to test her. Fairbairn took a cab to the campaign event, and later became good friends with her tormentor.

"To the credit of both Pearson and Diefenbaker, they said I should have the same access as the men," Fairbairn recalls. "But my mom was still worried by my chosen career. She thought, 'It's not just journalism, but *political* journalism!' She envisioned these smoke-filled rooms with men slugging back the Scotch and leering at me with lustful thoughts. The truth was that women simply didn't get into those places."[7]

Fairbairn, an avid builder of networks, left journalism in 1970 to become a legislative assistant and press aide to Pierre Trudeau. When the separatist FLQ kidnapped British diplomat James Cross in Quebec, Fairbairn found herself working closely with her new, intimidating boss, about whom she had once written some unflattering stories. "Our working relationship was defined by that crisis," Fairbairn says. "At one point he said to me, 'Let's keep on getting the job done during this time, and we'll figure out later if we get along.'" They did. Fairbairn stayed with Trudeau until 1984. He made her a senator just before he left office.

When she first took the job with Trudeau, Fairbairn says, "it was like going back in time. . . . There were no women advisors, no women in the upper echelons of government, because there was no history of women parliamentarians. I had the brutal sense of the struggle that lay ahead. It was an entrenched process of the old boys' network. I spent the first summer working feverishly to set up networks of my own." Trudeau wanted to move women into the corridors of power, Fairbairn feels, "but the mechanisms just weren't there."

Now, she says, "it thrills me to see the number of women around. We have a critical mass in the caucus room. It is a spirited caucus now, with old-timers like myself, and experienced women like Sheila Copps, Mary Clancy, and Sheila Finestone, and a flash of newcomers, many of whom are young. It's making a difference already. It's not women grabbing attention—now it's women and men working together. Instead of a handful of women, we're part of a whole group. The tone in the room changes."

"Where did we start from? Zip! I've been part of that zip. Now, the change is damned exciting to see. I sit back in caucus with the women and think, this is marvelous."[8]

Chrétien's decision to make Sheila Copps deputy prime minister was a striking gesture of respect for women. After all, the post had carried enormous power and prestige when Don Mazankowski occupied it for Brian Mulroney's Tories. But Ottawa insiders soon began to whisper, in hushed bureaucratic tones, that Copps was being "marginalized." Other ministers said that she was not effective at cabinet meetings, that she wasn't a team player, that she was secretive and only interested in building her empire. Many observers concluded that Copps did not have Chrétien's full trust and backing. *Globe and Mail* columnist Giles Gherson wrote on January 19, 1994: "One question mark: Deputy Prime Minister Sheila Copps, Mr. Chrétien's presumed heir. In the early going, the combative, controversial and exceedingly well-known Ms. Copps apparently hasn't shone around the cabinet table. Her environment portfolio isn't a priority. Insiders are making much of the fact that during Mr. Chrétien's European trip last week, cabinet wasn't presided over by Deputy PM Copps; it was cancelled."

Her troubles started during Chrétien's first absence the previous December. When the prime minister suddenly went on holidays, Copps stated the obvious: "I'm running the government. I'm here as deputy prime minister. I chaired the cabinet today and in terms of the issues that are going to be raised I'm in full control."

One writer instantly compared her to Alexander Haig, the chief of staff to former President Ronald Reagan, who blustered "I'm in charge here" after his boss was shot. But reporters failed to mention a crucial fact that made the comparison absurd: Haig was an unelected staff member, while Copps is the legitimate deputy prime minister, duly elected and sworn in. During Mulroney's many trips abroad, nobody in the press gallery trembled at the thought of Mazankowski's finger on the trigger of Canadian government, and he was certainly never mocked for assuming his responsibilities.

In some ways, Copps became an easy target for her many political foes as soon as she stepped into office. As a member of the government, she no longer had the freedom to snipe at opponents and speak her mind on issues. Her aggressive style had annoyed many people along the way, including other Liberals.

"Sheila Copps will have a very strong role, despite the fact that her personality is not one that he [Chrétien] finds it easy to get along with," says Sharon Carstairs, former leader of the

Manitoba Liberals. "But Sheila sometimes does dumb things politically. She interferes where she shouldn't." Copps's involvement in a Brandon federal riding before the 1993 election, Carstairs believes, probably cost a strong woman a nomination. "Sheila did none of the background, made no phone calls, she just got out on her high horse and did it herself—and she does this all the time. She tries to play the game the male way. She shouldn't. She should use her strengths as a woman."[9]

Chrétien is lavish in his praise of Copps, who opposed him in the Liberals' 1990 leadership convention in Calgary. "I like her very much," he says. "She's strong and witty and articulate and you'd better be ready to face her. She's probably the best woman politician in Canada at this time. She has more presence than anyone else by a long shot." Copps is tough, independent, and well able to take care of herself. If she doesn't enjoy Chrétien's full confidence, it is due to reasons other than her gender.

Given his firm view that women face no special barriers in politics, it's hardly surprising that the prime minister named so few women to his first cabinet. To his mind, not many have had the experience to do the job without making costly political blunders as they learn. (He appointed Anne McLellan, his greenest minister, because he wanted an Albertan to allay fears of another National Energy Program, but also because scores of Liberals had told him how bright and quick she is.) After surviving his own bitter trials through sheer persistence, Chrétien values caution and staying power above all else. McLellan says, "The prime minister runs a tight ship. You don't waste time in cabinet meetings. He gets to the point and expects you to do the same."[10]

Yet Chrétien has had a major influence over some of the most significant advances for Canadian women; he was justice minister when Bertha Wilson became the first woman named to the Supreme Court, and when women's equality was enshrined in the constitution in 1981. Clearly, he would like to have more women in cabinet as soon as they meet his demanding criteria. To that end, he named nine women to posts that provide valuable training for cabinet: three to non-cabinet secretary of state positions, and six as parliamentary secretaries to ministers. The plum went to Jean Augustine (Etobicoke-Lakeshore), who became Chrétien's own parliamentary secretary. She was likely to advance if she could show the ability to shift smoothly from city to federal politics.

"It's a marvellous opportunity," Augustine said. "I have a lifetime of experience as a mother and a working woman. I came to this country thirty-three years ago [from Grenada] and I started at what could be called the bottom and I worked my way up." When Augustine arrived in Canada, her first job was as a $100-a-month domestic worker.[11]

Chrétien was also advancing women along other tracks, some toward destinations nearly as important as cabinet. Chrétien's chief hand in charge of appointments was Penny Collenette, wife of Defence Minister David Collenette. A former executive director of the Liberal Party, she instantly had enormous influence for advancing women (although her first stated goal was to eliminate patronage, a regular promise of every new Canadian government). Chaviva Hosek, the former Ontario Liberal cabinet minister who once headed the National Action Committee on the Status of Women, was his director of policy and research. Hosek's influence is so great that when business people from Calgary were trying to convince the government to privatize the rest of Petro-Canada early in 1994, it was Hosek they met with in Ottawa.[12]

"I think it is not as surprising as it was ten or fifteen years ago to have women around, to have them take these prime leadership roles," says Hosek. She also believes that women can bring a different style of leadership as they work to produce solutions. "Most of us who are used to solving problems in the world know they are not solved by people screaming at each other. They are also not solved by assuming that everybody on one side is right and everybody on the other side is wrong. So there's a kind of unreality in the very black and white adversarial culture of politics that Canada tends to encourage."

Still, Hosek believes things are much improved for women politically. "I think there has been real change. I think it's partly generational. You've got men in their thirties and forties who have worked beside women in their professions and in their jobs. It's not as new to them. It depends on the background they come from and what women in those societies and communities have done."[13] Hosek notes, however, that woman are often surprised by the complexity of the problems they face once they are in office. "There's a lot of things you need to consider to make something happen—things that are a surprise for most people who enter public life. . . . In fact, when you start looking at the issues, it's really hard to make a difference. It's very hard to make change."

Chrétien's most startling move, the one that could mean more to women than all the others combined, was his appointment of Jocelyne Bourgon as Clerk of the Privy Council. When the announcement was made on February 24, 1994, the forty-two-year-old biologist was at once called "the most powerful woman in Ottawa." It was no exaggeration; a minister might influence hundreds or even thousands of civil servants in her or his department, but the clerk rules them all. Her influence extends into crannies of the civil service where even the prime minister cannot reach. She is also Chrétien's personal deputy minister, with power to intervene in departments on his behalf, even over the heads of ministers. Every bureaucrat knows that the Clerk almost always outlasts ministers and sometimes survives the death of a government. If a civil servant had to pick just one person in Ottawa to impress, most would choose the Clerk. Women will rise in Ottawa if Jocelyne Bourgon decides to make their advancement her mission.

She replaced Glen Shortcliffe, the hard-nosed Mulroney appointee who was extremely lucky to survive for three months under Chrétien. (He's said to be responsible for forcing Chrétien's nephew, Raymond Chrétien, now Canada's ambassador in Washington, to take the blame for the admission as a landed immigrant of a former Iraqi diplomat linked to Saddam Hussein's regime.) One story about Shortcliffe illustrates why Bourgon could be a useful corrective. When Kim Campbell was prime minister, she decided to meet with female deputy ministers—eight of

them—at Harrington Lake. By tradition, the Clerk is always noti-
fied of any formal meeting between the prime minister and a
deputy, so a Campbell aide called Shortcliffe at 7 p.m. to advise
him of the plan for the next day. Shortcliffe phoned back at 11
p.m. to say: "If you're going to do that with the women, I guess
I'll have to marshall my strength with the men." Campbell and the
female deputies had a lively meeting despite the Clerk's annoyance.
(At one point, the new prime minister apologized for not having
done enough for women.[14])

Nobody was happier with Bourgon's appointment than Brian
Mulroney. Two weeks before she got the job, he praised her and
said he hoped Chrétien would make her his Clerk. "I've been
positioning her and I hope that takes place," said Mulroney.
"She's superb, and she should be the Clerk."[15]

Despite Chrétien's efforts, some women from the Mulroney
cabinet find him but a pale echo of their boss. "He has taken no
risks and I think that's too bad," says former minister Barbara
McDougall. "In a way it's a kind of temporary setback, but it's
not the end of the world. There are so many [women] there that
they will have to come on sooner or later. They'll say after a
while, 'Come on, Jean, get serious.' . . . I think this is probably
personal to Chrétien. He surrounded himself with people who
were highly experienced from the *ancien regime* [of Pierre
Trudeau] and that has its good points and its bad points."[16]

Any momentum on women's issues will have to come from
within the government, because Chrétien faces very little opposition pressure in Parliament. The NDP won only nine seats in the
1993 election, down from forty-four, and the only woman in the
caucus is leader Audrey McLaughlin, who has announced her
intention to give up the job. The Bloc Québécois is too focused
on its main mission, sovereignty for Quebec, to have much
impact on any other national or social issues. And the Reform
Party, with seven women among its fifty-two MPs, simply
doesn't believe there is any such thing as a woman's issue.

The new Parliament is regionally fragmented, ideologically
split, and lacking consensus on almost everything. Brian

Mulroney faced two large opposition parties—the Liberals and the New Democrats—who at least pressed consistently for action on women's issues. Chrétien, as the leader of the only remaining national party, faces no such pressure. The opposition parties are also inexperienced: just six of Lucien Bouchard's colleagues have been in Parliament before; and only one Reformer, Deborah Grey, was an MP in the previous Parliament. This puts tremendous responsibility on Chrétien's women MPs.

Bloc Québécois leader Bouchard formed his party from the Quebec remnants of the Tories with the sole purpose of achieving independence for his province. His interest in women's issues appears minimal, although he had the sense to make Francine Lalonde, a former Quebec provincial minister for the status of women, responsible for such concerns in Ottawa. With eight women MPs out of fifty-four, the Bloc has a sensible policy on paper that reflects majority opinion in Quebec. "The Bloc will continue to defend women's rights as it relates to equal working conditions, income security, family rights, kindergarten services and violence against women," says a party policy document. But Bouchard's declarations on women were mostly limited to defending his wife, Audrey Best Bouchard, when she was called "a Valley Girl" in a *Toronto Star* article implying that she was merely a California beauty who answered the call of his mid-life crisis.[17]

Twenty-one years Bouchard's junior, she met him on a Paris–London plane when Bouchard was Canada's ambassador to France. Audrey Best was born in France and spent the first few years of her life there, but is American down to her blonde bob and deep tan. They now have two young children, and when the first was about to be born, Bouchard made sure that Audrey was raced across the river from Ottawa to Hull so the infant would first see the light on *terre natale*. Bouchard now says, however, that his wife is "pretty detached" about Quebec independence and wants the children to be Americans.[18]

Preston Manning's Reform Party, with most of its members from B.C. and Alberta, does not talk about "violence against women"; instead, the party refers to "family violence." Calgarian

Valerie Clark, a Reform member, expressed the party view: "The Reform Party prefers to categorize these so-called women's issues as equality issues, social welfare issues, and justice issues."[19] Reformers believe that if problems are linked to women, only women will be responsible for solving them, and they will be marginalized and resented as well. Much better, they argue, to have everyone acknowledge a stake in a social problem and work to eradicate it.

The Reform Party has a large quota of sexist men, but its women can be surprisingly strong (maybe because they have to put up with the men). Val Meredith, the B.C. Reform MP, stood up to male members of her riding executive who accused her of having an affair, calling their behaviour by its name: sexism. Deborah Grey, the first Reformer to be elected, was alone for four years in Parliament, scorned by other parties and often snubbed by other women MPs. Her brave conduct earned her a remarkable accolade from a political foe, Liberal senator Joyce Fairbairn. "In the last Parliament Deborah Grey had an extraordinarily difficult time, both personally and politically," says Fairbairn. "Yet she did a splendid and courageous job on her own."[20]

Jan Brown, a new Reform MP from Calgary with two master's degrees, wrote a cogent paper outlining the negative image faced by women politicians in Ottawa. "This stereotype, sustained by patriarchy, pictures women as servants, nurturers, motherly organizers who often give way to their emotions . . . ," she said. "Politics represents an overwhelming challenge for women. Not only are they struggling to rid themselves of a stereotypical social role, but they also have to re-establish themselves in a new environment; one that is quite foreign from the world in which they were initially socialized as children."[21] The same words could spring as readily from Sheila Copps or Audrey McLaughlin.

Nobody resents the image of Reform women as much as Sandra Manning, Preston Manning's wife of twenty-eight years. She showed her feelings once when Deborah Grey introduced her, intending glowing praise, as "the woman who stands behind the party leader." Sandra took the podium and gently corrected

Grey: "I stand *beside* him." On election night in 1993, when it was obvious that the party had won more seats than expected, Sandra rushed happily to the stage to welcome the well-wishers and introduce her husband. Some observers noted that it was odd, but pleasing, to see a leader's wife speak before her husband (or at all). An Edmonton lawyer who happened once to sit near the Mannings in an Ottawa restaurant was fascinated to note that Sandra did almost all the talking. "Preston couldn't get a word in," the lawyer said, "but I tell you, he was listening hard."

Sandra Manning feels that the public image of her and her family derives from knee-jerk reactions to Manning's Christian fundamentalism. "He has been summarily defined by the media as some sort of a Bible-thumping fanaticist. So then people think, 'Oh, he must have a little lady back at home who is probably pregnant with the fifteenth child and wears a bun on the back of her head, and recites Bible verses.' That's why I think there's a curiosity about what I am or who I am. But it's very definitely incorrect and erroneous."[22] She also rejects the stereotype that paints Reform women as feminist-haters. "I'm thankful for the progress that the feminist movement has made for me and for my daughters and for their daughters," she says. "At the same time, I have come out of a great deal of traditionalism for which I have to be thankful. It accounts for the security and self-esteem that I feel. I don't want either to leave that or destroy it as I move on." When it appeared briefly that Manning might be the opposition leader, Sandra said they would not live in Stornoway, the official residence. "We *have* a home," she said. "I know lots of women in abusive situations who might want to live there." Turn Stornoway into a shelter for such battered women, she urged.[23]

Although Preston Manning has no use for the feminist agenda, he wants to see more women in politics. The biggest difficulty, he says, is the male battle syndrome that discourages women from running. "The problem we found with women not wanting to run is the adversarial system," he says. "This bashing each other is a guy thing—the hunting mentality. Women attach a higher priority to relations, both within their family and with their colleagues. If the political system is not conducive to the relational approach, then women will be more reluctant to run."[24]

The Reform Party suggests several mechanisms to ease this problem, including freer votes, less division between front and back benches, and toning down Question Period. The partisan furor could be greatly eased, Manning claims, by placing MPs in a semi-circle instead of having them face each other across an aisle. But the Reformers' most interesting ideas come from their little-known but intense fascination with modern computer technology: by allowing members to vote electronically, sometimes from their ridings, women would be less bound to the House of Commons and freer to run. "Our current methods of voting are so archaic they're absurd," says Deborah Grey. "Electronic voting, for starters, would allow MPs more freedom. And what would be wrong with computer voting from home? Why not just dial in your vote?"[25]

None of this rhetoric persuades the women of the National Action Committee (NAC), who regard the Reform Party as parliamentary poison. When Reform MPs refused to meet NAC officials on June 13, 1994, the day of NAC's annual lobby of political parties on Parliament Hill, more than a hundred women tried to storm Preston Manning's office in the House of Commons. Faced with such an insult from the Reform Party, said NAC president Sunera Thobani, "we're not going to say 'Thank you very much' and go back home again."

Even if the Reform Party and the Bloc Québécois had a sudden *crise de conscience*, and began pursuing advances for women, they have little power to do anything but talk. They are not in a position to raise the level of women's incomes from two-thirds that of men's, enact policies to prevent violence, or move women toward numerical equality in government. Nor do they have specific programs to promote such needed change. The power rests entirely with Prime Minister Chrétien and his imposing Liberal majority. Even though he is not as obviously assertive about promoting women as Brian Mulroney was, Chrétien is not likely to ignore today's political realities. If he does, his female MPs will soon follow Barbara McDougall's advice and say: "Come on, Jean, get serious."

9

THE GREAT DIVIDE

"They wanted evidence that we were scummy politicians.
They wanted evidence that we were liars. They wanted to
know that we were sleazy. They really wanted some dirt."

Judi Tyabji
on the B.C. reporters who done her wrong

Every night at nine o'clock, Sue Hill waits in Okotoks, Alberta, for the daily phone call from her husband, Reform Party MP Grant Hill. He rings on the dot and they chat about events on Parliament Hill, scene of so many temptations for a lone male. The routine is part of their formula to make sure that the rookie MP doesn't succumb to the evil influences of politics by getting involved with another woman. Grant Hill says, "There are risks. We said, 'Let's face them openly and visibly. And let's take steps to prevent, rather than have problems after they occur. . . . Let's make sure we don't drift off and become a statistic in the political scene.'" Sue Hill interviewed both people that her husband hired for his staff—a man and woman—because, she states bluntly, "I was looking for somebody who I didn't feel threatened me." The Hills have a firm agreement that Grant will never dine alone with a woman, even for a business discussion.[1]

Rarely has there been a clearer expression of the widespread belief that women who cross the line from private life into public life have fallen, in more ways than one. Apparently they become so relentless that even a non-drinking, God-fearing Reformer will be transformed into a helpless mass of male jelly once they turn their sights on him. The moral blight extends even to women who work in the offices of Parliament Hill.

Another Reform Party MP, Val Meredith from B.C., sees this perception from the other side of the gender divide. After she won her riding in the 1993 election, members of the all-male riding executive accused her publicly of having an affair with her campaign manager. Meredith insists that the allegations are false and believes they spring from one source: the men don't like having a woman member of Parliament. Because it is no longer so acceptable to state clearly that women don't belong in politics, she believes, they tried to disqualify her by attacking her character.[2]

The public–private division is one of the oldest traditions in our culture, and the borderline is still stoutly defended by the guardians of morality. The demarcation rests on the assumption, enforced for centuries by religious leaders, that women's place is with home and family, while only men have a legitimate role in the public arena. Women who cross the line violate a powerful taboo and must be far more cautious than men about their personal conduct. Experienced women politicians know this well, and many live like nuns while they are in public life.

The attitude was expressed perfectly early this century in an editorial published in the *Toronto Mail and Empire* in 1909. "Nature has assigned to us all our duties in life," it declared. "To the man has been given the task of supporting the woman, of sustaining the home, of fighting the battles and of governing the family, the clan or the nation. To woman has been committed the charge of the home and the duty of exercising a moderating influence over all its inhabitants. The Suffragettes are at war with nature . . . they want the women to be too much like men."[3] Women who chose to fight nature, are, obviously, unnatural and therefore immoral.

This prejudice goes back to the very foundations of Western culture. In the original "democracy" of ancient Athens, the vote was denied to slaves, women, and anyone living outside the city walls. Six centuries before Christ, Pythagoras wrote: "There is a good principle which created order, light and man, and an evil principle which created chaos, darkness and women." Aristotle concluded three hundred years later: "It is a general law that there should be naturally ruling elements and elements naturally ruled. . . . The rule of the freeman over the slave is one kind of rule; that of the male over the female is another."

These views, always drawing their vague authority from "nature," "the gods," or "God," barred most women from public life for more than 2,000 years, far into the era of modern democracy. As the absolute authority of monarchs decayed at the end of the Middle Ages, political thinkers began to propound theories that remain the foundation of our modern political culture—and like all men of their day, they found the idea of women in public life simply unthinkable. As Janine Brodie notes in *Women and the Electoral Process in Canada*, liberalism produced a new politics based on the values of individualism, formal political equality, and equality of opportunity. But these values were assumed not to apply to women: "Liberal individualism denied that women could be citizens."[4]

As Western democracy matured, the ideas crystallized into a sharp and formal division between the private roles of women and the public roles of men. Only a man had the social mandate to cross the line—to be a public person at work and a private one at home. Women were confined entirely to "private" duties involving family and community. "Men and women learn to expect that only men should pursue a career in politics," Brodie says. "The cultural exclusion of women in political leadership roles . . . becomes self-reinforcing. The nearly exclusive election of males to public office creates the expectation that only males should seek office. . . . The gender-based division of political power is firmly entrenched, and is transmitted from generation to generation via the values and expectations of men and women."

The core belief that women should not be involved in politics has eroded only gradually even in this century. When Elsie Inman ran for office in Prince Edward Island during the First World War, men told her on their doorsteps that her husband should horsewhip her for this affront to true democracy.[5] More than fifty years later, as P.E.I. premier Catherine Callbeck first sought a seat in the legislature for the same province, she faced an identical attitude expressed in milder words. "I remember going around and talking to the poll chairman of the Liberal Party, trying to get the nomination," she said. "One poll chairman, who was an elderly gentleman, said to me, 'Look, I might as well tell you, I can't vote for you because you're a woman.'"[6]

Lise Bacon, the dynamic former deputy premier of Quebec, saw her political dreams popped when she planned to run in the 1970 general election. "People didn't think a woman could win in Trois-Rivières so they chose my brother, Guy Bacon, instead," she says. By the time the next election was called, in 1973, Lise Bacon was the Quebec Liberal Party's president, a post, she says, that "traditionally gets a safe riding." Instead, "I was offered a riding where I was unknown. I had to campaign hard, but I did win the seat." Bacon's perseverance paid off. She also earned a cabinet post as minister responsible for social affairs.[7]

Grace McCarthy, a former deputy premier of B.C. and later the province's Socred leader, heard a political echo at the other end of the country. "When I was on the parks board in 1960 I was also in business," she recalls. "One of my customers said, 'I sure would vote for you if you weren't a woman.' It was the strangest expression. I didn't let it bother me, but it was indicative of the attitudes toward women."[8]

In the early days after Canadian women were finally allowed to vote, their determination to take the first step into public life sometimes produced bizarre results. Elsie Inman dressed up a woman friend to disguise her from her husband, who had threatened his wife if she voted in the 1922 P.E.I. election. And when Inman went to accompany another woman to vote, the irate husband accused her of trying to lead his wife astray. "You're from a nice family, and have a good husband," he raged, "you should be ashamed of yourself."

Using disguise to cross the public–private divide already had a strange and revealing history in Canada. From 1871 to 1887, the representative for East Hastings in Ontario was a slight MP named John White—who was really a woman. Scholar John Akenson has shown that a woman named Eliza McCormack White successfully assumed the identity of her brother, who had died in their native Ireland. She glued on whiskers, dressed in men's clothing, practised male mannerisms, and even married a woman—all so successfully that she enjoyed a long political career which ended nearly thirty years before Canadian women would be allowed to vote. Akenson has observed: "When you look at it from a historical perspective, it makes sense. During that time, women could only really assume power in two ways. One was to be a part of the monarchy. The other was to be a man."[9] Disguise as a means of infiltrating male power structures still captures the imagination today, both in fiction and reality, because the public–private divide remains so sharp.

Embracing celibacy is a tactic that has allowed some women to be active in politics without violating the public–private taboo. Charlotte Whitton, the famous mayor of Ottawa in the 1950s and 1960s, preached this creed with special devotion. The first female mayor of any Canadian city, Whitton said that politics were her family, and argued that female sexual restraint brought special civic benefits. Her biographers P.T. Rooke and R.L. Schnell write: "Whitton and many of her contemporaries were committed to the cult of 'Blessed Singleness.' She believed that chastity was also power; that the choice of celibacy invested women's lives with a unique vocational meaning which enabled them to express female virtues and attributes through womanly service."[10] In 1947, Whitton said, "Women's natural sphere is home and motherhood . . . and natural too is consecration to celibacy in the service of mankind . . . and upon all women, but upon the 'secular unmarried' especially, rests responsibility for leadership and education of women for public life."[11] She argued that every woman has "motherly feelings," but that only the unmarried and celibate retained full power to use those divine sentiments for public benefit.

Whitton's choice did nothing to foster the political dreams of women who also want a husband and children—instead, it tended to lock them into their homes. But in her own career, Whitton's declaration gave her the freedom to be an irascible iconoclast who met men on their own terms and often punctured their pomposity. It was Whitton who made the unforgettable comment: "Whatever women do they must do twice as well as men to be thought half as good. Luckily, it's not difficult." She felt equally at liberty to chide women for their political inertia and their complicity in the male-dominated system as flunkies who cut sandwiches and served tea at auxiliary meetings.

Throughout her long career, Whitton operated outside the strict rules of femininity that constrained most women of the time. When a delicate matter came up for discussion in Ottawa city council, and male councillors suggested she should leave, Whitton snapped: "Whatever my sex, I'm no lady." She was both revered and feared for what a contemporary called her "adder-sharp tongue, keen satirical wit, terrifying memory and tremendous knowledge." Some of her attitudes probably arose from undeclared lesbianism—a delicate matter seldom more than hinted at in all the popular and academic writing about her. Whatever her reasons, Whitton's public declaration of celibacy freed her to operate in politics almost as an honorary man, immune to the usual charges that she had abandoned her family and children because of ambition. She managed to circumvent the public–private divide, but only by denying the most basic aspect of womanhood, her potential to be a mother.

The controversial B.C. MLA Judi Tyabji, by comparison, adopted no protective guise at all, and became a fascinating case study in the disastrous consequences of mixing public and private life. More than any woman in modern Canadian politics, Tyabji, who became the focus of national scandal for months, behaved as if the barrier simply didn't exist. Her whole being proclaimed: "I'm young, I'm a mother, I'm in love with a man who isn't my husband, and I'm also a talented politician who's going to have it all." A sharper contrast with Charlotte Whitton is hard to imagine—and it's instructive to note that Whitton enjoyed a long and honoured career in politics, while Tyabji's, awash in scandal, is likely to be short.

Tyabji's problems began on her very first day in the B.C. legislature in 1991. Her daughter, Tanita, had been born only three days earlier, and Tyabji was determined to make the point that a young mother can also be a politician. The Liberal MLA took her daughter to the office with a nanny in tow, proclaiming that if necessary she would leave the legislature to nurse. "I'm hoping it will set a good example and encourage even more young mothers to get involved," she had said just after the baby's birth. "I think one thing we are lacking in the legislature is a real cross-section of society. Just the fact that I'm the first to do this demonstrates that we have to get more women, more young mothers involved."

The governing B.C. New Democrats were quietly furious because Tyabji's defiant display of motherhood (she was the first B.C. MLA ever to give birth while in office) stole much of the media attention from their opening-day throne speech. Some news reports quipped about her "stunt." One reporter wrote: "From now on, when Tyabji says it's time for a change, she'll mean something other than most politicians." Some of B.C.'s leading female journalists were equally outraged. Columnist and former Social Credit candidate Nicole Parton fumed, "A house is not a home. Judi Tyabji has yet to learn that, but it probably won't take long.

Babies do not belong in the legislature. A cradle, a photocopier and a shredder shouldn't share the same room. . . . [She] should take a maternal leave of absence or put her ambition on hold." Women on the political left were just as hostile because they saw a threat to public day care if moms in other jobs followed Tyabji's example. "This is a great disservice to the rest of B.C.'s working mothers," wrote Jaqueline Kirby, a North Vancouver freelancer. "Think again, Judi." Another Liberal, former federal minister Iona Campagnolo, felt that Tyabji thrust her child too far into the world of politics. "When Judi brought her baby into the chamber, it was like saying this child is now in the public domain," Campagnolo said. "I would never allow my daughter to be put in the public domain. . . . Once you do that, you make that child part of your overall political persona."[12] And that, in Campagnolo's opinion, is an unwise and even dangerous thing to do.

Tyabji failed to realize that while babies on a Christmas card complete the well-rounded image of a male politician, they erode the political credibility of a woman. Toddlers become tiny demerits that provoke the instant outraged reaction: "Why isn't she home with the kids?" Or, if the politician brings her baby to the office, "That's no place for a kid!" Deputy Prime Minister Sheila Copps endured the same kind of hostility when she took her newborn daughter, Danelle, to her House of Commons office in 1987.[13]

But Tyabji's greatest mistake came two years later. She and her party leader, Gordon Wilson, believed that the public would put up with a political couple who at first denied they were having an affair, then confessed their attraction and expected simply to go on as before. They even felt that it was perfectly acceptable for Wilson, as the Liberal leader, to make Tyabji his chief deputy in the legislature. But when their affair became public, virtually the entire Liberal caucus went into open revolt, while the B.C. public and most of Canada smirked at the publication of Tyabji's famous "cerebral" love letter to Wilson. "I feel a love that is building," she wrote. "It is pure, and feels timeless. . . . Of course, the greatest magnet is our identical brains."[14]

Regardless of the organs involved, their political careers were virtually finished. All sympathy for Wilson vanished when he made his separation from his wife public without first telling her. "To hell with him," Elizabeth Wilson fumed. "I've never received any separation papers. I still do his laundry." Soon the Liberals turfed Wilson as leader, and he and Tyabji went off in a huff to form the Progressive Democratic Alliance, which quickly became marginal. By 1994, Wilson was advocating B.C.'s separation from Canada.

Nicole Parton's comment about Tyabji—that "she should put her ambition on hold"—ominously presaged what happened later. In March 1994, Tyabji lost custody of her three children to her former husband, Kim Sandana, who works full-time in a Kelowna grocery store. Justice John Spencer of the B.C. Supreme Court made it clear in his ruling that political ambition was part of the reason for her downfall. "The mother's attention as a custodial parent would be, to a degree, sidetracked by her career agenda. . . . At their present ages, the children will benefit more from their father's lower-key approach to life than from the mother's wider-ranging ambition."[15]

To women who might be thinking about a career in politics, the message was alarming: if you're ambitious enough to work long hours, and your marriage falls apart, you might lose the kids. "The custody decision smacked of the old world," says Campagnolo. She calls this "the Scarlet Letter syndrome"—the public branding of a woman who steps too far outside her "natural" private role. It is the ultimate price to pay for ambition. At the same time, Campagnolo and many other women conceded that the decision might have been best for Tyabji's three children, all of them under six years old. "Her ex-husband gets home and can take care of the kids after 6 p.m.," she says. "He also has an extended family to help. My bottom line is the kids." Despite the court's suggestion that ambitious female politicians had better beware, Campagnolo adds, "this is not really a blow to all women in public life."

The Wilson–Tyabji affair was such an extreme affront to public mores that in some ways it stands alone, more a cautionary tale than a precedent. But it also showed the grave personal and political dangers of ignoring—or being ignorant of—the long tradition that steers women away from the public arena. Women can cross the divide with some impunity in the 1990s, but only if they are scrupulously careful about their private lives. Tyabji was so disdainful of the line that it gradually curled and twisted until it became her political noose. Men usually have more leeway than women, but Gordon Wilson's judgment seemed so poor that he paid nearly as heavy a price, losing not only his marriage, but his leadership and his credibility. Yet neither admits to making any mistakes, and Tyabji sees herself as a victim of sexism, both from men in the Liberal Party and from B.C. women on the political left. It all happened, she believes, because of a love so pure that she and Wilson were powerless to deny it.

Tyabji feels that Liberals who fought to remove Wilson as party leader were motivated by sexism. When he wanted to appoint her House leader, she says, "One of them said he would no more take orders from me than he would from his daughter. . . . That was the attitude. They believed they could make the 'sleazy' label stick with me and 'fool for love label' stick with Gordon. You know, 'he fell for her looks, her womanly wiles.' That's what they thought they could get the public to believe, because even the people who worked with us didn't know that we were planning a permanent relationship, that we were madly in love. We never brought it into the office."[16]

While the right wing attacked Tyabji for her supposed lack of "family values," the left savaged her for refusing to support its ideological agenda. "The NDP have been particularly bitter toward me because I refuse to call myself a feminist," she says. "Look at my life—do I need a label? . . . I've gone out of my way to say that I don't consider myself a feminist, I consider myself a humanist, which means I fight for human rights. So when I was being publicly trashed, none of the women's groups spoke out. After I was turfed out as House leader, no one ever mentioned the extremely competent job that I did."

Later, Tyabji charged that some male Liberal MLAs were carrying on affairs, with no repercussions, even while her career was being ruined. "They were sometimes absent for debates because of their little trysts," she said in *Monday*, a Victoria news and entertainment weekly. "They were never exposed, but I lost my position."[17]

Unlike Tyabji, very few women in their twenties manage to cross the private–public barrier if they are also mothers. One survey by Janine Brodie shows that only 3.4 per cent of all female candidates fall into that category. But women in their twenties without children comprise the largest single group of female candidates: 42.4 per cent. More than 40 per cent of women surveyed said they delayed entering politics because their children were too young. In general, "women with no children were almost twice as likely as mothers to contest their first election before the age of 40; mothers more frequently entered the political field between the ages of 40 and 60."

Young women with children are more likely to confine their politics to the municipal boards, especially as councillors or school board trustees. Less frequently they venture as far as the provincial stage. In her extensive study of women candidates, Brodie found that 41 per cent of female candidates for municipal election were homemakers, while 26 per cent of provincial candidates fit that category. "Traditional gender roles appear to be more easily harmonized with municipal than with legislative candidacy," she concludes.[18] The phenomenon is even more obvious on the federal stage. In the final Mulroney Parliament, only four MPs out of 295 were women with young children. They were Sheila Copps, from Hamilton, and three Conservative members from southern Quebec—Lise Bourgault, Carole Jacques, and Marie Gibeau. All were within easy commuting distance from home, at least as Canadian MPs measure these things. Even so, says Senator Janis Johnson, "I know them all and they were completely wrecked all the time." Adds Reform Party MP Diane Ablonczy, "As an MP it's hard enough to feed and water a marriage, let alone a family."[19] There's no question that our vast geography inhibits many women from seeking federal office. In B.C. or Newfoundland, women with young children simply find the challenges of travel too daunting to consider political life in Ottawa. Distance alone tends to confine family women to local politics.

Women who try to harmonize elected office with family life often suffer from a phenomenon called "role strain"—extreme tension between the demands of office and those of the home. "Female politicians, not unlike female professionals, are much more likely to suffer private-versus-public role strain than their male counterparts," Janine Brodie observes. "Because of their breadwinning role, males generally benefit from unambiguous norms that divide their time between public and private roles. Except in very unusual circumstances, the demands of work come first. The female, however, often has to resolve her private role demands before she can consider adopting a public role." Even when women do opt for politics and they have supportive husbands at home, they often feel a weight of guilt and duty that whispers to them, "Go back—you're neglecting your *real* job."

Lyn McLeod, leader of the Ontario Liberals, still feels this strain, even though the two younger of her four children were in high school when she was first elected in 1987, and her husband backs her career with enthusiasm. "It is that much more difficult for women," she says, "because we are still asked that stereotypical question—whether or not we are deserting our homes. It comes back to the sense that somehow it's not quite natural. I don't think you would ever have had the question asked of a male in politics: 'How is the family managing in your absence?' But women face it all the time."

McLeod says that her decision to go into politics brought "a difficult family adjustment. My daughters were marvellous and my husband was equally supportive. It's been fine for our family. . . . But there's still that feeling that it isn't quite right for it to be the woman, the mother, who is out of the home, living away from home five days a week. It's just accepted that it's perfectly natural for a male to be in that role. We do see it as being less natural for women."[20]

Alexa McDonough, Nova Scotia's NDP leader, deals with an even more traditional, Maritime attitude toward her private responsibilities. "I'm very often tied to the so-called significant men in my life," she says. "People describe me or identify me in relation to who my father is, who my brother is, who my husband was. Nobody ever does that to male politicians. Nobody ever says, 'I don't know anything about Donald Cameron's mother.' So why is it relevant who my father is?"

McDonough went through three elections as NDP leader "with the traditional Nova Scotia family—a spouse and two kids. But then my husband and I split up, and going into this latest election I really struggled a lot with all of the prejudices that are inherent against a separated or divorced woman in politics. I knew perfectly well I would find myself in situations where there would be a great attempt to portray my two opponents as good family men surrounded by their adoring, dutiful families."[21] When McDonough's two grown sons learned that she was thinking of quitting because of this, they were appalled. They told her she couldn't succumb to the very sexism she had always fought. Because of them, she decided to run again, and won.

Some female politicians deal with "role strain" by delegating part of their family function to another woman, often a relative. When Iona Campagnolo was elected, her younger sister dropped her career to come to Ottawa. "I could not have done the job had my sister not left her job as a chartered accountant and come to care for my daughter. She acted as my hostess, she took in my dry cleaning, got my shoes fixed and did all those things. I owe her such a debt. She's ten years younger than me. I'll always be making up my debt to her because she looked after my only daughter when I couldn't."

Senator Janis Johnson's saviour was her aunt. "If she hadn't happened to retire at the same time I was asked to go into the Senate, I couldn't have done my job," Johnson says. "She came into my home in Winnipeg and looked after my son and dogs, and my son's friend who lived with us for four years. And still it has been very difficult because I don't like being away that much."

When Céline Hervieux-Payette was a minister in the Trudeau government, she relied on her mother. "My children were fourteen, sixteen, and seventeen when I was first elected," she says. "They would have lunch with my mother because they went to a private school right next to her house. My mother became more or less my assistant. It was a good support for me to have her there. . . . But this is the worst age that you can be away from home. They were absolutely, the three of them, little devils. They were awful. It was a revolution at home."[22]

For many years, Parliament simply did not recognize such typically female problems, so thoroughly male was its adminstration. Senator and former Tory MP Pat Carney managed a small victory in 1979 when she went "on strike" by refusing to enter the Commons chamber. She was annoyed that MPs were allowed air fares to bring their spouses to Ottawa but the benefit was not transferable to children. Carney, a single mother with a teenage son in Vancouver, felt this was blatantly unfair and sexist because a higher percentage of female MPs were single parents. Other women joined her protest and the male MPs, sensing embarrassment and even scandal, changed the rule.[23]

Janis Johnson faces similar problems today in the Senate. "There's no provision for parental leave for any reason," she says. "I'm having to chart new territory in the Senate because most of the people in there, until me and a few others, don't have children at home—they have grandchildren! My latest crusade has been a parental leave policy, so you can be absent if your kid is really sick when you're needed for a vote." This happened to Johnson in January 1993, when her party Whip wanted her in Ottawa. "I said to the Whip, 'I can't come—I don't just up and leave my child when he's ill!' And the Whip was saying, 'What do you mean?' Then I had to sit down and write this letter in a rage to say that women are there and you're going to have to cope with this and accommodate us."[24]

When Céline Hervieux-Payette was in cabinet, she was the only minister with dependent children still at home. "All of the rest of my colleagues were single, like Monique Bégin, or they had grown-up children," she says. "I was the only one who would receive a phone call when there was a war at home. I have seen male colleagues devoting all their time and attention to their career in politics, but I always tried to strike a balance between my family responsibility and my career. I think it's more specific to women. If I was in a cabinet meeting, and if my children had some emergency, I always said not even the prime minister was more important than my children. If they needed me, they could call me twenty-four hours a day, seven days a week, wherever I was. They were always my top priority, and my children knew that."

Ontario NDP minister Evelyn Gigantes speaks poignantly of how her decision to pursue a political career hurt her relationship with her young daughter. "When I was first elected in 1975, leaving my daughter during the week was really hard on our relationship. She was eight at the time, and it took a long time to get that relationship rebuilt. There's no doubt in my mind that she felt resentful. All that is behind us, and we have a wonderful relationship. But it was very tough, and there were many times when I thought I really made the wrong decision."[25]

With all this tension over public and private responsibilities, it's hardly surprising that boyfriends or husbands of female politicians, supportive at first, often fail to stand by their mates for very long. Most men simply can't take the demands of office or the attention lavished upon the women. The role reversal eats at their egos, crumbles their sense of self-worth, and makes them feel unmanly. Journalist Robert Fife reports that Kim Campbell's second husband, Howard Eddy, was judged harshly, at least in Ottawa terms, when he went out to political dinners with his wife: he was said to be boring.

"There are very few men who can stand the stress," says Iona Campagnolo. "There are very few men who could even date a female cabinet minister. When you go into a room, you just take all the oxygen out. You're the one everyone wants to talk to. Suddenly, at the end of the evening you're looking around for your escort to try to take the poor soul out the door with you.

It's embarrassing; it's also what men have done to women since time immemorial, but a woman can't do it."

Alexa McDonough is blunt about the end of her marriage several years ago. "It's intensely personal but I don't mind addressing it," she says. "There's no question that there was an element of this in the break-up. There aren't very many men that are intact enough, confident enough, to be able and willing to really support a woman in public life. But to be fair, you have to acknowledge that if you really have a passion for politics, and you really are wholeheartedly committed to fighting for change, it takes a lot of time and energy.

"So if you have a partner who isn't completely caught up in the same process, then it can become a real source of tension and ultimately division. Most people who know me and know my husband would agree that that was a big factor. He was very supportive on a personal level. He was absolutely my best campaigner, and a wonderful door-to-door canvasser. He loved it and was good at it. But in terms of being as caught up in the political process on a day-to-day basis, he just wasn't—and it took a toll."

For many Canadian political women, the unlikely model of the dream man is Denis Thatcher, husband of former British prime minister Margaret Thatcher. "Unfortunately, no one has replicated the Denis Thatcher mould," says Jodi White, former aide to Kim Campbell.[26] Thatcher stood by his wife even though he was constantly portrayed in the British media as a wimpish buffoon whose main job was to fall down drunk at state functions. *Private Eye*, the British model for *Frank* magazine, carried a regular "letter" from Denis Thatcher, in which he complained about being bossed around by his wife and hounded about his favourite hobbies, drinking and lounging at his club. His manliness was so often belittled, in fact, that he must have been quite a man to take the abuse. Yet the media could see this successful political marriage only in one way: she must be the battle-axe and he, the victim.

Brian Mulroney, who met Denis Thatcher at many conferences, came to know a very different man. "At first I saw him as a caricature because that's the way he was always portrayed," Mulroney recalls. "But after seeing him many times I realized he was absolutely indispensable to his wife. He provided her with advice, encouragement, love, and sanctuary. We talked once about this at a meeting in Kuala Lumpur and he said, 'Brian, I'm not only happy to do this, I'm honoured to help Margaret do her work.'"[27] Denis summed up his attitude when *The Los Angeles Times* asked him who wears the pants in his family. "I do," he said, "and I also wash and iron them." In her memoirs, Thatcher paid her husband the ultimate compliment for his loyalty. "Being prime minister is a lonely job. In a sense, it ought to be: you cannot lead from the crowd. But with Denis there I was never alone. What a man. What a husband. What a friend."[28]

The beleaguered and patient Denis Thatcher, a rare bird indeed, has achieved cult status among female politicians. Hardly any have someone like him. It's far more common for senior women to be single (Monique Bégin, Flora MacDonald, Judy LaMarsh, Mary Clancy); divorced (Sheila Copps, Kim Campbell, Pat Carney, Audrey McLaughlin, Iona Campagnolo, and many others); or widowed (Barbara McDougall, whose husband died years after they separated). Public–private tension is the acid that eats away at relationships.

A few women politicians are lucky enough to have their own Canadian versions of Denis. Ontario Liberal leader Lyn McLeod leaves a supportive husband in Sudbury when she goes to the legislature in Toronto. Former Manitoba Liberal leader Sharon Carstairs says with amusement, "whenever I've been on the platform I've had the adoring male by my side. But that is the very reason I chose never to go into federal politics—because my life is very much a part of his life and vice-versa. I have to say that when I've been in campaigns he has been there every single step of the way. He goes around my constituency, knocking on doors, saying he hopes they're going to vote for 'Beauty Wonder.' It seems to me quite appropriate that he should be by my side on election night. But it sure kept me out of federal politics, I can tell you."[29]

Even when a female politician is both highly successful and happily married, as Carstairs was, the pull of private life tends to limit her career. Carstairs was always annoyed by the assumptions people made about her husband because he was married to a famous female politician. "John was very successful in his own right and never thought I was a threat," she says. "But I was always infuriated when people assumed that he couldn't be too bright to be married to this very bright woman, or that he really couldn't be quite a man to put up with this dominant woman. What was really offensive was that people in my own party treated him that way. And he was raising all the corporate financing! Without John Carstairs the Liberal Party in Manitoba would be in debt up to its eyeballs."[30]

Other women troop off to Ottawa with happy relationships and high hopes. Anne McLellan, Chrétien's natural resources minister, lives with prominent Edmonton lawyer John Law. Deborah Grey was married not long before the 1993 election (after raising seven foster children as a single woman). Senator Joyce Fairbairn is married, and so is Health Minister Diane Marleau, who has three children. Sheila Copps, after having had one marriage fail while she was in Parliament, embarked on another to Ottawa labour consultant Austin Thorne. Given the dismal survival record of such relationships, one can only wish them all the best of luck.

Campagnolo eloquently describes the more common reality: "The stereotypical view of the politician is the familial picture of the man with the wife lovingly staring in Nancy Reagan fashion at the platform, and two or three kids on the postcard at Christmas. But all the women I've known in political life, we've been alone. [Former Liberal MP] Simma Holt had a husband but no children. Jeanne Sauvé [the late Liberal cabinet minister and Governor-General] had one son and her husband had been an MP before her. The rest of us were all either divorced or never married."

Every one of these women would have warned Judi Tyabji to be careful, not to get involved with another politician, to draw a careful line between her public and private lives. But the young B.C. politician, while proclaiming her determination to shatter stereotypes, fell into the most damaging one of all: in the public's eye she became the younger woman who wrecked marriages by running off with the boss. True or not, that's what the voters saw, and the image made short work of Tyabji's promising career.

But there is another, more encouraging example for women in the 1990s—Sheila Copps. She became deputy prime minister in spite of a long career of standing up to men while refusing to deny her sexuality. Like Tyabji, she was reviled in some quarters for taking her baby to the office, and she still provokes many men beyond endurance. When a male journalist spoke to a group of businessmen at a private club in Calgary, he was astounded by their reaction to his suggestion that Copps might someday be prime minister. "They laughed, they hooted, and they actually got angry at me for even making the suggestion," he says. "They absolutely hate her, and it's not just because she's a Liberal. She's too mouthy for them, that's the problem. Besides, they'd already had their little experiment with a female political leader—Kim Campbell. For guys like that, one per century is plenty."[31]

But while Copps often seems to step dangerously close to the public–private divide, she always knows exactly where the line is, and has an innate sense of how much the majority of Canadians will tolerate. She learned her lessons the hard way, in the crucible of Ontario provincial politics, the federal back benches, and during her run for the federal Liberal leadership in 1990. That campaign taught her the power of the impulse to relegate women to private life. "I analyzed the coverage by male journalists very carefully," she says. "I was never taken seriously—in fact, I was completely marginalized. They concentrated more on my clothes and my hair than on what was inside my head. What I was wearing was far more significant than what I was saying. I had felt that this was happening during the campaign, but when I actually saw the proof I was appalled and very angry."[32] Significantly, her male opponents saw this publicity as working to her advantage. Prime Minister Jean Chrétien says, "At least she got ink—in politics, it's very important. The worst thing that can happen to you is when nobody talks about you. I don't say it's an advantage, that she got ink for that. But I never got any for *my* clothing, so she had an advantage over me in a way."[33]

Unlike the inexperienced Judi Tyabji, Copps understands the great public–private psychological divide, often far better than her male opponents do. She has made a career of turning men's prejudices back on them in ways they find infuriating. Over the years, she has saved some of her shrewdest barbs for John Crosbie, the former Conservative minister who could never resist "joking" with her. Once Crosbie spotted Copps in the House of Commons when she was eight and a half months pregnant—a waddling embodiment of the threatening woman who has crossed the traditional line dividing her private world from her public ambitions. Crosbie looked her up and down for a moment and then grumbled, "Well, I suppose this is about the time you're getting more bitchy." Copps paused, gave Crosbie her sweetest smile, and said, "You know me, John—I'm *never* bitchy." She went on to become the first member of Parliament to give birth while in office, an achievement she could be sure John Crosbie would never match.

10

THE LAST GATEKEEPERS

"They asked me what a woman's issue was. One guy who couldn't believe it after I'd spoken looked at me and said, 'I don't mean to be rude, but I don't know what you're talking about.'"

Senator Janis Johnson,
describing a talk with male Tories

Before the 1993 federal election, nobody tried harder to find female candidates than the NDP did. On election day, through its unique affirmative action program, the party ran women in 113 ridings, a record number for any party in any election. But the campaign quickly became a mad dance to socialist oblivion, as the voters rejected 112 of the women officially "designated" by the once eager and idealistic party. Only NDP leader Audrey McLaughlin won her riding, and the dubious right to preside over a dispirited caucus of eight men.

At the same time, Prime Minister Kim Campbell was stumbling toward her own political precipice, dragging with her every female Tory candidate but one (Elsie Wayne, the former mayor of Saint John, N.B.). Sixty-six Conservative women lost. The men, of course, fared even worse: 227 were defeated in the catastrophe that left only Jean Charest standing, dazed, amid the smoking rubble. Two of Canada's major parties had elected a grand total of two women. The only female prime minister in Canadian history was humiliated by a furious electorate. She fell in ignominy, apologizing for her campaign blunders one day, joking about her expanding posterior the next.

A pessimist could easily see this as a disastrous setback for women, a retreat to the dark ages of medieval gender roles. But there was another reality: women who stood for the parties that succeeded fared extremely well. The victorious Liberals ran sixty-four female candidates; thirty-six of them won. Eight of the ten Bloc Québécois women candidates became members of Parliament. Even the Reform Party, whose detractors envision women chained to the coffee pot at political meetings, elected seven of its twenty-three female candidates. Reform women did far better, in fact, than their male counterparts. Female Reformers, a tougher breed than they seem, proved adept at grabbing nominations in winnable ridings in Alberta and British Columbia.[1] And female Bloc candidates enjoyed a remarkable success ratio—80 per cent—compared to the party's men.

When the heads were counted after the voting, women had scored more individual victories than in any previous Canadian election. Fifty-three female MPs were elected, compared to thirty-nine in 1988. The percentage of women members in Parliament rose from 13.4 to 18. In less than a decade since the 1984 election, this vital measure of women's participation had nearly doubled from 9.6 per cent. As recently as 1968, in the first Trudeau sweep of the country, only one woman (New Democrat Grace MacInnis) was elected. In 1993, more than

one-third of all the women ever elected to Parliament were sitting in the Commons. This steady progress hasn't yet reached
levels that would make Scandinavian women envious, but it is
real progress nonetheless. Audrey McLaughlin says, "When I go
to some international meetings, including in the United States,
they just envy us. They think this is Nirvana. They can't believe
that women are where they're at here."

And yet, during the 1993 campaign, there was almost no
debate about legitimate women's issues: child care, abortion,
wife and child abuse, pay equity, tax inequity, and a host of
others. During the 1984 campaign, by contrast, women's groups
forced a full debate by the party leaders on these same issues. In
1988, despite the heavy campaign focus on free trade, there were
still questions on women's concerns. Then came the laminated
silence of 1993—yet at the same time, more women than ever
before were being elected. The voters, it seemed, were both
more willing to elect women and less interested in discussing
their traditional issues.

The problem for women today, obviously, is not the
Canadian voters. (See Appendix 1, Table 4.) It is major political
parties that are still reluctant to give at least half of their nominations to women. The residue of prejudice still lingers in our parties long after most Canadians have shaken it off. "I don't think
there's a gender barrier with the electorate," says Liberal MP
Mary Clancy. "If anything, there's an edge to being a woman.
Certainly that's true with an urban electorate. . . . The problem
is that men in political parties just don't want to share power!"

Iona Campagnolo met that reluctance in its purest, angriest
form when she decided to run for the presidency of the Liberal
Party in 1980. After losing her House of Commons seat in the
1979 election, she felt that this would be a good way to use the
experience she had accumulated as an MP and minister. But the
campaign took a frightening turn that she hadn't expected. "The
night of the vote I had to get off the convention floor, the hatred
was so palpable," she recalls. "I had done what wasn't done in
the party; I had challenged an incumbent [Norman McLeod]. In

the morning I found little bits of paper, full of hate, misogynist hate, at my door. It was as if outside my door that night I was in Salem, not in the Château Laurier in Ottawa." Campagnolo won (with Pierre Trudeau's backing) and became the first female president of her party, but the experience shook her badly.

Academic researchers have known for years that the parties are the gatekeepers that control, and usually block, women's entry into elected politics.[2] Traditionally, all the parties have been very reluctant to allow women into elite policy-making roles like the one Campagnolo was seeking. As late as 1990, only 22 per cent of riding presidents in the Ontario Tory party were women, while 66 per cent of the secretaries were female. Even the Ontario NDP, which worked hard to find female riding executives, still showed a significant gap in 1990: 35 per cent of the presidents and 49 per cent of the secretaries were women. Women are most likely to be riding presidents where their party is inactive and has little chance of winning. In Ontario in the early 1980s, many of the female riding presidents for all three parties held power that was only symbolic.

Women usually work in the "pink ghetto" posts—as office secretaries, envelope stuffers, coffee fetchers and phone canvassers. "Women perform stereotypically feminine types of party work at the local level," Sylvia Bashevkin finds. "The few Canadian women who are involved in urban party activities tend to work harder than their male colleagues, and, at the same time, expect fewer tangible rewards for their commitment."[3] Anybody who has ever seen a Canadian campaign office at work has experienced these realities first-hand. Jean Chrétien acknowledges this. "If you want something done in politics," he says, "you'll always do better with a woman than a man, in general terms. Men tend to discuss a lot and they all want to be generals. They all want to be the big shots. At the grassroots level there's no comparison. Women are the best."[4] Despite this, women remain the foot-soldiers of party work in most Canadian ridings. Like female civil servants, they find that their very competence at lower-level jobs tends to freeze them in place: if they moved up, the generals might have to do some real work.

Long before the academic researchers began to analyze these problems, Judy LaMarsh captured their essence with her usual clear eye and earthy language. "The dirty jobs of politics, the ones of no glamour, often fell to me," she wrote. "Like a good soldier, I did my part. Women are much more realistic about this than men—we know that much of life is made up of dirty, tough jobs that someone has to do. Someone has to clean off a sticky bottom when a diaper needs changing, someone has to wash the cold eggy plates, flick off the accumulated dust, and look after sick people. Women understand that men must often be kept from soiling themselves with the little dirty details of life in order to accomplish the big shiny jobs unimpeded. And women in politics have generally accepted this role—to do all the humdrum, tedious, must-be-done jobs. Pity the party without enough woman power. . . ."[5]

The relegation of women to the "little dirty details" for many years produced the results desired by the party fixers; far fewer women than men ran for office, and among those who did, the success rate was much lower. In all federal elections between 1921 and 1965, only 2.4 per cent of candidates for Parliament were women, and 0.8 per cent of MPs were female. By the 1988 election, the totals had risen substantially; 13.4 per cent of MPs were women,[6] and that figure rose again to 18 per cent in 1993. But women's success rates were still lower than those of men; 12.9 per cent versus 20.1 per cent in 1988. In 1993, although more women candidates were elected than ever before, their success ratio dropped to 11 per cent. This fall was partly due to the huge number of women who ran for the NDP and lost, but the fact remains that women candidates still win far less often than men. "The experience of women in western liberal democracies has been almost universal," writes Janine Brodie. "More women have been running for legislative office but their gains in representation have been slow and tentative."[7]

The numbers are deceptive, however, because so many women run for parties that have no chance of electing anyone. In 1993, 198 women were candidates for parties like the Greens, the Marxist-Leninists, and the Natural Law Party, which claims to be able to solve the world's problems through yogic flying. Nearly 42 per cent of all female candidates—198 of 475—fell into this fringe-party category. Yet this was an improvement of sorts: before the 1984 election, the clear majority of women candidates ran for fringe parties. In 1993, the NDP ran 113 women at the moment of its lowest popularity in thirty years. (Cynics within the NDP suggest that women were welcome to nominations *because* the men knew they would lose.) In the end, 311 of the 475 female candidates—or 65 per cent—had virtually no chance of winning. Audrey McLaughlin is the only one of the 311 who actually did win, thus saving this benighted group from being completely shut out.

The electoral achievements of women running for other parties, even if we include the unpopular Tories, are much more impressive. A total of 164 women ran for the Liberals, Tories, Reform, and Bloc Québécois. Fifty-two of them, or 31 per cent, won their ridings—a higher ratio than men running for the same parties. Again, the conclusion is inescapable: when more women run in desirable ridings for popular parties, their numbers in the House of Commons will skyrocket. And the only barrier to this inevitable progress is within the parties themselves.

The male power brokers in the parties have used many tricks to give the appearance that women are involved, without actually giving up their power. Even after Brian Mulroney told his party in the clearest terms that he wanted women candidates, resistance among Tory men persisted. In 1984, many Conservative women wanted the nomination in Toronto's choice St. Paul's riding to go to Barbara McDougall. Senator Marjory LeBreton recalls that senior campaign officials wanted the riding to go to Mike Wadsworth. "They tried to sideline Barbara, and women in the party like myself and my sister, and quite a number of us went to the leader and he put his foot down. If it were not for women and his help, Barbara McDougall might have been denied that opportunity."[8]

Women have always been welcome to run, however, where their parties were almost certain to lose. In federal and provincial elections between 1945 and 1975, 63 per cent of the women nominees ran in ridings where their party had won none of the previous five elections. The Liberals put up a woman candidate against John Diefenbaker in Prince Albert in 1965. In 1968, the year of Trudeaumania, the Tories ran a woman against the prime minister in Montreal's Mount Royal riding.[9] Nominations are tougher to get when the chances are better. Janine Brodie has found that a woman who seeks nomination in a desirable, competitive riding is more likely to be the victim of "dirty tricks," such as voting irregularities, backstage opposition from the party hierarchy, or active searching for a male to oppose her nomination.

Many excuses have been used to deny nominations in winnable ridings to women. New Democrat Dawn Black recalls what happened to Pauline Jewett when she ran for the Liberal nomination in Ontario's Northumberland riding. "She was at an all-candidates debate for the nomination," says Black. "The fact that she wasn't married had become a huge issue. People were saying, 'It's one thing to vote for a woman, but to vote for a woman who's never been married, that's different.' Suddenly a farmer got up from the back row and stood there in a no-nonsense manner and said, 'Oh, for God's sake, if that's such an issue *I'll* marry Pauline!'"[10] In that case, humour won the day, Jewett won the nomination and became an MP in 1963—only the fourteenth woman elected in Canada to that time.

The NDP was often no better, despite its fine words. When former NAC president Judy Rebick tried for a Toronto NDP nomination in 1988, she lost to a man who had far less chance of winning the election. "If I'd taken the nomination, the women's movement would have mobilized," Rebick says. "Everyone agreed I was the better candidate. The nomination was affirmative action for men—which is what they've always been. Since then, I've gotten so disillusioned with the NDP that I wouldn't run for them."[11]

Such attitudes have discouraged women from seeking the

most desirable ridings because few have the stomach for a pitched battle with the party establishment. They have allowed themselves to become sacrificial candidates whose main function is to make the parties' claims for "women's involvement" as well as national representation look more impressive than they are. Women ensure the party is truly national by often running in the ridings where the party has no chance of winning (the "sausage seats" where the party is squeezed out). But there is growing evidence that when women compete head-on for prized nominations, they can do very well. Lynda Erikson and R.K. Carty found that in nominations for the 1988 election, women won 54 per cent of the nomination fights they contested. "When presented with the choice, local activists were no more likely to choose male than female candidates," they conclude. The parties' key failure, they say, is to search out and encourage top women candidates to run. Women are more likely to run if search committees approach them.[12] One of the key barriers is veteran MPs; when they run again their nominations are rarely contested, and most incumbents, of course, are men.

Another handicap is women's traditional occupations. For more than a century, Canadian parties have nominated candidates mainly from the executive, professional, and business middle class—groups dominated by men. Even the NDP, which fights this tendency, has a smaller number of candidates from lower-income groups than comparable parties in Britain and Australia. In the 1988 election, only 1 per cent of all candidates were "homemakers," an occupation almost monopolized by women. The results are predictable: in 1988, 19 per cent of federal candidates were women, and in 1993 the figure rose only marginally, to 22 per cent. Women have come some distance in the two decades since 1974, when only 9.4 per cent of candidates were female. But they are still a very long way from equality before the voters on election day.

Money, or the lack of it, is another long-standing problem. Women candidates have always had less success than men in raising the substantial amounts required to run effective campaigns.

"Men have an advantage because of their closer links with the business community and with their higher average incomes," Sheila Copps said in 1990.[13] Men have always been ready, and usually eager, to tap their old network of friends from school, sports, and business. Peter Lougheed, Alberta's former premier, used to comb the lists of all the football and baseball teams he'd ever played for in his search for volunteers and donors. "A lot of these people were completely apolitical," he says. "Certainly my group were. But they're also competitors. That affinity to the team sport, in many cases, allows men to have a network that they can call on."[14]

But these male connections are starting to break down, Lougheed says, while women's networks are expanding. Women have become extremely effective fundraisers for schools, communities, and charities. Unlike men, however, they are reluctant to tap their funding sources to further their own political goals. Many female politicians say that one of the hardest things for them to do is ask friends for money. If they ever hope to equal men's success, they will have to start.

There's no doubt that the parties finally recognize all these problems and are making some effort to improve their dismal record. By the early 1980s, women militants of all three "traditional" parties—Liberals, Tories, and New Democrats—were fed up with being denied the rewards of their hard work within the parties. The 1982 constitution, with its guarantee of women's equality, prompted many to speak out against the parties' traditional barriers against women.

Opinion pollsters also began to see the first glimmerings of a "gender gap" and a group of voters who would support a party only if it were sympathetic to women. The significant thing about a gender gap, say Lise Gottell and Janine Brodie, "is not so much that men and women perceive the issues of the day differently, but that these political preferences might provide the margin of victory for one party or another."[15] Motivated by the only thing that really moves our parties—electoral self-interest—all three created funds and programs to encourage the selection of high-profile female candidates in desirable ridings. Before and during the 1993 campaign, there was also a great deal of media hype about the parties' all-out "scramble for female candidates."[16] The results, a mere 3 per cent increase in the number of women running, show that the public relations victory was much more impressive than the progress for women.

Only the NDP adopted true affirmative action: the party promised that 50 per cent of its candidates in the 1993 election would be women. (It also sought out visible minority and aboriginal candidates.) Once the women were found and approved, nominating meetings were scheduled and members informed. The candidates then received $1,200 each from the NDP's Agnes Macphail Fund. (Macphail was also a founder of the Co-operative Commonwealth Federation.)

The Tories and Liberals had their own ambitious plans to attract more women. The Liberals' Judy LaMarsh Fund, established in 1984, provides women candidates with an organizing network, training, seminars on campaigning, and modest funding. In the 1993 election, thanks in part to this "Judy Campaign," Liberal women had an impressive success ratio of 56 per cent. Yet only 21 per cent of the Liberal Party's candidates were women, well short of Jean Chrétien's already modest pre-campaign goal of 25 per cent. Had the Liberals nominated women in just 100 of the 295 ridings, it's very likely that enough would have been elected—perhaps 50 to 60—to bring about a truly shattering break with the past.

Before the 1993 campaign began, Chrétien surprised many people inside and outside his party by directly appointing nine female candidates. He was determined to raise the percentage of women running for his party, but he had a second goal as well: to keep anti-abortion Liberals out of his caucus. In at least three of the ridings, Chrétien's appointment of women headed off strong challenges by members of Liberals for Life. When he named Jean Augustine, chairman of the Metro Toronto Housing Authority, to run in Etobicoke-Lakeshore, the pro-lifers were furious. Thwarted candidate Dan McCash called Chrétien "a tired old man who doesn't know how to lead the party." In the end, it was McCash who crashed politically.

There were also bitter hoots from Canada's right wing. Reform Party MP Deborah Grey jeered, "I want to work with *good* women, not someone that Jean Chrétien appointed." If Reform leader Preston Manning had anointed her without a nomination meeting, she says, "I'd feel like some wimp or something."[17] Conservative Mary Collins, then the minister responsible for the status of women, called the move dictatorial. The most hypocritical reaction came from the NDP's Nelson Riis, whose party had "designated" many of its 113 women candidates. "There are ways and means to ensure that women candidates are successful in nominations without the leader stepping in and using this draconian measure," Riis trumpeted. In fact, the NDP's selection meetings were tamer than the Liberals' only because so few people wanted the party's nominations.

Chrétien makes no apologies for his elevation of women candidates. "We had a goal of having 25 per cent, hopefully, but not only in ridings where they have no chance to win. It's easy to have 50 per cent but you put them in ridings where there is no chance. I refuse to do that. I have helped women to get selected, and I have appointed women to make sure.

"In the old days it was not done the way I do it. One of my problems is that I wanted to do it in the open. I've been around and I know how you do it: you break arms and legs and you manoeuvre in a way that your candidate is selected. I changed that; I said, 'If I have to do it, let's do it in the open.' It was not backroom manipulation, it was me." Asked if he feared a backlash, he said, "I live with backlash, but you turn the page. I do something, and if I feel I've done it right I keep going."[18]

The tactic certainly didn't hurt the Liberals on election day, when six of the nine appointed women won their ridings. They helped Chrétien's Liberals, with thirty-six women in caucus, shatter the Tory record for the largest number of women in a federal government caucus (twenty-one in 1988). Politically,

Chrétien is much better off than he would have been with several pro-life males in their place. His controversial move was an unqualified political and public relations victory—so successful, in fact, that hardly anybody considered what it said about the Liberal Party: that in order to get sixty-four women to run in 1993, the leader still had to appoint nine of them. Chrétien knew that his party had not changed very much since 1988, when it nominated only thirty-seven women.

Female candidates for the Conservatives had support from the Ellen Fairclough Foundation. Once again, the results—one victory for sixty-seven women—demonstrate the obvious truth that candidates can only win in substantial numbers when their parties are popular. (In 1984, when the Tories were in high favour, an extraordinary nineteen of their twenty-three women candidates won.) The Reform Party had absolutely no program to encourage women candidates in 1993; indeed, the party denies the existence of women's issues. Yet Reform nominated twenty-three and seven of them won. (If the party had a fund to help women, says MP Deborah Grey, "I wouldn't take a dollar of it. It's tokenism.") Luckily for the Reformers, the party's relative popularity did the work of affirmative action. The Bloc Québécois, which also had no plan to find and support women candidates, nominated ten, eight of whom won their ridings.

It's clear that mechanisms for choosing women candidates, whether it's the NDP's affirmative action, Reform's free-for-all, or the Bloc's benign neglect, are largely irrelevant. What matters is that all parties offer equal numbers of female and male candidates. Yet party prejudice runs deep and is hard to root out. Tory senator Janis Johnson remembers the stunned incomprehension of her party and many MPs when Brian Mulroney made her the party's national director in 1984. "When I went to the first caucus meeting as national director, I was received with sort of this hushed silence as I entered the room. I was young, a woman, and from the West. I think some people thought he [Mulroney] had taken leave of his senses. . . . They asked me what a woman's issue was. One guy who couldn't believe it after I'd spoken looked at me and said, 'I don't mean to be rude, but I don't know what you're talking about.' And that was only ten years ago."[19]

Much has changed in that decade. There are more women in Parliament than ever before, after an election that offered the most female candidates ever. Gradually, but with increasing confidence, women are taking major roles in their parties, both at the national and local levels. By 1992, polls conducted by Insight Canada Research showed that a woman candidate had a 2 per cent better chance than a man of winning a given riding in an election. "People perceive women candidates as more honest and more trustworthy," said Insight chairman Michael Marzolini. Experienced politicians like Barbara McDougall now feel that being female is an advantage, although women "must still go that extra mile. Sexism lies there just under the surface."[20]

One highly encouraging sign is that more female delegates are attending party conventions. In 1967, only 19 per cent of delegates at the annual Tory meeting were women, while the Liberals drew just 18 per cent the following year. By 1989, 46 per cent of federal Tory delegates were women. At the 1990 Liberal convention in Calgary that chose Jean Chrétien as leader, 47 per cent of the delegates were women.[21]

For a few brief months in 1993, the prime minister was a woman and so was her chief of staff, Jodi White. NDP leader Audrey McLaughlin dumped a male chief of staff and gave the job to Saskatoon lawyer Sandra Mitchell. McLaughlin's caucus research director was Tessa Hebb, and her party president was labour activist Nancy Riche.[22] In this new climate, few men in any of the parties, let alone a member of Parliament, would have the bravado to say to a woman like Janis Johnson, "I don't know what you're talking about." Women are slowly changing the alien political culture in the only way they can—through sheer numbers.

In the 1990s, voting patterns clearly show that Canadians do not discriminate against female aspirants for office. They only discriminate against candidates who run for parties they dislike—women or men. The major stumbling block to women's political aspirations today is not the voters, but the parties that still refuse to nominate equal numbers of competent women. Many women are increasingly frustrated and angry about this stubborn paternalism. One radical response is to form parties that nominate only women. In Manitoba, women began working in March 1994 to create such a party in time to run in the next provincial election. Charging that the four women in the Manitoba NDP caucus "look just like a bunch of men in jeans," party organizer Marcelle Marion argued that "it's not enough to elect women to the legislature; there has to be an acknowledgment of the women's agenda as well." She said that men would be welcome to participate in the party at some level (possibly serving coffee) but would not be allowed to stand as candidates.

With its Icelandic influence, Manitoba is the ideal place for such an experiment.[23] In the 1980s, Iceland's Women's Alliance held the balance of power after an election, and was invited to join a coalition with the main parties. It refused, but continued to have strong influence on the government, often running third among six parties in public opinion polls. Canadians might not be attracted to gender-exclusive parties (although we had them for a century when the beneficiaries were men), but their formation is a clear message to the old parties: open up the gates to women, or get ready for competition.

11

CLOSER TO HOME

"I work in a very hostile workplace."

Marion Boyd,
Ontario attorney-general

"It's terrible, but you have to show them you can be rough and tough and beat them up if you need to."

Janice MacKinnon,
Saskatchewan finance minister

As male MPPs shouted accusations of "rape" and "gang rape," their cries flying like knives across the floor of the Ontario legislature, Frances Lankin found herself upset to the point of tears. The provincial NDP minister realized that the opposition had hit upon a legitimate issue, sexual harassment of female trainees at the Bell Cairn school for jail guards in

Hamilton. She also knew exactly what the members were talking about. As a guard at Toronto's tough Don Jail earlier in her career, Lankin had often felt victimized and harassed by other guards. But today she saw that male opposition members were exploiting the issue with too much enjoyment, casually bellowing words that strike many women as sharply as blows. They were hardly considering the feelings of female MPPs, some of whom sat hunched in their seats, oppressed by the din that masqueraded as a defence of their gender. And if the charges were true, Lankin felt, the men who made them certainly were not being sensitive to female guards who had been raped.

"I was hurt by the way they took this issue and sensationalized it, and proceeded day after day to yell about gang rape," she recalls. "There are more women in the Ontario legislature than there have been in the past. More than one of us has been a victim of violence and assault or sexual assault. . . . This was dragging me down to the point where I didn't know whether I was going to explode in tears or in rage. I was one of three women who first started working at the Don Jail in Toronto and experienced tremendous acts of harassment and violence. So it hit me in a personal way."

Beginning to break down in tears, Lankin left the chamber. After a time the legislature grew increasingly rowdy and the Speaker called a break. "I pulled myself together," Lankin says, "and I went across to the room behind the opposition area and I found the Tory member who was being most outrageous in his language. I don't know where it came from inside, but I went up to him and said: 'You have got to stop this, stop this provocative language, this exploitation. If you really care about this, stop grabbing the headlines and deal with the issue. There are women on my side of the house who are survivors of assault. The way you are characterizing this, there are people in anguish in the legislature, and there must be some on your side too.'

"He went quite ashen and said, 'You're right, I'm sorry.' And he actually changed his language."[1]

The male MPP was Conservative member Bob Runciman, from Leeds-Grenville riding, who first brought the training school scandal to the legislature. No friend of the New Democrats, Runciman believes they can be unduly touchy and "politically correct" about other people's language. "Sometimes I see a real lack of sincerity in their complaints," he says. But on this day, he realized at once that Frances Lankin was serious. "She was really upset and she certainly meant what she was saying. I don't think I'm an insensitive lout. I told her, 'Okay, fine,' and I didn't refer to the issue in those terms again."[2]

The episode underscores how women politicians, when in sufficient numbers, can begin to change both the tone and the substance of debate. Yet the struggle smoulders on, and every gain must be won against generations of inborn tradition and prejudice. As Lankin's colleague Marion Boyd has pointed out, the workplace is still hostile. But there are now women in provincial legislatures all across Canada who coax and prod the men into considering points of view they have never recognized before. Slowly, as their numbers increase, they are changing the language of politics.

Progress toward equality is still distressingly slow in some provinces (see Appendix 1, Table 2)—only 6 per cent of members in Newfoundland's House of Assembly are women, and in the Nova Scotia legislature the total is 10 per cent. But in several provinces, women legislators are nearing the "critical mass" of one-quarter to one-third. Because many women feel more comfortable running for office close to home so they can be near their families, it's likely that further major advances will occur in these legislatures before filtering up to the national Parliament.

Recent elections in several provinces have brought substantial gains for women. In British Columbia, the 1991 vote won by the New Democrats raised the quota of female legislators from 13 per cent to 25 per cent. Prince Edward Island, where both the premier and opposition leader are women, saw an equally impressive jump in female representation—from 9 per cent to 25 per cent in the 1993 election. Next come Ontario and Manitoba, both at 21 per cent, up from 15 per cent and 16 per cent, respectively, in their previous general elections. These provinces are substantially ahead of the federal Parliament, where women MPs hold 18 per cent of the seats, up from 13 per cent in Brian Mulroney's final government.

Even in Newfoundland, where the idea of women's political equality is lightly rooted, female representation has tripled, from 2 per cent to 6 per cent. Most important, some of the biggest gains are being made in larger provinces, especially B.C. and Ontario. Quebec's female representation before the September 12 election was equal to Ottawa's at 18 per cent, and included extremely strong women such as deputy premier Monique Gagnon-Tremblay, and former deputy premier Lise Bacon. (See Appendix 1 tables for full statistics on provincial and federal representation.)

Sometimes, however, the election of more women coincides with less progress on issues that matter to women. Alberta provides a telling example: In the 1993 election, female representation in the provincial legislature climbed from 15 per cent to 19 per cent, even though Tory leadership candidate Nancy Betkowski had been defeated by Ralph Klein in a campaign with blatantly sexist overtones. (One provincial cabinet minister, asked later by a former government worker to support Kim Campbell, said bluntly, "I didn't back a woman for provincial leader. Why the hell would I support one for federal leader?") With the defeat and subsequent resignations of Betkowski and another strong female leadership candidate, Elaine McCoy, the beleaguered feminist element was blown out of the government caucus. Newly powerful Tory ministers such as Dianne Mirosh and Pat Black stated proudly that they are not feminists, and they have no impulse to extend any special help to women. Mirosh's main contribution to the dialogue between the sexes was her performance in a skit at a provincial Tory convention, when she played a nurse who repeatedly squealed about the "hammer" in a male minister's pocket.[3] Despite polls that showed high public support for pay equity legislation, Mirosh said, "People in this province are sick and tired of constant legislation forcing issues." Her close friend Ken Kowalski, the deputy premier, called pay equity "a communist approach" to meeting the salary demands of working women.

After the Conservatives were re-elected under Klein in mid-1993, Mirosh was demoted and several promising new female MLAs joined the Tory caucus. Despite rumours that the Women's Secretariat would be abolished, the government left it in place. There is no lack of women's activism in Alberta: seminars of Winning Women, the group dedicated to electing more women of all political views, are packed with eager participants, including Conservative MLAs. The Alberta spirit that launched the Persons Case is still very much alive. But drastic government spending cuts in all sectors have tended to push women's concerns off the public agenda. With the very survival of schools and hospitals at stake, many women have quickly set aside their own goals and organized campaigns to maintain the quality of health and education programs.

Ontario's approach under Bob Rae's New Democrats is the polar opposite of Alberta's. Soon after he was elected in September 1990, Rae gave notice that he intended to advance women aggressively, first by naming twelve women to his twenty-seven-member cabinet. At 44 per cent, this was by far the largest female contingent ever to enter the inner circle of a Canadian government. The move was all the more striking because there were only nineteen women in the entire NDP caucus of seventy-three. Rae later reduced the size of his cabinet to twenty, but there were still eight women ministers, or 40 per cent of the total. The premier compensated for the slight drop in female cabinet members by naming three women (Marion Boyd, Frances Lankin, and Ruth Grier) to the seven-member committee on priorities and planning.

"In the old traditional sense, he didn't have to do any of that," says Evelyn Gigantes, veteran NDP member and former housing minister. "There weren't as many NDP women elected as men. A lot of the women who were elected weren't as experienced as some of the men he left out of cabinet. He made a very deliberate choice there, and I'm sure there were men who felt they were owed a place in cabinet. But many of those same men were fully supportive of the notion that women have to be represented."[4] With Lyn

McLeod leading the Liberal Official Opposition, the powerful presence of women in the legislature was impossible to ignore.

Despite the goodwill perceived by Evelyn Gigantes, some male New Democrats did resent being excluded from cabinet. One female minister told *The Toronto Star*, "We battle, as many women do, this attitude from some that we are here only because of affirmative action; that we've taken jobs some men think more rightly belong to them."

From the start, the NDP women, with Rae's support, were determined to change not just the tone of government, but every core policy affecting women. The New Democrats have passed strict pay equity laws that forced major adjustments across the public and private sectors, increased day-care spaces, begun campaigns against sexual assault and wife abuse, tried to curb sexism in beer advertising, introduced mandatory payroll deductions for child support, increased access to abortion, raised the minimum wage to $6.70 an hour, recognized midwifery as a medical profession, and ensured that half of all new judges and crown attorneys are women. In a time of recession and high deficits, the government has not hesitated to pump money into these programs. In 1994 alone, it will spend $99 million on measures to prevent violence against women. Since 1990, it has increased funding on subsidized child care by 45 per cent, and the new pay equity law means that the NDP will spend $568 million to raise wages in some of the lowest-paid women's jobs.[5]

Most of these moves have been met with fierce opposition from business, and some of them—especially pay equity— brought howls of outrage from public agencies such as health boards. The New Democrats made themselves vastly unpopular by launching an expensive social reform, almost a revolution, in the midst of the deepest recession since the 1930s. Businesses found many ways to circumvent the new law guaranteeing equal pay for women. They placed employees on contract, forced unpaid overtime and shorter work weeks, and hired part-time workers.[6] The government's employment equity campaign aimed at hiring more women, often by posting advertisements that bar men from applying, has made many men angry and resentful. Even Thomas Walkom, *The Toronto Star's* fair-minded Queen's Park columnist, called the decision to hire on the basis of race and sex "wrong, unwise and unfortunate." Women should be "given the nod" when applicants are of equal merit, he argued, but excluding any group from applying is dangerous. "The government has merely succeeded in creating a new victim: the able-bodied white male."

The policies created almost as much turmoil at the heart of Rae's inexperienced young government. Some NDP men argued that, if implemented too quickly, the policies would create a serious backlash and hurt the government badly. They were partly right, but the women countered that the chance to make fundamental changes could not be squandered. With Rae's support, the women usually won.

In the everyday life of the legislature, male New Democrats also made many blunders that showed they were not immune to stereotypes. NDP member Drummond White, while chairing the legislature justice committee, once referred to a feminist lawyer as "Mrs." She said she would rather be addressed as "Ms." White retorted: "I always want to give the benefit of the doubt." He was hissed by committee members, including New Democrats.

The presence of a large and powerful group of female ministers led to cabinet battles over issues that once would have been settled over lunch. For instance, a noisy cabinet argument erupted over a proposal to create jobs by spending $700 million on roads and sewers. The female ministers pointed out, perhaps for the first time in a Canadian cabinet meeting, that almost all the money would go to male construction workers. One minister snapped, "You're not going to fight this recession on the backs of women."

There were deep divisions within Rae's government when the federal Tories proposed to make abortion a criminal offence except in cases when a doctor certifies that pregnancy threatens a woman's emotional and physical well-being. Feminists in cabinet pressed Rae to say he would not enforce such legislation, but Howard Hampton, then the attorney-general, was said to reject any such threat to the "rule of law." On this issue the feminists eventually won: the bill was narrowly defeated in Ottawa, and Marion Boyd later became Ontario's attorney-general, the first non-lawyer, as well as the first woman, ever to hold the job.

In the legislature, opposition members often demeaned female members by mocking their voices and blowing kisses. But as Frances Lankin showed by confronting a male MPP, the NDP women now had more latitude to oppose behaviour and language that offended them, and they enjoyed added clout because every MPP in the legislature knew that the premier was behind them. Rae deserves considerable credit for this support, even though he has suffered for it just as the admirable Denis Thatcher did. Gradually Rae was dressed in the "wimp" cloak that seems to fall over the shoulders of every political man who supports women's causes. In the eyes of many Ontarians he began to appear captive to the women and there-fore less than a man. (*Frank* magazine took to calling him "Norma Bob Rae.")

Even women on the left began to turn against Rae during acrimonious contract negotiations with the civil service. The real-ity is that Rae, far from being a wimp, has been resolute in the face of implacable opposition and warnings that he would destroy his government. The changes that benefit women are being woven into Ontario's everyday fabric, so that if the NDP loses the next election, a new government is likely to leave much of the legislation in place.

But even with all the women in government, and the good-will of most of the men, the struggle remains a daily trial. As Frances Lankin says, "Politics in general is a very male culture, and the legislature is another example. I have said in the past— and I know this drives some members of the legislature crazy, on all sides of the house—that I experience it almost as abuse or violence. The yelling and the antics and the grabbing the thirty-second clip. I find that after being there for so long it's starting to get to *me!* They're starting to transform *me!* As long as they keep fighting, you become part of that institutional culture. . . .

"There are a number of men in our cabinet who have made a major contribution there. But when it comes to the legislature, I don't think we've been able to change the political culture. . . . I can't believe the bombastic, synthetic outrage that is displayed there. They're red in the face, they're shaking their fist, then they sit down, and once the camera is off them they wink and laugh and smile."

Evelyn Gigantes has a milder impression, at least of some male legislators. "When I was first elected in 1975," she says, "the men MPPs didn't have the same role in the family as they do now. The average age of the legislature has dropped significantly, and there are a lot of young fathers now. Their view of their role in their children's lives, and their relationships with their spouses, is very different. So I feel more kinship with the men than I used to."[7] From her longer perspective, the behaviour is at least improving.

Attorney-General Marion Boyd notices a profound difference in style and priorities that goes far beyond surface antics. "I think women come from a more practical perspective," she says. "It's very important to us to know if something will work—not whether it sounds good, but how's it actually going to work. If you've had to run a household, hold down a full-time job, and raise children, and maintain relationships, you have to be very clear about time management. We often laugh on Wednesday mornings at cabinet, because the people who arrive first and are sitting around the table ready for the meeting are mostly the women. We're tempted to start early, as soon as we get a quorum."[8]

Boyd believes that the only way to make progress in this environment is through patience and understanding of the other viewpoint. Rooted traditions cannot be challenged head on all the time, she says. "It's the issue we always face as feminists—can we manage to work within an institution, or can we only be activists outside of institutions? If we can work within the institution to make change, of course we must do that. But that change doesn't happen overnight. The more venerable the institution, the harder it is, because there are real traditions that matter a great deal to people. People often equate stability and strength with maintaining what has existed in the past. Anyone who is considering going into politics mustn't be naive about how strong those traditions are. . . .

"I work in a very hostile workplace. Some of that hostility is very direct and is couched in party political terms. It comes from those who assume that the people who have always exercised power should continue to exercise power." Because of this, Boyd says, it is still difficult to convince other women to come into politics. "It's hard to go out and say to women, 'Come on in and maybe we can change it from the inside.' We know exactly how hard it is to change it from inside. Until there are a sufficient number of women to give each other support so that we don't slide into the other kind of behaviour—which is always dangerous for us—then it's hard to say to women that we wholeheartedly encourage them. The truth is, this is not a very healthy environment."

Boyd took her concerns to a legislature committee in 1992, arguing that women were special targets of "demeaning and insulting" comments in the legislature. She charged, for instance, that male MPPs intentionally raise the level of heckling when women members are speaking. "These tactics are employed primarily against women in an attempt to intimidate us, diminish our authority and to reinforce the idea that the House is not meant to be our home," Boyd told the committee.

Ontario's NDP women have tried to change the very vocabulary of politics, often with results that can seem hilariously picayune, as well as annoying to voters who don't like being told how they should talk. But Boyd makes no apology for trying to create a language that offends no one. It's vitally important, she believes, to consider people and name them as they want to be named. To her, "political correctness" is a term invented by those who want to demean the powerless when they ask to be treated equally. With no sense of irony, Boyd describes cabinet debates over the word "grandfathering" as it applies to legislation. "For a while people were saying that maybe you should use 'grandmothering,' and I'd say, why don't we just say 'grandparenting'?

There's very seldom a meeting that goes by when we don't remind each other that the language we've agreed to use is 'grandparenting.' And it's hard. We forget, we all do."

In 1993, an agency of the government, the Ontario Women's Directorate, caused an uproar when it produced a pamphlet called "Words That Count Women In." The publication suggested hundreds of replacements for words that imply gender bias: underwater technician for frogman, terminator for hatchet man, seducer for femme fatale, Renaissance type for Renaissance man, sustaining earth for mother earth, average citizen for John Q. Public, native language for mother tongue, honour system for gentleman's agreement, dead zone for no-man's-land, monkey business for tomfoolery, skilled for masterful, and synthetic for man-made. The document also suggested replacing "balls" with "moxie" or "guts." It provoked an avalanche of commentary from columnists like Rosie DiManno, whose name, one *Toronto Star* reader quipped, should be changed to "DiPersonno." DiManno hated the pamphlet, while others, including *Toronto Star* columnist Michelle Landsberg, found the directory's ideas good-humoured and inoffensive. The pamphlet went through several printings after a flood of orders from corporations, schools, and media. In May 1994, the government unleashed another public furor by introducing Canada's first legislation intending to give equal rights of marriage, adoption, and benefits to gay couples. The legislation was defeated amidst much controversy.

For all their considerable power to push such issues—the most that political women have ever exercised in Canada—the Ontario NDP women are often exhausted and frustrated. Boyd and Lankin say the demands of cabinet are so heavy that it's difficult to maintain their women's network within the government. They are always being pulled back to the routine details of their ministries, and keeping up the pressure on women's issues is a constant struggle. In a way their role is hardly different from that of Judy LaMarsh or Flora MacDonald; they are expected to do all the regular chores of government, and the "women's work" as well. Still, they have male colleagues who accept some of the responsibility, and the gains they have made would have been incomprehensible (or even offensive) to a Judy LaMarsh. But their burden is largely the same: in politics as in the home, women end up assuming extra chores.

The effect on personal lives is profound and often devastating. Lankin says that when she was in the labour movement, she began trying to integrate work with private activities. "I was becoming a more balanced person. As soon as I got into politics, it was shot all to hell. The expectation of being on top of all things at all times really makes it difficult to have a balanced life. I'm a single person, and destined to stay that way, I'm afraid."

Many of these experiences sound familiar to Lyn McLeod, leader of the Official Opposition, and head of the province's Liberals. The Sudbury politician, who was Ontario's energy and natural resources minister when David Peterson was premier, often had to endure headlines such as "New Natural Resources Minister Doesn't Fish," as well as snickering about her height (she is barely five feet tall). Like many women politicians before her, she has had more problems within her party than with the electorate.

"In the leadership race," she says, "I started to run into those stereotypical questions, such as: 'is she strong enough to do this job?' There's a tendency to think of women as being more consensual, and the consensual style is seen as not being tough enough to deal with tough times. We have to be careful not to assume that this is necessarily gender, because the question is also asked of a male who is more consensual in his approach. But as a woman, if you have an image of toughness, you are often accused of stridency, and that's not seen to be acceptable either. . . .

"The whole challenge is breaking down these stereotypes. Behind them there's a hint of the thought: 'the little lady shouldn't trouble her head with business.'" When McLeod first ran for the school board in her community, she was told she wouldn't be interested in sitting on the budget committee. "I went from there to being on the economic policy committee of [Peterson's] cabinet. I was the only woman on that committee, and it took me twenty years to get from one to the other. Progress was a little slow."[9]

For a time, McLeod seemed to have a chance to become Ontario's first female premier. Opinion polls showed the Liberals running ahead of the New Democrats and Conservatives through most of 1993 and into 1994. But her popularity took a dip in June 1994, when she was accused of hypocrisy during the emotional clash over the NDP's same-sex marriage bill, which was intended to extend spousal benefits to homosexuals. McLeod joined the majority in voting against the bill, even though a year earlier she had urged Premier Rae to bring in same-sex legislation.

McLeod promises that if she is elected, she will reverse or rewrite much NDP legislation that she believes has robbed Ontario of its competitive advantage. The NDP, she says, shows "a strong distrust of the private sector," along with an "orientation and an imbalance towards the labour sector." Few will argue with that, but it's hardly likely that McLeod would uproot all the equity laws and feminist changes firmly implanted by the New Democrats. Against the will of many, including some within their own party, NDP women have succeeded in demolishing many of the barriers faced by Ontario women for more than a hundred years. For a province that did not elect a single female MPP until 1943, this is a huge accomplishment. A new government would have to be very impetuous—and foolish—to try moving back in time as we approach the year 2000.

Under Mike Harcourt's NDP government, elected in B.C. in 1991, the Victoria legislature has an even stronger female presence than Ontario's: more than 25 per cent of the MLAs are women. Seven of Harcourt's nineteen ministers—nearly 37 per cent—are women, and he quickly named Penny Priddy as Canada's only minister responsible solely for women's equality. Priddy's first deputy minister was Dr. Sheila Wynn, a skilled and seasoned bureaucrat who had fostered women's issues in Alberta, a much more fragile environment, and in Ottawa's bureaucratic jungle, before going to Victoria. Priddy produced a blizzard of initiatives, many of them controversial in B.C.'s highly polarized society: increased funding for day care, programs to fight violence against women, employment equity in the civil service, revamped labour laws that made it easier for women to organize, and an aggressive policy to find female appointees for provincial boards and commissions. In a move that enraged the province's voluble right wing, the government also changed the Limitations Act to allow survivors of childhood sexual abuse to take legal action regardless of the time that had passed since the abuse occurred.[10]

None of this serious purpose inoculated the New Democrats against the zaniness that is never absent from B.C. politics. Early in her tenure, Priddy took eighty-five of her bureaucrats to a policy brainstorming session at a posh Vancouver Island resort. To warm up for the discussions, the feminists made abstract sculptures and mobiles from knitting needles and drinking straws. In 1994, the new social services minister, Joy MacPhail, spent nearly $3,500 on a weekend retreat at Tigh-Na-Mara, a wooded seaside resort on Vancouver Island, where she and eleven bureaucrats discussed ways to help the poor. Premier Harcourt, when he heard about the retreat, helped her identify more closely with the poor by ordering the participants to pay back the money. MacPhail's share was $1,656. "You learn and grow from each experience," said the minister. "And I certainly have done that and I actually consider that a positive aspect."

For the women in Harcourt's government, there's no shortage of learning experiences. Anne Edwards, the minister of energy, mines and petroleum resources, finds that she has to establish her credentials every time she holds a meeting with the men who control the industry. "People want to satisfy themselves that I know something about the business," she says. "That part is always explored very carefully before we get down to any serious talk about anything. I'm always introduced as a graduate in English from the University of Saskatchewan, so everybody wonders what in hell I have to do with mines in B.C."[11]

The men will have to get used to it because, as Edwards points out, for a time the four largest provinces all had women in the "dirt porfolios"—in charge of mines, energy, or natural resources. The others were Pat Black in Alberta, Ontario's Shelley Martel, and Lise Bacon in Quebec. Later, Anne McLellan took on the equivalent job in Ottawa for the Liberal government. Edwards says, half joking, that this is appropriate because "there's always a bit of mothering to be done, and our resources certainly need some." But she notices a universal phenomenon: men in the industry won't make eye contact with her until they understand that she has the power to make decisions. "It's a symptom that they're not really sure of what's going to happen. They wonder: 'Have you really got any authority, or should we go and talk to the premier to get something done?'" Once Edwards establishes that she's the boss, the dealings become frank and direct. But the stereotypes are still powerful: in deference to her gender, the machinery and exhibits at a mining trade fair were once explained to her as if they were dresses in a fashion show.

Mike Harcourt gave another vital non-traditional portfolio—finance—to Elizabeth Cull, her reward for two difficult but successful years in the health ministry. Cull also became one of only two female deputy premiers in the country, along with Monique Gagnon-Tremblay in Quebec.[12] Even enemies of the NDP concede that Cull, a former urban planner, is an exceptionally intelligent and able politician. During a bitter fee dispute with B.C. doctors, one physicians' representative said of her, "We don't like her, but if I was on the other side I would think she was great. Throughout our fight, she stuck to her guns. And we're no pushovers." By the time Cull assumed finance, hardly anyone complained that a woman should not do a job reserved exclusively for men for more than a century.

Canada's first female finance minister was Cull's NDP colleague in Saskatchewan, Janice MacKinnon, who took over the job in early 1993 after the former minister, Ed Tchorzewski, cited job stress and moved up to deputy premier. It was an understandable reaction: Saskatchewan was nearly bankrupt, and Ottawa had actually made plans to revert the province to its pre-1905 status as a ward of the federal government. MacKinnon has the added disadvantage of being an elegant and attractive blonde. Her qualifications for the job were questioned immediately, even though she had been a university history professor, and had written two books and many articles, some on the free trade agreement with the U.S. Her most recent academic achievement is a study showing that loyalist women, far from being weak and dependent, were active participants in the American Revolutionary War. She presented a paper on her research at a conference in Vancouver in May 1994, while she was finance minister.

In that post, MacKinnon quickly and competently got to work in a difficult situation: she raised taxes, cut the annual deficit in half, and laid out a four-year plan to eliminate overspending entirely. When the Tories criticized her performance, the *Moosomin World-Spectator* handed her the ultimate in backhanded compliments: "Even if the Tories are correct and MacKinnon is horrible at her job, she can certainly be no worse than the various finance ministers in the Devine government. The woman deserves a chance. The Tory critics deserve a spanking."[13]

For a province with a long NDP history, women's representation in the Saskatchewan legislature is surprisingly low, at 18 per cent (although far better than the pre-1991 figure of only 8 per cent). Nor is female cabinet representation very impressive in the government of Roy Romanow. Four of nineteen ministers, or 21 per cent, are women. But MacKinnon's powerful presence—as finance minister, she is third on the status list behind Romanow and Tchorzewski—makes up for a good deal.

She handles the oddities of being a woman in charge of public money with a shrewd eye and keen humour. "After I read the budget," she says, "I got letters that male finance ministers have never received around here. People said, 'I liked your dark blue suit. It looked very businesslike.' Or, 'Your white blouse was nice, and your hair was good, not too short, not too long. I noticed you didn't wear any bright nail polish. I would like to have you as a neighbour.' And then they go and make a comment. One man said I looked very nice and then added, 'Why did you bring out a budget like that? I can't believe somebody as nice as you would bring out such a budget.' The positive side is that I've had a lot of women come up to me and say things like, 'Oh, you're doing a very good job. Are you okay? Are you surviving all right?' They're very supportive. The vast majority of women, when they see another woman there, they want her to succeed."[14]

There is another type of woman, though, and MacKinnon met one at a cocktail party shortly after she became finance minister. "It was all men and their wives," she recalls. "A woman came up to me, an older woman, and said in a kind of imperious way, 'Oh, and who are you, dear? And who are you with?' A friend saw me sort of steeling up. I said who I was but she didn't hear me and just wandered off. Her husband took her aside and said, 'What is the matter with you? That was the minister of finance.' You get some women who treat you like that, too."

MacKinnon's favourite incident occurred just after she became social services minister following the NDP victory in 1991. "I was at a head table in Prince Albert. There were about twenty people and they were all being introduced, but not in any particular order. And I realized that I hadn't been introduced. I looked around and saw that I was the only woman up there. The person who was introducing us said the Mayor of Prince Albert had brought his wife. I looked around and asked myself, 'Where is she?' Then the Mayor, who was sitting right next to me, looked over and said, 'They think you're my wife.' "

When MacKinnon looks across the aisle of the Saskatchewan legislature, she sees Lynda Haverstock, the province's outspoken Liberal leader. Although she was elected as her party's only MLA in 1991, Haverstock's caucus now includes an NDP defector and a woman who won a Regina by-election for the Liberals. Haverstock suspects she won her party's leadership largely because it was going nowhere. This usually happens, she says, "when a party is in such a state that it's possible for a woman to take over." But Haverstock, who sometimes criticizes her party and rejects "traditional" politics, has raised her party substantially in the polls, and enjoys high personal popularity.

Haverstock recognizes a kindred spirit in MacKinnon. "It's a major breakthrough that we have a woman finance minister," she says. "I think it is interesting to see how often people will undermine her because she is a woman. People say, 'How much work does she actually do for herself, and which decisions does she actually make?' I find that interesting because they never ask that of a man."[15]

Unlike most female politicians, Haverstock is bluntly critical of women who can't accept their own kind as leaders. "I'm fortunate in that I'm a tall person," she says. "It has a bearing on the way people treat me. I'm taller than a lot of men, and because of that, they don't dismiss me readily. I've received more discrimination from women than from men. I don't find men as uncomfortable, if I'm in their presence for business meetings, as I have found women. There does seem to be some kind of discomfort, a lack of acceptance."

Haverstock isn't the first female professional to notice resentment from women whose role in life, as she says, is "to keep the home fires burning," and expect other women to do the same. This is one reason why she believes that politics remains "astonishingly narrow—it is one of the things in our society that has not evolved. Politics is so steeped in the old ways of doing things that it is years behind where the general public is going."

Haverstock feels that her "difficult life" equips her well for politics. She had a baby at age sixteen, and arthritis confined her to a wheelchair for a time when she was younger. She earned a doctorate in clinical psychology, lectured at the University of Saskatchewan, held popular public seminars on farm stress, and three years ago married a provincial civil servant. The birth of her granddaughter, she says, was "the thrill of my life." Sometimes she wonders why she forfeited a stable profession and an increasingly happy personal life to enter a field that often appalls her. "If there's any place where I have been dismissed and treated in an unwarranted manner, it's within my own party," she says. "And that's because of my commitment to a new politics. Some of the party people who have a desire to keep the politics of patronage are very much frustrated by someone like me."

By early 1994, however, her standing in the polls had risen so significantly that the party dissidents stopped sniping.

When Prince Edward Islanders went out to vote on March 29, 1993, they had a choice that women across the country could envy, and one that had never been offered to electors in Canadian history: the leaders of the only parties with a chance of winning were women. Catherine Callbeck, the Liberal leader, became Canada's first elected female premier. (Rita Johnston of B.C. was the first woman to be a provincial premier; she took over the Socred Party leadership from Bill Vander Zalm, but her party was crushed by Mike Harcourt's New Democrats in the 1991 election.) Lynda Haverstock believes that "Catherine Callbeck's election in P.E.I. was extraordinary for the very reason that it didn't seem extraordinary. It was the first time ever that gender simply was not an issue."

The P.E.I. Conservatives managed to snatch just one seat from Callbeck's victorious Liberals, and it went to their party leader, Patricia Mella. There was another momentous advance as well: female representation in the thirty-two-seat legislature rose from only 9 per cent to 25 per cent. Tiny P.E.I., with its population of 130,000, quietly became a laboratory for female political progress in Canada. The Legislature's Clerk Assistant, Charles A. MacKay, proudly lists the achievements: P.E.I has women serving as Lieutenant Governor (Marion Reid), Legislature Speaker (Nancy Guptill), Deputy Speaker (Elizabeth Hubley), Premier, and Opposition Leader.[16]

Premier Callbeck is not a feminist, however, and she has no special agenda for advancing women. When she named her cabinet, only one woman, Jeannie Lea, made the list, as a minister without portfolio. Female presence in cabinet was only 20 per cent (two of ten ministers), less than in the legislature as a whole, although it could be argued that Callbeck's job gives her the power of several ministers.

There is certainly no doubt that she's the boss. When Callbeck succeeded Joe Ghiz as Liberal leader and premier, she was already a veteran of Island politics. From 1974 to 1978, she served in the provincial cabinet of Liberal premier Alex Campbell. Callbeck then left elected politics for ten years to look after the family business, but in 1988 she ran in the federal election and became Liberal MP for Malpeque. When she decided in late 1992 to enter the provincial leadership race, she had built up a large group of friends and supporters the way women often do: by volunteering for many years on local boards, agencies, committees, and charities. Callbeck is an example of how these women's community activities, once a closed circle, can now lead to higher elected office.

She faced plenty of discimination early in her career, largely from men who didn't think she should run for office. But now, she says, "I honestly believe that people vote for the person they think can best do the job. We've reached that point in our society. There are just so many positions I can point to now that are held by women. Fifty years ago, it was unheard of."[17] When Callbeck was younger, she often found herself working in mainly male groups. "I was the only woman in my class in commerce at Mount Allison, the only woman teaching Business Administration at the Saint John Institute of Technology, and later the only woman in the cabinet of Premier Alex Campbell. So I really don't think in terms of whether I'm the only woman here or whether I'm not. I'm just used to that type of situation."

To become a politician, Callbeck overcame a disadvantage that afflicts many women. "I was extremely shy as a child," she says. "Even in my early twenties I would have been intimidated at the thought of entering public life. What changed this was getting involved in community activities. In 1973, we had our centennial year for the province, and I was asked to chair a committee of celebration. I really had to push myself to take that on, but I wanted to overcome this shyness. There were wonderful people on my committee, and the result was a great success. After that, one door just started to open after another.

"So my advice is that whatever you get into, give it your best. People recognize that. And those other people sitting around the table may be on another board or committee. They see that you'll give it all you have, so they want you on their board. One thing leads to another. Your name gets known as somebody who is hard-working and concerned."

Callbeck concedes that as a single woman, her track was probably smoother than that of most women who aspire to politics. "If a woman is married and has a family," she says, "it must be very difficult to balance your family obligations with the political ones. I'm sure it's difficult for men, too. But women have traditionally been the nurturers, so they have added problems. In politics you have to be really, really focused if you're going to do the job. It's demanding; it takes a lot of time and effort and energy. There are days when you're just going practically around the clock."

Callbeck does not bring what the Ontario New Democrats call "a feminist analysis" to politics. Her priorities are not driven by sexist language, male behaviour in the legislature, or gender inequities in society. Her rise to office will not bring a revolution to P.E.I., and as a result, she does not create strong emotions among the voters. "The odd person will say that the women are taking over, just jokingly," she says. "But I can honestly say I haven't felt any backlash." Traditional male politicians will say of a Catherine Callbeck: "She's okay—we can work with her." This is one reason why, as Callbeck notes, she has enjoyed "fantastic support" from party networks for most of her career.

Some Canadian women might wish she were more militant, or leading a larger province. But this rather wary woman is already a pivotal figure in the history of Canadian women in politics. Prince Edward Islanders, when they glance at their society, now see a competent power structure with a distinctly female face (even the chancellor of the University of Prince Edward Island is a woman). Whether this approach will better the lot of women in the long run remains to be seen.

With the sole exception of P.E.I., the record of the Atlantic provinces is by far the worst in the country when it comes to electing women. Newfoundland, with its 6 per cent female representation in the House of Assembly, seems hopelessly locked in the Jurassic age. New Brunswick, at 17 per cent, is closer to national trends, and Elizabeth Weir leads the New Democrats while holding their only legislature seat. But Nova Scotia's female representation level is, and always has been, dismal. Only ten women have been elected to the legislature since Gladys Muriel Porter secured a seat in 1960. Five of those won their places in 1993, when John Savage's Liberals took the government, but they still accounted for less than 10 per cent of the fifty-two-member house. Like Newfoundland, Nova Scotia still runs on exclusively male networks of patronage and privilege.

One of the bravest political figures in Canada is Alexa McDonough, the Nova Scotia NDP leader, an ardent feminist who has battled the provincial elite in the legislature for nearly fifteen years. She has been elected four times since 1981 in her Halifax Chebucto riding, often to sit as the only New Democrat in the legislature. (She now has two male MLAs in her caucus.) From a well-to-do establishment family, McDonough was once a Liberal and might have become a cabinet minister with ease; but in the 1970s, she grew disgusted with the government of Gerald Regan, joined the NDP, and in 1980 won the party leadership. Thus began her long odyssey as a feminist politician in a sea of patriarchy.

The journey often leaves her discouraged. "I wish I could say there have been dramatic changes for women in politics over the last decade," McDonough says. "But frankly, I don't see them. There are some small symbolic changes, but from a Nova Scotia perspective it's hard to be enthusiastic about that."

McDonough's most alarming experience with angry sexism came during the negotiations for the Charlottetown Accord, when she supported gender parity in a reformed Senate. "It was just ugly. I got hate mail from both men and women, screaming and yelling about how anti-male the idea was. They said that all kinds of important, deserving, powerful men in our society would be denied their rightful ascent to office if you put women in their way. It was awful stuff. People made threatening phone calls. I had a young man come storming in here who was so aggressive and agitated that my staff was actually very nervous. There were a number of strange incidents that made you remember how far we are from breaking down the prejudices and barriers. It probably did more to reinvigorate my own feminist commitment than anything else that's happened in a long time."

But McDonough admits that, for all the trials they endure, female politicians are highly favoured compared to other women. "In the early years of the legislature I often felt intimidated by the raving sexist attitudes," she says. "But I always reminded myself that I'm in a much more privileged position than some women when it comes to fighting back. Those men don't have any power over my job. They're not my boss, they can't fire me, they can't demote me, and they can't stand in the way of my promotion. Only the public gets to do that.

"When my male co-workers engage in overtly sexist practices, they do it in a fishbowl, and I damn well have the ability to fight back. I can expose them for what they are. How many women have the opportunity to do that?" Besides, Alexa McDonough laughs, "politics is one of the few areas where you get equal pay."[18]

Few of Canada's elected women, and none at all in provincial politics, have caught the public's eye as quickly and surely as Sharon Carstairs of Manitoba. Leader of the province's Liberal Party from 1984 to 1994, Carstairs nearly upset Gary Filmon's Conservatives to take the government in 1988. Largely because of her example, female representation in the Manitoba legislature stands at 21 per cent, the same as in Ontario, second only to B.C. and P.E.I. After the Meech Lake fiasco, and her admission that she had taken tranquillizers in order to sleep, the Liberals plunged in the polls and won only seven seats in the following election. In Manitoba, Carstairs seemed a spent political force. But her ten years on the stage left indelible memories in the minds of everyone who follows Canadian politics.

Her prominence was due partly to appearance and style. Carstairs' coke-bottle glasses and unique voice—she sounded like a tape on permanent fast-forward—made her impossible to ignore. She had a ready laugh, a quick and sometimes bitter wit, and a long memory for political slights. Like Judy LaMarsh before her, Carstairs didn't hesitate to attack the powerful people within her own party. Her autobiography, *Not One of the Boys*, hit the market in late 1993, just as the federal party swept back into office. This didn't prevent her from calling Lloyd Axworthy, the newly influential Winnipeg minister, "conceited and arrogant . . . my nemesis throughout my leadership." She also attacked the male "bullies" who rule politics and revealed that a relative had sexually abused her when she was a child. In her book, and in a later interview, Carstairs discussed the occupational hazards of being a woman at work: "when I was teaching I had a principal who came up to me and licked my ear at a cocktail party. I couldn't believe it."[19] Her political persona was shaped by her refusal to be bullied any longer.

Carstairs always resented the reaction to her voice and appearance. "I'd get letters, all too often from women, that were attacks on my hair, or my clothes, or my voice," she says. "The first couple of years you kind of ignore them. But as they go on and on, you feel diminished as a human being. That takes its toll, and it's something male politicians don't have to put up with. I was stopped by party people and told that I needed a haircut. I mean, we even had a caucus discussion on whether I should colour my hair! It was done in a bit of fun, you know, but half of them thought I should!

"We need sufficient numbers of women so that this stuff will stop being an issue. We need at least a quarter of any caucus to make significant changes. You also have to have women who are prepared to stand together, and that's not necessarily happening. We have to get women to be better friends with one another when they're younger. Until we get that mutual respect as human beings, and not as rivals for some male plumage, I feel that we won't cross those barriers."

When Carstairs announced her resignation as Liberal leader, she was replaced by Paul Edwards, a thirty-three-year-old lawyer who had absorbed many of her messages. "I am not Sharon

Carstairs, nor will I ever be," he said. "Sharon was an extremely charismatic, forceful person who did enormous things for our party. Those are shoes I will never fill in the same way." This admission prompted many people to snicker that Paul Edwards would look odd indeed in his predecessor's red pumps, and stranger still if he tried to become Sharon Carstairs. But these glib reactions merely demonstrated how men, and many women, still think first of gender (or of sex). Paul Edwards showed not a trace of this limiting attitude; instead, he could talk about a female leader without any reference to her gender. Edwards was able to consider only her leadership qualities, not just in his words, but in his whole attitude. It's a hopeful sign that a younger breed of leaders, drawing on their experience of strong female models, can at last begin to leave stereotypes behind.

In Quebec, it's possible for an observer as shrewd as columnist Francine Pelletier to say, "The battle is over, and feminism won." By some measures the statement seems exaggerated; as Quebec headed toward the 1994 provincial election, only 18 per cent of members of the National Assembly were women, and Premier Daniel Johnson's cabinet had just four female members out of twenty-one (19 per cent). But these appearances were misleading. The energetic deputy premier, Monique Gagnon-Tremblay, also held the most powerful levers of government as president of the Treasury Board and minister responsible for the public service. Another woman, Lise Bacon, had been deputy premier until she decided to retire when Robert Bourassa resigned because of ill health. The governing Liberal Party had an exceptionally high level of female participation: women accounted for 49 per cent of the party members and 38 per cent of those sitting on executive party bodies.[20] Quebec political women have a strong tradition of militancy dating back to Thérèse Casgrain's struggle for the vote and Monique Bégin's days at *La Fédération des Femmes du Québec*. In 1980, federalist women, reacting against their portrayal as traditional, house-bound *Yvettes*, organized huge rallies that helped carry the referendum for the No side.[21]

Perhaps most important, Québécois in general show an exceptionally high level of support for feminism. A 1992 Gallup poll found that 67 per cent of the Quebec population backed feminist goals. (The figure was 60 per cent in Ontario, 58 per cent in Atlantic Canada, 54 per cent on the Prairies and 52 per cent in British Columbia.) By 1994, an astonishing 85 per cent of the Quebec population championed the goals of the women's movement, and the support was split evenly among women and men. There was a widespread consensus that full implementation of pay equity would be the best way to help women reach true equality. "It's only a matter of time before women are a majority in the national assembly," Francine Pelletier says confidently.[22]

Quebec women have also reached high levels of credibility in the media. Pelletier, Lysiane Gagnon of *La Presse*, and Lise Bissonnette of *Le Devoir* have long been as influential as any commentators in the province. Often they combine lively writing with an intellectual depth that is all too rare in English Canada. (For instance, Pelletier once wrote: "There has always been a strange kind of kinship between Québécois and their politicians. A feeling that no matter how much you might hate them, they are part of the family."[23]) Peering past gender, Pelletier was one of the first female journalists in the country to question "Kim Campbell's Tinkerbell spell."

Despite all these encouraging signs, Quebec is far from a feminist paradise. In 1993, the government-appointed Quebec Status of Women Council decried the low number of women in public life, business, and university teaching. Lise Bacon, who had to struggle for her first party nominations, noted just before she retired: "To this day, when I speak out on an issue, reporters will refer to my 'curt tone' or say I was 'ruffled.' In other words, they use emotion-laden adjectives to describe me, whereas my male colleagues are called 'determined.'"[24]

Nationalism and feminism are often an uncomfortable match in Quebec, and feminism tends to take the rumble seat when emotions rise. There are also disturbing hints of anti-feminist backlash, says Francine Pelletier, "now that women are seen to have an advantage." Lise Bacon sounds like female politicians anywhere in Canada when she says: "We cannot rest on our laurels, as some were tempted to do in the late 1980s. We cannot be satisfied with our political gains. We must always continue working to push back the frontiers; we must keep after the political parties to seek out more qualified women candidates; we must continue pressing our concerns in the political arena."

Canada's North has never been chilly to female politicians who aspire to high office. In the Northwest Territories, Nellie Cournoyea was quietly serving as the elected "premier" before Catherine Callbeck won her victory in Prince Edward Island. Cournoyea, an Inuvialuit woman who was the CBC station manager in Inuvik, helped form the Inuvialuit land claims organization COPE (Committee for Original People's Entitlement). In 1979, Cournoyea put her broadcasting and land claims experience to the best political use, and won a seat in the N.W.T. legislature. Her tenacity and political acumen were instrumental in the federal government's land claim award of over $240 million to the Inuvialuit. As government leader, and minister responsible for four powerful portfolios, Cournoyea uses her consensual, no-nonsense style ("She doesn't differentiate between male and female politicians," says her assistant Art Sorensen) to oversee expansion of government services into more communities.[25] "By taking control of our own government, we have won control of our resources," writes *Up-here* editor Rosemary Allerston. "Cournoyea has signalled a historic shift: she's telling Canada we're open for business—on our own terms. And she's inviting Canadians to share the Northern Dream, thereby fulfilling our destiny as a Northern nation."[26] Audrey McLaughlin realized her own northern dream and was quickly accepted by Yukoners when she moved to Whitehorse from Toronto in 1979. She helped organize the Yukon election campaigns of her friends Margaret (Joe) Commodore and Norma Kassi, who, in turn, gave McLaughlin moral as well as political support. Commodore, from Whitehorse North, was minister of justice and minister responsible for the Women's Directorate. She was the first aboriginal woman to be appointed to Tony Penikett's NDP cabinet. Kassi, from Old Crow, was Deputy Speaker in the last legislature.[27]

Political life, says Commodore, "is a bit lonely at times, but certainly my life is fulfilling. Audrey and I have spoken a lot about the lack of partners in our life. I think we've both decided it's easier not having to think about who's worrying at home if you have to travel somewhere. I'm now a single politician. I wasn't when I started. I found I had to work twice as hard in trying to achieve what I wanted to whether I had a husband sitting beside me or not."[28]

Rosemarie Kuptana, President of the Inuit Tapirisat of Canada, became one of the key figures in negotiations for the Charlottetown Accord. The only women to sit at the constitutional table, in fact, were the northern "Mothers of Confederation": Kuptana, Cournoyea, and Mary Simon, former president of the Inuit Circumpolar Conference, who acted as Kuptana's advisor. Mary Sillett of Labrador co-ordinated the Inuit Committee on National Issues and now sits on the Royal Commission on Aboriginal Peoples. Without these accomplished women in high positions, who have become role models to northern and southern women alike, the vacuum in leadership would be as immense as the tundra.[29]

Canada's North, like the early West, offers less structured societies where southern social barriers are buried by the snow. "Because our communities are small and more tightly knit, politicians are more clearly accountable. People, not expert manufacturers of opinion, own the political process," says *Up-here* editor Allerston. And because they do, female leaders like Cournoyea, Kuptana, Simon, and Ethel Blondin-Andrew, MP for the Western Arctic, are readily accepted.

Kuptana likes to call herself "a village Eskimo," and she has a close bond with her community. A small, striking woman of fierce determination, she can remember holding the flashlight while her grandmother shot a marauding polar bear in the dead of night. "Unlike Canadian girls who grow up hearing the story of Little Red Riding Hood, Kuptana learned first-hand that you don't have to wait for a man to save you from dangerous animals," says Yellowknife writer Marina Devine. Kuptana sees threats to her culture with a clear eye and uses her experience as a broadcaster to describe them in vivid language. When television came to the North, Kuptana once told a CRTC hearing, it hit with the impact of a neutron bomb. "Neutron bomb television is the kind of television that destroys the soul of a people, but leaves the shell of a people walking around."

With leaders like her, the North has quickly shed its image as a placid ward of the Canadian state. The picture of Kuptana standing up to the male negotiators of the Charlottetown deal struck a chord with women all over Canada, and caused them to ask: Why can't we do the same?

The largest gains for women in Canadian politics are being achieved at the municipal level. In the 1980s, women moved out of school boards, community groups, and hospital boards to flood municipal councils. This is a natural path of advancement: Young mothers, especially, tend to organize or join groups that directly affect their family and require little time away from the children. They move from neighbourhood and school issues to larger community ones. The obvious place to express this growing concern, while still staying close to home and family, is the local elected council. Women can run for such positions without having to vault over the "gatekeepers"—political parties' apparatchiks that control access to higher levels of government but are often cool toward women candidates.

Several women have become mayors of major cities; they include June Rowlands in Toronto, Jan Reimer of Edmonton, Ottawa's Jacquie Holzman, Moira Ducharme of Halifax, and Gloria McCluskey in its twin city of Dartmouth. Shanni Duff, the dynamic mayor of St. John's, is known throughout Newfoundland for fostering culture and the environment. Hazel McCallion, the mayor of Mississauga, promotes fiscal responsibility.

Some of these women carry their experience into provincial

and federal politics. After her stint as mayor of Ottawa, Marion Dewar stood for federal office. Gretchen Brewin, a former mayor of Victoria, moved to the B.C. legislature as an NDP MLA. Elsie Wayne left the mayor's office in Saint John to become a Tory MP (one of only two) in the 1993 federal election. In future, many female councillors are likely to follow these paths to higher levels of government.

In 1992, women held an average of 31 per cent of the seats on the councils of Canada's ten largest cities. The total in Edmonton was a remarkable 54 per cent, even though far fewer women than men had run in the previous election. Forty per cent of Calgary councillors were women, while Ottawa council had 37 per cent, Montreal 32 per cent, Toronto 29 per cent, and Vancouver 27 per cent. Hamilton was very much the exception at a low 12 per cent. In all the others, the totals are higher than those achieved in the House of Commons or provincial legislatures.

As they gradually move upward from local councils, women are beginning to erode the old tradition of "the higher, the fewer"—the tendency of women to vanish from office as the stakes of power increase. Enthusiastically reversing this rule ("the lower, the larger"), women are gaining the networks, experience, and funding sources they need to advance to higher office. For these reasons, astute political observers like former prime minister Joe Clark, and Alberta's former premier Peter Lougheed, expect to see more women reaching high office in Canada.

Any woman who wants to succeed in politics, says Aline Chrétien, "should get involved locally first. They should become known in their own place by working hard—and then working hard some more."[30] Women are taking this sound advice and turning it into action. Today, one of the most encouraging signs for women in Canadian politics is the rapid growth of their power base within their communities and provinces, closer to home.

12

BEYOND THE GILDED GHETTO

"You don't have to be a magician to be in politics. You just need to be an individual with the desire to do something— the desire to make a difference."

Elaine McCoy,
former Alberta cabinet minister

In January 1991, Liberal senator Joyce Fairbairn was worried that the Conservatives' new abortion bill might become law, and like many other Canadian women, she decided to act. "Everyone was saying there was no hope, it was going to pass," she recalls. "I got out a list of the senators and started asking myself: has anyone ever asked them what they think and how they intend to vote? I got on the phone and started calling people. I even phoned someone who was in South America. I called one guy who was on a tractor in his field. His wife said, 'Get on that plane and vote against it.'"[1] Fairbairn and thousands like her were about to prove in the most dramatic way that women can make a difference in politics.

This crisis of conscience arose in response to the introduction by the Tories of an abortion bill, C-43, seven months earlier. A new law was necessary, the Conservatives felt, because the Supreme Court had ruled in 1988 that Canada's abortion legislation violated a woman's right to security of the person, as defined by the Charter of Rights and Freedoms. With the abortion issue suddenly in legal limbo, physicians and provincial governments were unsure of what action to take. The intent of the bill, piloted in the crucial later stages by Justice Minister Kim Campbell, was to control access to abortion once again by making the procedure a criminal offence, except when a doctor certified that a woman's physical or emotional health was threatened.

Millions of Canadian women were outraged and profoundly disappointed that a female minister had defended such legislation. The anger embraced both pro-choice women who objected to the criminalization of abortion and pro-life advocates who thought the bill didn't go far enough. But Bill C-43 passed the House of Commons, with its loyal Tory legions, after emotional debate. It was also expected to slip through the Senate, where the Tories had enjoyed a majority since late 1990, when Prime Minister Brian Mulroney installed eight new Conservative senators to ensure passage of the Goods and Services Tax.

Senator Fairbairn, an ardent pro-choice supporter, knew she had to do something—anything—to influence the result. Some female Tory senators were equally adamant. Pat Carney was suffering severe arthritis in Vancouver, but she got out of bed to fly to Ottawa and vote against her government's bill. (Within a week, Lowell Murray, the government leader in the Senate, dumped her from a Senate constitution committee, claiming she was "unreliable." She called him "disgusting" in response.) Janis Johnson, appointed just months earlier in the GST-inspired inflation of the Senate, also broke ranks with her party to oppose the bill. "Some were in tears at the end," Fairbairn says. "Everyone thought their vote was the deciding one."

And in the end, everyone was right. The outcome in the emotion-charged chamber was a tie: 43 votes in favour of the bill, 43 opposed. Under Senate rules, the abortion legislation was defeated. It was the first time in more than thirty years that the Senate had formally killed a government bill on the floor of the Red Chamber. "I was a limp rag after that vote," says Fairbairn. "I was sitting at my desk, and I don't shed tears, but they were coming after that."

Across the country, women of many political and social opinions were relieved that a policy disaster had been averted. Campbell, who had annoyed almost all of them, was left to mend her shattered fences. Fairbairn was astounded when, soon after the vote, Campbell's office phoned her staff. "They said she was pleased it was defeated!" Fairbairn recalls. "There are times you must be true to yourself. You know where you hit and where there are no compromises. You ask yourself, 'Do I bend on this or is this one where I can't?'" For many women who had assumed that Campbell was a moderate pro-choice feminist, she had bent too far, and the deadly blurring of her image had begun.

The abortion dispute showed what can happen when women unite on principle across party lines. There is little doubt that without women in the Senate, the abortion bill would have passed, just as the original 1969 Criminal Code abortion amendments had been jammed into law with little consideration of women's views. At that time, New Democrat Grace MacInnis was the only woman in the House of Commons; four women sat in the Senate. These women had virtually no impact on the debate, and the abortion law that resulted was a reflection of male attitudes. Decisions on "therapeutic abortions" were to be made by a three-member committee of doctors, and when they met, the woman being discussed was not allowed to attend.

Outraged women were left to protest outside Parliament, as they had little voice within it. An Abortion Caravan, organized by "women's liberation" groups, made its way from Vancouver to Ottawa, where women chained themselves to the visitors' gallery of the House of Commons.[2]

By 1991, however, women had considerable power in the two chambers of Parliament: thirty-nine sat in the Commons, fifteen in the Senate. When they began to mobilize (ironically, against an abortion bill sponsored by a woman), they had a powerful effect on the debate. Because of their lobbying, male legislators learned of the problems with the bill and they worried, quite properly, about the effect on the government's popularity. The pressure applied by women swayed voters and ultimately defeated the bill by the narrowest margin possible. After that one tense moment on a January evening in 1991, it was very clear that in the right circumstances, women in politics *do* make a difference.

Canada's women politicians have a greater impact, in fact, than do their counterparts in the United States, as U.S. women's activist Gloria Steinem acknowledged during a 1992 speech in Toronto. (She cited sexual assault legislation that better defines consent; recognition that sexual harassment can lead to stress-related illness; and some provision for abortion.) One reason for the greater effectiveness of Canadian women is simply the numbers. Eighteen per cent of House of Commons seats are now held by women, while they make up only 10 per cent of the U.S. House of Representatives.[3] Obviously, American women are still a greater distance from the "critical mass" required to have a major impact on decisions, and this has handicapped them seriously at crucial moments. When U.S. women lobbyists fought in the early 1980s for passage of the Equal Rights Amendment, they often appeared before committees of Congress and the state legislatures. There were so few elected women to support them, one observer reported, that the atmosphere seemed "surreal and circus-like."[4] And who can forget the spectacle of Anita Hill testifying before an all-male committee during Supreme Court confirmation hearings for Judge Clarence Thomas?

Canadian women also benefit from a better-organized national women's movement with access to government money. "We funded women to lobby against us," Jean Chrétien once observed, referring to fierce lobbying by women during the 1981 constitutional debate. That struggle, which ended with a declaration of full women's equality in the Constitution, provides another sharp contrast with the American women's movement. As the Canadian constitution became law in 1982, the Equal Rights Amendment was being defeated in the United States, after falling three states short of the three-quarters needed for ratification. Canadian women achieved their enormous victory after one year of lobbying, during which they took brilliant advantage of Pierre Trudeau's desire to patriate the constitution from Britain. American women had been fighting for the ERA since 1923, only to lose at the last moment. Their 1982 defeat was crushing, and the sapped energy that remains today is now directed to electing more women to Congress and the state legislatures.

Another factor in women's gains in Canada is the proliferation of women's groups across the country. Winning Women and the Committee for '94, who are devoted to electing more women at all levels of government, hold regular meetings and seminars to discuss basic political skills such as organizing and fundraising. In Quebec the same goal is pursued by FRAPPE (*Femmes regroupées pour l'accès au pouvoir politique et économique*). *La Fédération des Femmes du Québec*, formed in 1966 by Thérèse Casgrain and her protegée, Monique Bégin, among others, still has more than 100,000 members. The Canadian Advisory Council on the Status of Women, appointed by the government, often performs a crucial advisory role. On the other side of the political spectrum, REAL Women (an acronym for Realistic, Equal, Active, for Life) lobbies hard for "traditional" values and against abortion. "Feminist demands for equality with men will lead to gender-free legislation that treats women as severely as men," one speaker said at a REAL Women convention.

Chaviva Hosek feels that "anti-feminist women now have a larger, more visible target for their attacks. It's a sign of our power and of the building social consensus around our issues."[5] Hosek, now a key advisor to Prime Minister Chrétien, is a former president of the NAC, which has long been a powerful voice for women's progress.

NAC often annoys female politicians with its constant demands and criticisms; no matter what governments achieve, NAC is always there to ask for more. But while elected women grumble, they also see NAC as a handy lever to use against their male colleagues. With NAC pounding at the doors for radical solutions, a female cabinet minister can often convince the men to go along with a more moderate option that brings substantial progress. NAC has been a catalyst for pay equity laws, anti-harassment measures, funding for battered women's shelters, and the creation of women's bureaus and secretariats by provinces across the country. And the women politicians, although irritated by the role, end up serving as go-betweens. For obvious reasons, neither NAC nor the politicians admit to this reality; but their curious dynamic is one of the most productive in Canadian politics.

Judy Rebick, past president of NAC, cogently expresses the organization's view: "The political system is so patriarchal and so hierarchical—it is such a male culture. What happens to women politicians is they either get sidelined within it, or they get co-opted into it. It's very difficult not to do one or the other. And there are very few opportunities where women can work together to change things.

"If you look at the Ontario cabinet, for example, you see very strong feminists and they've managed to do a few good things on women's issues. But Frances Lankin, when she first went in there, was going to do everything to counter the ridiculous formalism and hierarchy. She hasn't been able to do any of that because it's a very centralized, very patriarchal system—both the bureaucracy and the political parties.

"So women haven't been able to change at all the way the things function. They are 'Madam Minister' and they have the same kind of centralized power that the men have. It seems to be almost impossible to make any structural changes."

Ontario attorney-general Marion Boyd, from her perch within the government, regards this attitude with frustration. "NAC has always taken the position that it is politically unaligned," she says. "It does that so it can criticize any government or any party as it sees fit. As a political person, I don't think that's always the most appropriate step, because it leads you, as an activist group, always to be in a critical mood. You seldom recognize or praise the steps that are taken—the many smaller steps that people want. It's very hard for women in politics when women who share the same beliefs and values never recognize the changes that are made, simply because the millenium hasn't been reached. You constantly feel that no matter how hard you work, it's never recognized."

The problem is even more annoying when female ministers lose the closed-door arguments within government, because the doctrine of cabinet solidarity prevents them from stating their position in public. They must pretend to agree with the male majority even when the men make decisions that adversely affect women. Often these female ministers find themselves being called traitors and sell-outs by the very women whose views they supported in the private debate.

Activists like Rebick and her successor as NAC president, Sunera Thobani, believe that only one kind of elected woman has a chance to do any good—a firm feminist who makes it her business to enact legislation that eradicates inequality. "As long as women politicians refuse to address issues like poverty, child care, violence, and women's unemployment," says Thobani, "women haven't made advances."[6] This view is almost uniform among women on the left in Canadian politics. "I don't think that simply electing more women is going to change much," says NDP leader Audrey McLaughlin, "unless those women are *committed* to change. Margaret Thatcher didn't change much for women in Britain—except for worse."

Alexa McDonough, Nova Scotia's NDP leader, is even more adamant on this point. "I don't know if there is a magic number," she says. "You don't have to look any further than Prince Edward Island to see a good example of how it doesn't make much difference when the women support the same policies as the men who came before them. If they're not prepared to be feminists and activists, then I don't really think it makes any difference. Sometimes I think it can actually be counter-productive, because if women are going to carry on the old boys' traditions, then the system becomes hostile to progress that the majority of women really need. I don't think there's anything about P.E.I. politics that I could point to as being progressive, with or without the women.

"I just believe so strongly that the formula of 'X' women and 'Y' men misses the point. There's no question that my male colleagues in caucus [John Holm and Robert Chisholm] have been much more aggressive and effective on behalf of women's equality than have the women in the other two caucuses. Those women by and large are quite happy to be queen bees in the old boys' world."

Various studies have shown that when there are few women legislators, they are treated as tokens and swallowed up by the party system. "Female politicians may sympathize with and support the women's movement," writes University of Alberta professor Linda Trimble in "A Few Good Women," her exhaustive study of female politicians in the Alberta legislature. "They are less likely to speak for women in the formal institutions of political power. And *acting* for women is quite another matter."[7]

Trimble found that between 1972 and 1985, when all the women in the legislature were members of the governing Conservative caucus, they did not often raise issues of concern to women. "The Tory women were not outspoken on these matters, and confined their remarks, for the most part, to statements of support for their party's policies." Opposition MLAs—all men—raised such issues twice as often as the women did. Even government men spoke out more often than the women. But this changed sharply in 1986 with the election of ten women, including three for the NDP. Trimble found that women's concerns were suddenly legitimate subjects for discussion and debate. Finally these issues were raised most often by women, although "opposition women were much more vocal than governing party women . . . and women on the Conservative backbenches were virtually silent about gender equality."

No wonder. The Alberta legislature was still one of the most sexist institutions in Canada. Pam Barrett, the former NDP House leader, recalls being hugged at a reception by one Tory MLA after another.[8] This was meant to look friendly but in fact was highly aggressive and demeaning, she says. A female Tory cabinet minister, who would rather not see her name in print, was shocked once when a male colleague squeezed her breast. In 1992, the provincial Treasurer, Dick Johnston, referred to Health Minister Nancy Betkowski as "Miss Pretty Minister."

Perhaps because of such experiences, a subtle bond began to form among the female MLAs across party lines. The opposition women, especially, sometimes ignored party discipline and quietly followed up each other's questions. During debates, women of all parties stuck more closely to the issues and engaged in less partisan mudslinging. There were also modest advances in policy relating to job-site inequality, violence against women, harassment, and other problems. Under Elaine McCoy, the Tory labour minister responsible for women's issues in the early 1990s, the government began an effective publicity campaign to highlight women's concerns and combat violence. McCoy, an adept minister, quickly learned how to manoeuvre her priorities through cabinet without setting off the men's alarm bells. She never referred to herself as a feminist, instead calling herself "an advocate for women." McCoy ignored the men's jibes in the interests of getting the job done. (They often called her "The Dragon Lady" as she sat in the cabinet room, coolly wreathed in her own cigarette smoke.)

In 1991, McCoy told an audience, "Women politicians do make a difference . . . and that's why I believe our agenda for the 1990s—the agenda of women and women's organizations—must be to encourage and help more women get into politics. . . . If more of us take seats in the legislature, at the cabinet table and in the top ranks of the public service, then gradually issues of concern to half the human race will no longer be ghettoized as 'women's issues.'" After retiring from politics in 1993, McCoy became involved with Winning Women, the non-partisan group devoted to electing more women to all levels of government.

Linda Trimble concludes that even in Alberta's highly conservative climate, a growing number of women legislators of all parties have changed both the style and substance of debate. Women not only bring their concerns to the table, she argues, "they begin to transform the table." They change the tone of discussion, introduce issues that would not otherwise be considered, and influence legislation, both directly and indirectly.

This phenomenon is occurring across the country. In a study of the Quebec legislature, 78 per cent of female MNAs agreed with the statement: "Women who have been elected have a special responsibility not only to their constituents, but also all the women of Quebec."[9] Even within an overriding context of French-Canadian nationalism, female MNAs of both parties— Liberals and Parti Québécois—aggressively bring women's concerns to the legislature.

Various studies, as well as testimony from many elected women, suggest that there *is* progress when enough women are elected, even if those women do not call themselves feminists. This progress may not be as dramatic as it is, for instance, under an NDP government in Ontario. It will not always please women with strong and urgent convictions about progress; but it occurs nonetheless. "Women are not a monolith," says Mildred Istona, editor of *Chatelaine* magazine. "Like men, we hold views that span the political spectrum. As more women from various parties run for public office, we'll have more ideological choice and elect more women."[10]

All those women, whatever their policy differences and decision-making styles, do bring one unique quality to politics—a life experience that men simply cannot share. That experience becomes part of the system, expanding the government's awareness, as soon as there are enough women politicians to express it with confidence.

How many women? Most academics now agree that when

female representation reaches about 15 per cent of the total number of legislators, they begin to make a significant difference. And after women achieve representation of more than 25 per cent, as in countries like Norway (34.5 per cent) or Finland (40 per cent), their influence is impossible to resist. (See Appendix 1, Table 5.) Indeed, when Gro Harlem Brundtland became prime minister of Norway in 1986, her cabinet comprised equal numbers of men and women.[11] The women ministers may not always win on issues, but the men risk serious problems of solidarity in parliament if they consistently ignore or offend such a significant group. Moreover, a simple human dynamic begins to operate both in government and within parties: it is much easier to understand and sympathize with a person who is actually sitting next to you. No country, not even in progressive Scandinavia, has yet reached 50 per cent female representation in a legislature, but as we near that goal, the effect is certain to be profound.

Most Canadian legislatures, and Parliament as well, have already passed the minimum "critical mass" of 15 per cent, but none has yet reached the 30 per cent required for major, sustained influence. Although progress is accelerating, it has been agonizingly slow for generations. The impatience of women who want only declared feminists in office is understandable; in Manitoba, with its Icelandic influence, some women have even formed a women's party. But Canadian women have not yet seen the benefits of full equality with men in elected bodies. This must surely remain a major goal of women who want to put an end to paternalism.

Numbers are not the only problem, of course. Those women who are elected, in their efforts to make a difference, quickly confront two barriers that have nothing to do with gender: regionalism and party discipline. Canada's elaborate system of regional bartering often overrides every other issue, especially at times of constitutional crisis. In Ottawa and the provinces, women politicians are expected to share these concerns (and their parties' solutions) before they consider anything else. Often they are required to cheer while male leaders thump their chests in the country's endless turf wars. Party discipline, stronger in Canada than in most other countries, makes it extremely difficult for women to introduce gender issues at such times. As Lisa Young notes, "female MPs often find themselves negotiating space for gender concerns within the constraints of both partisanship and regionalism."[12]

In recent years, however, women have become increasingly skillful at finding that space. In 1981, for instance, they used the constitutional wrangle to force full female equality into the basic law of the land. The tactics amounted to rhetorical blackmail. "Give us this," women said, "and you can play your regional games. But deny us and we'll make you pay." Male politicians knew that they faced a nearly solid wall of gender power (breached only by a few groups like REAL Women, which actually argued against the equality provision.) In the women's movement and within the halls of Parliament, women learned the powerful lessons of guerrilla politics: find the opponent's weakness, apply maximum pressure to the sore point, and refuse to stop until he relents. In later constitutional rounds for the Meech Lake and Charlottetown accords, women pressed their demands with increasing confidence. They forced into the debate many suggestions for achieving gender parity, including proportional representation (a major reason for the high women's representation in Scandinavian countries), equality in the Senate, and more radical notions such as electing two MPs, a woman and a man, from each riding. The Charlottetown round, with its large public forums, produced a fountain of such novel ideas—all rejected by the male leaders who negotiated for the provinces and Ottawa. In the fevered drive to find a solution that governments could accept, the men ignored half the voters, many of whom might have supported the deal if it had advanced women toward full equality. Instead, the voters were offered the Charlottetown Accord, a cold-blooded redistribution of jurisdictional powers.

The struggles continue in the daily affairs of Parliament and the provincial legislatures, where women have learned to use subversive tactics to increase their influence beyond their numbers. Mostly they undercut party discipline with quiet co-operation across party lines on key issues, talking among themselves and then arguing their points within their party caucuses. Their male colleagues often feel threatened when they discover that women in their own party are saying the same thing as their "opponents." To many men, this smacks of disloyalty and hints at a breakdown of the all-powerful party system under which they have operated comfortably for so long. But as the number of women legislators increases, the men have little choice but to adapt.

In Ottawa, such cross-party women's co-operation has slowly worked its way into formal structures such as the Association of Women Parliamentarians, formed mainly to discuss women's common experiences, including difficulties in combining family and political life. Though AWP members are always careful to say they do not discuss policy, there is no doubt that the discussions lay the groundwork for a larger consensus on major public issues. The Sub-Committee on the Status of Women did substantial policy work on violence against women, sexual assault laws, gun control, and breast cancer, before being automatically disbanded when the Liberals took office in 1993.

Moreover, women's concerns are now more prominent in the House of Commons itself. After the Federal Court of Appeal ruled in 1994 that parents who receive child support payments should not have to pay income tax on the money, the government went to the Supreme Court to appeal the decision. The potential loss of revenue—said to be about $330 million a year—was of grave concern to financial planners. But the Commons, voting on a motion introduced by Liberal MP Beryl Gaffney, called for changes to the Income Tax Act that would make the payments deductible. The motion was not binding, and the government did not change its position, but the vote showed the growing influence of women. Indeed, the Liberal Women's Caucus Association has more potential clout than any previous women's group in Parliament. And with the highest numbers ever in the House of Commons, women have more power to make their views known and influence colleagues. Male MPs must now think very carefully before they oppose pro-women legislation such as the strong anti-stalking law passed in June 1993.

Finally, with no blast of trumpets, women have slipped into the mainstream of Canadian politics. Their concerns are no longer completely "theirs," but part of the vast flowing river of public issues open for debate by women and men. Even some feminists concede that women's problems are "people problems" shared by the whole population. Women politicians are more often seen as competent or incompetent on the basis of their personal qualities, not their gender. In 1993, a woman became prime minister, albeit briefly, and another was leader of the federal New Democratic Party. Catherine Callbeck of Prince Edward Island, who was once told by a Liberal poll captain that she shouldn't seek a nomination because she's a woman, became the first woman ever to be elected as premier of a province. Janice MacKinnon was finance minister of Saskatchewan, Marion Boyd was attorney-general of Ontario, Nellie Cournoyea was leader of the Northwest Territories government. Scores of others were in influential positions all over the country.

After struggling up the steep slopes of Canadian politics for generations, these women clambered onto a plateau, looked around anxiously, and found that few wanted to push them down again. They were free to stay at their new forward base or to keep climbing. The route to the top was still steep and difficult, fraught with many more dangers than men would face, but for the first time in our history the summit was in view. Glenda Simms, president of the Canadian Advisory Council on the Status of Women, warns women not to fear the heights. "We have made significant strides," she says. "The backlash tells me that. Backlash comes only when you're gaining. But don't give in to that backlash. It's difficult to stand firm, but you must."[13] Only by taking that advice will Canada's elected women at last emerge from their gilded ghetto into the broader world of true political authority.

Appendix 1

STATISTICS

TABLE 1

WOMEN WIN THE VOTE

Province	Vote granted	Eligible to hold office	First woman elected
Manitoba	Jan. 28, 1916	same	June 29, 1920
Saskatchewan	Mar. 14, 1916	same	June 29, 1919
Alberta	Apr. 19, 1916	same	June 7, 1917
British Columbia	Apr. 5, 1917	same	Jan. 24, 1918
Ontario	Apr. 23, 1917	Apr. 4, 1919	Aug. 4, 1943
Nova Scotia	Apr. 26, 1918	same	June 7, 1960
New Brunswick	Apr. 17, 1919	Mar. 9, 1934	Oct. 10, 1967
Prince Edward Island	May 3, 1922	same	May 11, 1970
Newfoundland[1]	Apr. 13, 1925	same	May 17, 1930
Quebec	Apr. 25, 1940	same	Dec. 15, 1961
Canada[2]	**May 24, 1918**	**July 7, 1919**	**Dec. 6, 1921**

SOURCES: Catherine Cleverdon, *The Woman Suffrage Movement in Canada*, Toronto, University of Toronto Press, 1974, p. 2; Sylvia B. Bashevkin, *Toeing the Lines: Women and Party Politics in English Canada*, Second Edition, Toronto, Oxford University Press, 1993, p. 5; and Jill McCalla Vickers and Janine Brodie, "Canada," in Joni Lovenduski and Jill Hills, eds., *The Politics of the Second Electorate: Women and Public Participation*, London, Routledge & Kegan Paul, 1981, p. 71.

[1] *While men could vote at twenty-one, women had to wait until they were twenty-five. This legislation remained until Newfoundland's entry into Confederation in 1948.*
[2] *Women who had served in the military or who were closely related to servicemen could vote in 1917. The Dominion Elections Act of 1920 confirmed women's eligibility to vote and hold office.*

TABLE 2

WOMEN ELECTED TO PROVINCIAL LEGISLATURES AND PARLIAMENT AS OF AUGUST 1994

(PER CENT OF TOTAL)

Place	Current	Previous election
Federal House of Commons	18	13
British Columbia	25	13
Alberta	19	15
Saskatchewan	18	8
Manitoba	21	16
Ontario	21	16
Quebec	18	14
New Brunswick	17	14
Nova Scotia	10	6
Prince Edward Island	25	9
Newfoundland	6	2
Northwest Territories	8	8
Yukon	19	25

SOURCES: The provincial legislatures and Elections Canada.
NOTE: Figures are rounded to the nearest whole number.

TABLE 3

WOMEN CANDIDATES AND MPs IN FEDERAL ELECTIONS

(PER CENT OF TOTAL)

Election	Candidates Total	Women candidates No.	%	Women elected No.	%
1921	632	4	0.6	1	0.2
1925	579	4	0.7	1	0.2
1926	530	2	0.4	1	0.2
1930	543	9	1.7	1	0.2
1935	888	16	1.8	2	0.2
1940	665	9	1.4	1	0.2
1945	952	19	2.0	1	0.1
1949	848	11	1.3	0	—
1953	897	47	5.2	4	0.5
1957	867	29	3.4	2	0.2
1958	831	21	2.5	2	0.2
1962	1,016	26	2.6	5	0.5
1963	1,023	40	3.9	4	0.4
1965	1,011	37	3.7	4	0.4
1968	967	36	3.5	1	0.4
1972	1,117	71	6.4	5	1.8
1974	1,209	137	9.4	9	3.4
1979	1,424	195	13.8	10	3.6
1980	1,504	217	14.4	14	5.0
1984	1,449	214	14.5	27	9.6
1988	1,574	302	19.2	39	13.4
1993	2,155	475	22.0	53	18.0

SOURCE: Elections Canada.
NOTE: Figures include incumbents.

TABLE 4

SUCCESS RATES FOR WOMEN AND MEN CANDIDATES BY FEDERAL PARTY, 1974–1993

Year Gov't	LIBERAL		CONSERVATIVE		NEW DEMOCRAT		REFORM		BLOC Q	
	Women Won/Ran	Men Won/Ran	Women Won/Ran	Men Won/Ran	Women Won/Ran	Men Won/Ran	Women Won/Ran	Men Won/Ran	Women Won/Ran	Men Won/Ran
1974 LIB.	8/20 40%	133/244 55%	1/11 9%	94/253 37%	0/42 0%	16/220 7%				
1979 P.C.	6/14 43%	107/266 40%	2/21 10%	135/261 52%	2/47 4%	24/234 10%				
1980 LIB.	10/14 71%	137/268 51%	2/23 9%	101/259 39%	2/33 6%	30/247 12%				
1984 P.C.	5/44 11%	35/238 15%	19/23 83%	192/259 74%	3/64 5%	27/218 12%				
1988 P.C.	13/37 35%	70/257 27%	21/53 40%	148/242 61%	5/84 6%	38/211 18%	0/8 0%	0/64 0%	—	—
1993 LIB.	36/64 56%	140/231 61%	1/67 1.5%	1/228 0.4%	1/113 0.9%	8/81 4%	7/23 30%	45/184 24%	8/10 80%	46/65 71%

SOURCE: Elections Canada.

NOTE: If the party is popular, the public readily votes for its female candidates. The parties, not the voters, keep women from reaching equality in the federal Parliament.

TABLE 5

WOMEN IN NATIONAL LEGISLATURES

(PER CENT OF TOTAL)

Country	Women members
Finland	40.0
Sweden	38.1
Norway	34.5
Denmark	32.4
Germany	22.5
Iceland	22.2
Canada	**18.0**
New Zealand	16.5
Italy	12.9
United States	10.3
Belgium	8.5
United Kingdom	6.8
France	5.9

SOURCES: Doris Anderson, *The Unfinished Revolution,* Toronto, Doubleday, 1991; and Sylvia Bashevkin, *Toeing the Lines,* Toronto, Oxford University Press, 1993, pp. 153–54.

Appendix 2

WOMEN IN PARLIAMENT

IN THE HOUSE OF COMMONS

MACPHAIL, AGNES CAMPBELL. Progressive, United Farmers of Ontario—Labour. Grey South East, Ont., 1921, 1925, 1926, 1930. Co-operative Commonwealth Federation, Grey Bruce, Ont. 1935. 1921–1940.

BLACK, MARTHA LOUISE PURDY. Conservative. Yukon Territory. 1935–1940.

NIELSEN, DORISE WINNIFRED. Unity (New Democracy). North Battleford, Sask. 1940–1945.

CASSELMAN, CORA TAYLOR. Liberal. Edmonton East, Alta. 1941–1945.

STRUM, GLADYS GRACE MAY. Co-operative Commonwealth Federation. Qu'Appelle, Sask. 1945–1949.

FAIRCLOUGH, ELLEN LOUKS. Progressive Conservative. Hamilton West, Ont. 1950–1963.

AITKEN, MARGARET. Progressive Conservative. York-Humber, Ont. 1953–1962.

BENNETT, SYBIL. Progressive Conservative. Halton, Ont. 1953–1956.

SHIPLEY, MARIE ANN. Liberal. Timiskaming, Ont. 1953–1957.

WADDS, JEAN CASSELMAN. Progressive Conservative. Grenville-Dundas, Ont. 1958–1968.

LAMARSH, JULIA VERLYN (JUDY). Liberal. Niagara Falls, Ont. 1960–1968.

MACDONALD, MARGARET MAY. Progressive Conservative. Kings, P.E.I. 1961–1963.

HARDIE, ISABEL. Liberal. Mackenzie River, N.W.T. 1962–1963.

JEWETT, PAULINE. Liberal. Northumberland, Ont. 1963–1965. New Democrat. New Westminster-Coquitlam, B.C. 1979–1988.

KONANTZ, MARGARET MCTAVISH. Liberal. Winnipeg South, Man. 1963–1965.

JONES, ELOISE MAY. Progressive Conservative. Saskatoon, Sask. 1964–1965.

RIDEOUT, MARGARET ISABEL. Liberal. Westmorland, N.B. 1964–1968.

MacInnis, Winona Grace. New Democrat. Vancouver-Kingsway, B.C. 1965–1974.

Bégin, Monique. Liberal. Saint-Michel, Que. 1972–1979. St. Léonard-Anjou, Que. 1979–present.

MacDonald, Flora Isabel. Progressive Conservative. Kingston and the Islands, Ont. 1972–1988.

Morin, Albanie. Liberal. Louis-Hébert, Que. 1972–1976.

Sauvé, Jeanne. Liberal. Ahuntsic, Que. 1972–1979. Laval-des-Rapides, Que. 1979–1984.

Appolloni, Ursula. Liberal. York South, Ont. 1974–1979. York South-Weston, Ont. 1979–1984.

Campagnolo, Iona. Liberal. Skeena, B.C. 1974–1979.

Campbell, Coline M. Liberal. South Western Nova, N.S. 1974–1979. South West Nova, N.S. 1980–1984, 1988–1993.

Holt, Simma. Liberal. Vancouver-Kingsway, B.C. 1974–1979.

Nicholson, Aideen. Liberal. Trinity, Ont. 1974–1988.

Pigott, Jean. Progressive Conservative. Ottawa-Carleton, Ont. 1976–1979.

Killens, Thérèse. Liberal. St. Michel, Que. 1979–1983. St. Michel-Ahuntsic, Que. 1983–1988.

Hervieux-Payette, Céline. Liberal. Mercier, Que. 1979–1984.

Stratas, Diane. Progressive Conservative. Scarborough Centre, Ont. 1979–1980.

Mitchell, Margaret Anne. New Democrat. Vancouver East, B.C. 1979–1993.

Beauchamp-Niquet, Suzanne. Liberal. Roberval, Que. 1980–1984.

Côté, Eva Lachance. Liberal. Rimouski, Que. 1980. Rimouski-Temiscouata, Que. 1980–1984.

Erola, Judy. Liberal. Nickel Belt, Ont. 1980–1984.

Carney, Patricia. Progressive Conservative. Vancouver-Centre, B.C. 1980–1988.

Cossitt, Jennifer. Progressive Conservative. Leeds-Grenville, Ont. 1982–1988.

McDonald, Lynn. New Democrat. Broadview-Greenwood, Ont. 1982–1988.

Bertrand, Gabrielle. Progressive Conservative. Brome-Missisquoi, Que. 1984–1993.

Blais-Grenier, Suzanne. Progressive Conservative. Rosemont, Que. 1984–1988. Independent. 1988.

Blouin, Anne. Progressive Conservative. Montmorency-Orleans, Que. 1984–1988.

BOURGAULT, LISE. Progressive Conservative. Argenteuil-Papineau, Que. 1984–1993.

BROWES, PAULINE. Progressive Conservative. Scarborough Centre, Ont. 1984–1993.

CHAMPAGNE, ANDRÉE P. Progressive Conservative. St.-Hyacinthe-Bagot, Que. 1984–1993.

COLLINS, MARY. Progressive Conservative. Capilano, B.C. 1984–1988. Capilano-Howe Sound, B.C. 1988–1993.

COPPS, SHEILA. Liberal. Hamilton East, Ont. 1984–present.

DUPLESSIS, SUZANNE. Progressive Conservative. Louis-Hébert, Que. 1984–1993.

FINESTONE, SHEILA. Liberal. Mount Royal, Que. 1984–present.

JACQUES, CAROLE. Progressive Conservative. Mercier, Que. 1984–1993.

LANDRY, MONIQUE. Progressive Conservative. Blainville-Deux-Montagnes, Que. 1984–1993.

MCDOUGALL, BARBARA JEAN. Progressive Conservative. St. Paul's, Ont. 1984–1993.

MAILLY, CLAUDY. Progressive Conservative. Gatineau, Que. 1984–1988.

MARTIN, SHIRLEY. Progressive Conservative. Lincoln, Ont. 1984–1993.

PÉPIN, LUCIE. Liberal. Outremont, Que. 1984–1988.

SPARROW, BARBARA. Progressive Conservative. Calgary South, Alta. 1984–1988. Calgary Southwest, Alta. 1988–1993.

TARDIF, MONIQUE BERNATCHEZ. Progressive Conservative. Charlesbourg, Que. 1984–1993.

VÉZINA, MONIQUE. Progressive Conservative. Rimouski-Temiscouata, Que. 1984–1993.

DEWAR, MARION. New Democrat. Hamilton Mountain, Ont. 1987–1988.

MCLAUGHLIN, AUDREY. New Democrat. Yukon. 1987–present.

ANDERSON, EDNA. Progressive Conservative. Simcoe Centre, Ont. 1988–1993.

BLACK, DAWN. New Democrat. New Westminster-Burnaby, B.C. 1988–1993.

BLONDIN-ANDREW, ETHEL. Liberal. Western Arctic, N.W.T. 1988–present.

CALLBECK, CATHERINE. Liberal. Malpeque, P.E.I. 1988–1993.

CAMPBELL, A. KIM. Progressive Conservative. Vancouver Centre, B.C. 1988–1993.

CATTERALL, MARLENE. Liberal. Ottawa West, Ont. 1988–present.

CLANCY, MARY. Liberal. Halifax, N.S. 1988–present.

DOBBIE, DOROTHY. Progressive Conservative. Winnipeg South, Man. 1988–1993.

FELTHAM, LOUISE. Progressive Conservative. Wild Rose, Alta. 1988–1993.

GAFFNEY, BERYL. Liberal. Nepean, Ont. 1988–present.

GIBEAU, MARIE. Progressive Conservative. Bourassa, Que. 1988–1993.

GREENE, BARBARA. Progressive Conservative. Don Valley North, Ont. 1988–1993.

GUARNIERI, ALBINA. Liberal. Mississauga East, Ont. 1988–present.

HUNTER, LYNN. New Democrat. Saanich-Gulf Islands, B.C. 1988–1993.

LANGAN, JOY. New Democrat. Mission-Coquitlam, B.C. 1988–1993.

MAHEU, SHIRLEY. Liberal. St.-Laurent, Que. 1988–1993. St.-Laurent-Cartierville, Que. 1993–present.

MARLEAU, DIANE. Liberal. Sudbury, Ont. 1988–present.

PHINNEY, BETH. Liberal. Hamilton Mountain, Ont. 1988–present.

ROY-ARCELIN, NICOLE. Progressive Conservative. Ahuntsic, Que. 1988–1993.

STEWART, CHRISTINE. Liberal. Northumberland, Ont. 1988–present.

VENNE, PIERRETTE. Progressive Conservative. St.-Hubert, Que. 1988–1991. Bloc Québécois (August 12, 1991). 1991–present.

GREY, DEBORAH. Reform. Beaver River, Alta. 1989–present.

ABLONCZY, DIANE. Reform. Calgary North, Alta. 1993–present.

AUGUSTINE, JEAN. Liberal. Etobicoke-Lakeshore, Ont. 1993–present.

BAKOPANOS, ELENI. Liberal. Saint-Denis, Que. 1993–present.

BARNES, SUSAN. Liberal. London West, Ont. 1993–present.

BEAUMIER, COLLEEN. Liberal. Brampton, Ont. 1993–present.

BETHEL, JUDY. Liberal. Edmonton East, Alta. 1993.

BRIDGMAN, MARGARET. Reform. Surrey North, B.C. 1993–present.

BROWN, BONNIE. Liberal. Oakville-Milton, Ont. 1993–present.

BROWN, JAN. Reform. Calgary Southeast, Alta. 1993–present.

BRUSHETT, DIANNE. Liberal. Cumberland-Colchester, N.S. 1993–present.

CHAMBERLAIN, BRENDA. Liberal. Guelph-Wellington, Ont. 1993–present.

COHEN, SHAUGHNESSY. Liberal. Windsor-St. Clair, Ont. 1993–present.

COWLING, MARLENE. Liberal. Dauphin-Swan River, Man. 1993–present.

DALPHOND-GUIRAL, MADELEINE. Bloc Québécois. Laval Centre, Que. 1993–present.

DEBIEN, MAUD. Bloc Québécois. Laval East, Que. 1993–present.

FRY, HEDY. Liberal. Vancouver Centre, B.C. 1993–present.

GAGNON, CHRISTIANE. Bloc Québécois. Quebec, Que. 1993–present.

GUAY, MONIQUE. Bloc Québécois. Laurentides, Que. 1993–present.

HAYES, SHARON. Reform. Port Moody-Coquitlam, B.C. 1993–present.

HICKEY, BONNIE. Liberal. St. John's East, Nfld. 1993–present.

JENNINGS, DAPHNE. Reform. Mission-Coquitlam, B.C. 1993–present.

KRAFT SLOANE, KAREN. Liberal. York-Simcoe, Ont. 1993–present.

LALONDE, FRANCINE. Bloc Québécois. Mercier, Que. 1993–present.

MCLELLAN, ANNE. Liberal. Edmonton Northwest, Alta. 1993–present.

MEREDITH, VAL. Reform. Surrey-White Rock-South Langley, B.C. 1993–present.

MINNA, MARIA. Liberal. Beaches-Woodbine, Ont. 1993–present.

PARRISH, CAROLYN. Liberal. Mississauga West, Ont. 1993–present.

PAYNE, JEAN. Liberal. St. John's West, Nfld. 1993–present.

PICARD, PAULINE. Bloc Québécois. Drummond, Que. 1993–present.

RINGUETTE-MALTAIS, PIERRETTE. Liberal. Madawaska-Victoria, N.B. 1993–present.

SHERIDAN, GEORGETTE. Liberal. Saskatoon-Humboldt, Sask. 1993–present.

SKOKE, ROSEANNE. Liberal. Central Nova, N.S. 1993–present.

STEWART, JANE. Liberal. Brant, Ont. 1993–present.

TERRANA, ANNA. Liberal. Vancouver East, B.C. 1993–present.

TORSNEY, PATRICIA. Liberal. Burlington, Ont. 1993–present.

TREMBLAY, SUZANNE. Bloc Québécois. Rimouski-Temiscouata, Que. 1993–present.

UR, ROSE-MARIE. Liberal. Lambton-Middlesex, Ont. 1993–present.

WAYNE, ELSIE. Progressive Conservative. Saint John, N.B. 1993–present.

WHELAN, SUSAN. Liberal. Essex-Windsor, Ont. 1993–present.

IN THE SENATE

WILSON, CAIRINE REAY. Liberal. Rockcliffe, Ont. 1930–1962.

FALLIS, IVA CAMPBELL. Progressive Conservative. Peterborough, Ont. 1935–1956.

FERGUSSON, MURIEL MCQUEEN. Liberal. Fredericton, N.B. 1953–1975.

HODGES, NANCY. Liberal. Victoria, B.C. 1953–1965.

JODOIN, MARIANNA BEAUCHAMP. Liberal. Sorel, Que. 1953–1966.

INMAN, FLORENCE ELSIE. Liberal. Murray Harbour, P.E.I. 1955–1986.

IRVINE, OLIVE LILLIAN. Progressive Conservative. Lisgar, Man. 1960–1969.

QUART, JOSIE ALICE DINAN. Progressive Conservative. Victoria, Que. 1960–1980.

KINNEAR, MARY ELIZABETH. Liberal. Welland, Ont. 1967–1973.

CASGRAIN, THÉRÈSE FORGET. Independent. Mille-Isles, Que. 1970–1971.

BELL, ANN ELIZABETH HADDON HEATH. Liberal. Nanaimo-Malaspina, B.C. 1970–1986. Independent. 1986-1989.

LAPOINTE, LOUISE MARGUERITE RENAUDE. Liberal. Mille-Isles, Que. 1971–1987.

NORRIE, MARGARET ROSAMOND FAWCETT. Liberal. Colchester-Cumberland, N.S. 1972-1980.

NEIMAN, JOAN BISSETT. Liberal. Peel, Ont. 1972-present.

ANDERSON, MARGARET JEAN. Liberal. Northumberland-Miramichi, N.B. 1978–1990.

BIRD, FLORENCE BAYARD (ANNE FRANCIS). Liberal. Carleton, Ont. 1978–1983.

WOOD, DALIA. Liberal. Montarville, Que. 1979–present.

ROUSSEAU, YVETTE. Liberal. De Salaberry, Que. 1979–1988.

BIELISH, MARTHA. Progressive Conservative. Lakeland, Alta. 1979–1990.

COOLS, ANNE CLARE. Liberal. Toronto Centre, Ont. 1984–present.

MARSDEN, LORNA. Liberal. Toronto-Taddle Creek, Ont. 1984–1992.

FAIRBAIRN, JOYCE. Liberal. Lethbridge, Alta. 1984–present.

ROBERTSON, BRENDA. Progressive Conservative. Riverview, N.B. 1984–present.

ROSSITER, EILEEN. Progressive Conservative. P.E.I. 1986–present.

SPIVAK, MIRA. Progressive Conservative. Man. 1986–present.

COCHRANE, ETHEL. Progressive Conservative. Nfld. 1986–present.

CHAPUT-ROLLAND, Solange. Progressive Conservative. Que. 1988–1994.

CARNEY, PATRICIA. Progressive Conservative. B.C. 1990–present.

TEED, NANCY ELIZABETH CLARK. Progressive Conservative. N.B. 1990–1993.

DEWARE, MABEL MARGARET. Progressive Conservative. N.B. 1990–present.

LAVOIE-ROUX, THÉRÈSE. Progressive Conservative. Division of Quebec. 1990–present.

JOHNSON, JANIS. Progressive Conservative. Division of the Western Provinces. 1990–present.

ANDREYCHUK, RAYNELL. Progressive Conservative. Sask. 1993–present.

COHEN, ERMINIE JOY. Progressive Conservative. N.B. 1993–present.

LEBRETON, MARJORY. Progressive Conservative. Manotick, Ont. 1993–present.

Courtesy of the Library of Parliament, Information and Technical Services Branch, March 1994.

ENDNOTES

1/ THE GILDED GHETTO

[1] Interview with Jean Pigott, June 9, 1993.

[2] Punham Khosla, "Review of the Situation of Women in Canada, 1993," a report published by the National Action Committee on the Status of Women.

[3] Interview with Deborah Grey, May 28, 1993.

[4] Judy LaMarsh, *Memoirs of a Bird in a Gilded Cage,* McClelland & Stewart, Toronto, 1968, pp. 302–3.

[5] Interview with Anne McLellan, June 2, 1994.

[6] Interview with Glenda Simms, Nov. 18, 1993.

[7] Interview with Maude Barlow, Nov. 22, 1993.

[8] See Charlotte Gray's perceptive article about McDougall, "A Woman's Place," in *Saturday Night,* May 1987.

[9] Punham Khosla, "Review of the Situation of Women in Canada, 1993."

[10] Chantal Maillé, "Primed for Power: Women in Canadian Politics," a background paper published by the Canadian Advisory Council on the Status of Women, 1990. The paper's estimate is calculated on the rate of progress that prevailed between the 1984 and 1988 election. This rate was constant in 1993.

[11] Susan Crosland of the *Sunday Times of London* gives more examples in a fascinating article reprinted in *The Globe and Mail,* July 10, 1993.

[12] See Barbara Presley Noble, "The Debate Over *la Différence*," *New York Times*, Aug. 15, 1993.

2/ TINKERBELL SPELL

[1] Quoted in *The Edmonton Journal*, wire service story, Mar. 20, 1993.

[2] For a biting, perceptive, and often hilarious account of Mackenzie King's amazingly twisted sex life, see Heather Robertson, *More than a Rose: Prime Ministers, Wives, and Other Women*, Seal Books, Toronto, 1992, pp. 194–218. Robertson's retelling of Margaret Trudeau's famous adventures is equally compelling. See "The Multiple Lives of Maggie T.," pp. 316–47.

[3] Campbell later said that this remark, published in an article by Judy Steed in *The Toronto Star*, hurt her deeply. See Susan Riley's article in *This Magazine*, "Ms. Representing Feminism: The Troubling Ascent of Kim Campbell," May 1993.

[4] Her inner circle referred to the former Russian as Moscow on the St. Lawrence.

[5] *Edmonton Journal*, wire service story, Mar. 20, 1993.

[6] Robertson, *More than a Rose*, pp. 343–45.

[7] Interview with Audrey McLaughlin, Oct. 27, 1993.

[8] Interview with Alexa McDonough, June 8, 1993.

[9] I was the writer who received this memo. The request to inquire about any lesbian links in McLaughlin's past was absurd. There was never a shred of evidence to merit asking such a personal question that is dubious under any circumstances.

[10] See Barbara Woodley, *Portraits: Canadian Women in Focus*, Doubleday Canada, Toronto, 1992, p. 64.

[11] *Globe and Mail*, Mar. 12, 1993.

[12] Interview with Judy Rebick, June 24, 1993.

[13] Peter C. Newman, "Kim Campbell," *Vancouver* magazine, May 1993, p. 34.

[14] *Calgary Herald*, Southam News Service, May 19, 1993.

[15] *Vancouver* magazine, May 1993, p. 33.

[16] *Vancouver Sun*, July 31, 1993.

[17] Interview with Janis Johnson, June 28, 1993.

[18] Interview with Iona Campagnolo, May 3, 1993. Campagnolo also placed female solidarity over partisanship by giving money to Flora MacDonald's Tory leadership campaign in 1976.

[19] Southam News story, Dec. 8, 1993.

[20] *Maclean's*, "The Number Two," Dec. 6, 1993.

[21] Interview with Audrey McLaughlin, Apr. 6, 1993.

[22] McDougall was part of a post-election panel chaired by Stevie Cameron, at the Canadian Association of Journalists meeting, Nov. 13, 1993, in Winnipeg. McDougall appeared with Sharon Carstairs, former head of the Manitoba Liberals, and Margaret (Joe) Commodore, then Yukon minister of justice. Called "Politicians in Pumps," the session was a frank and often hilarious recounting of female politicians' experiences with reporters.

[23] Interview with Pat Carney, Apr. 1, 1993.

[24] Interview with Marjory LeBreton, July 25, 1993.

[25] See John Sawatsky's excellent account of Mulroney's formative years in *Mulroney: The Politics of Ambition*, Macfarlane Walter & Ross, Toronto, 1991, especially "Part One: The Seeds of Ambition."

[26] The best account of Campbell's development as a politician is found in Robert Fife's *Kim Campbell: The Making of a Politician*, HarperCollins Publishers, Toronto, 1993.

[27] Interview with Brian Mulroney, Feb. 10, 1994.

[28] Interview with Janis Johnson, June 28, 1993.

[29] Interview with Jodi White, Jan. 25, 1994.

[30] This well-known story is recounted in Fife, *Kim Campbell*, pp. 147–48.

[31] Interview with Marjory LeBreton, July 25, 1993.

[32] Interview with Brian Mulroney, Feb. 10, 1994.

[33] Interview with Judy Rebick, June 24, 1993.

[34] Interview with Deborah Grey, May 28, 1993.

[35] Fotheringham recounted this episode on April 29, 1994. The celebrated columnist for the *Sun* and *Maclean's* is an eternal source of the best stories on the Ottawa circuit.

[36] Interview with Flora MacDonald, June 7, 1993.

[37] Interview with Brian Mulroney, Feb. 10, 1994.

[38] Interview with Wanda O'Hagan, Oct. 27, 1993.

[39] Interview with Maude Barlow, Nov. 22, 1993.

[40] Interview with Glenda Simms, Nov. 18, 1993.

[41] She also emphasized this point in an interview with the author.

[42] *The Globe and Mail*, Apr. 6, 1993.

[43] Interview with Audrey McLaughlin, Apr. 4, 1994.

3/ TESTOSTERONE TABERNACLE

[1] Interview with Audrey McLaughlin, April 6, 1993. McLaughlin also recounts this story in her book, *A Woman's Place: My Life and Politics*, Macfarlane Walter & Ross, Toronto, 1992, pp. 27–28.

[2] For a succinct but amusing account of Parliament's many bizarre traditions, see Heather Robertson's *On the Hill: A People's Guide to Canada's Parliament*, McClelland & Stewart, Toronto, 1992, especially pp. 10–11 and 120.

[3] All these venomous words and many others are duly recorded in issues of *Hansard*, the official record of House of Commons debates. See especially, Commons debates of June 7, 1985, p. 5528; June 30, 1987, p. 7867; Oct. 29, 1987, p. 10532; March 18, 1988, p. 13906; June 6, 1988, p. 16167; July 4, 1988, p. 16999; and Dec. 19, 1989, pp. 7216–17.

[4] See Sheila Copps's submission to House of Commons, "Minutes of Proceedings and Evidence of the Special Committee on Electoral Reform," Jan. 26, 1993, p. 8:113.

[5] See Heather Robertson's wonderfully lively account of Macphail's career in *More than a Rose*, pp. 218–32.

[6] Interview with Dawn Black, June 9, 1993.

[7] Interview with Iona Campagnolo, May 3, 1993.

[8] Interview with Pat Carney, Apr. 1, 1993.

[9] Interview with Flora MacDonald, June 7, 1993.

[10] Mia Stainsby wrote an excellent account of the political manoeuvring behind the bill in the *Vancouver Sun*, Oct. 3, 1991.

[11] Lisa Young of the University of Toronto wrote a superb analysis of the efforts of female MPs to co-operate across party lines in "Fulfilling the Mandate of Difference: Cross-Party Co-operation Among Women in the Canadian House of Commons," a paper prepared for the annual meeting of the Canadian Political Science Association at Carleton University, June 6–8, 1993. Mary Clancy's statement, taken from *Hansard*, is on p. 9.

[12] Ibid., p. 11.

[13] Sydney Sharpe and Don Braid, *Storming Babylon: Preston Manning and the Rise of the Reform Party*, Key Porter Books, Toronto, 1992, p. 146.

[14] See *Maclean's*, Apr. 4, 1994, p. 18.

[15] Interview with Audrey McLaughlin, Apr. 6, 1993.

[16] Sheila Copps, *Nobody's Baby*, Deneau, Toronto, 1986, p. 29.

[17] *Hansard*, Dec. 14, 1987, p. 11760. Crosbie was at least trying to be funny

when he insulted Copps, and sometimes he was. Often others were simply vicious.

[18] Recounted in Robert Fife and John Warren, *A Capital Scandal: Politics, Patronage and Payoffs—Why Parliament Must Be Reformed*, Key Porter Books, Toronto, 1991, p. 216. This book is a useful guide to every episode of political venality, cupidity, and stupidity in the past half-century.

[19] Interview with Jean Pigott, June 9, 1993.

[20] From the "Report of the Special Advisory Committee to the Speaker: Recommendations for Amendments to the Standing Orders on Unparliamentary Language and the Speaker's Authority to Deal with Breaches of Decorum and Behaviour," June 22, 1992.

[21] Interview with Joe Clark, Apr. 4, 1993.

[22] Interview with Mary Clancy, June 15, 1993.

[23] Interview with Dawn Black, June 9, 1993.

[24] Heather Robertson, *On the Hill*, pp. 113–14.

[25] *Beneath the Veneer: The Report of the Task Force on Barriers to Women in the Public Service*, Minister of Supply and Services, 1990, Vol. 1, "Report and Recommendations," Foreword, p. 2.

[26] Ibid. For a wealth of charts, graphs, and statistics on women's employment in the civil service, see Vol. 1, Ch. 3, "Where the Women Are," pp. 16–38.

[27] LaMarsh, *Memoirs of a Bird in a Gilded Cage*, p. 36.

4/ HOLLOW CHIVALRY

[1] Doris Anderson, editor's column in *Chatelaine* magazine, May 1972.

[2] Doris Anderson, *The Unfinished Revolution: The status of women in twelve countries*, Doubleday Canada, Toronto, 1991, p. 18.

[3] Sheila Rowbotham, *Women in Movement: feminism and social action*, Routledge, New York, 1992, p. 23. For an examination of the subjection of women in history, see Mary R. Beard, *Women as a Force in History*, Collier Books, New York, 1962; for a historical sourcebook on attitudes toward women, see Rosemary Agonito, *History of Ideas on Women: A Source Book*, Perigee, New York, 1977.

[4] Trevor Lloyd, *Suffragettes International: The world-wide campaign for women's rights*, Library of the 20th Century, London, 1971, p. 69. This slim volume is a treasure-chest of photos, drawings, cartoons, and descriptive writing about women's movements in the nineteenth and early twentieth centuries.

[5] Ibid., p. 60.

[6] See Manon Tremblay, "Gender and Society: Rights and Realities," in David Thomas, ed., *Canada and the United States: Differences that Count*, Broadview Press, Peterborough, 1993, p. 271.

[7] Eleanor Flexner, *Century of Struggle: The Women's Rights Movement in the United States*, Atheneum, New York, 1968, p. 77.

[8] Quoted in Flexner, *Century of Struggle*, pp. 258–59.

[9] Linda Witt, Karen M. Paget, and Glenna Matthews, *Running as a Woman: Gender and Power in American Politics*, Maxwell Macmillan Canada, Toronto, 1994, p. 56.

[10] Janine Brodie and Jill McCalla Vickers, "Canadian Women in Politics: An Overview," Canadian Research Institute for the Advancement of Women, Ottawa, 1982, p. 39. For a spirited examination of the rivalries within the Canadian suffragist movement, its ultimate failure to influence women to run for office, and the reasons for the decline of feminism after the vote was won, see Carol Lee Bacchi, *Liberation Deferred? The Ideas of the English-Canadian Suffragists, 1877–1918*, Toronto, University of Toronto Press, 1983. For an overview of the suffragist movement as well as an understanding of the regional problems involved, see Catherine L. Cleverdon, *The Woman Suffrage Movement in Canada*, University of Toronto Press, 1974.

[11] Sandra Burt, "Legislators, Women, and Public Policy," in Sandra Burt, Lorraine Code, and Lindsay Dorney, eds., *Changing Patterns: Women in Canada*, McClelland & Stewart, Toronto, 1988, pp. 129–30. This article is an excellent summary of the policy assumptions that underpinned early laws affecting women.

[12] This passage appears in Mary Beard's analysis of Blackstone and his effect on Western law and society in *Women as a Force in History*, p. 89.

[13] L. Kanowitz, *Women and the Law: The Unfinished Revolution*, University of New Mexico Press, Albuquerque, 1969, p. 35. Quoted in Gwen Matheson, ed., *Women in the Canadian Mosaic*, Peter Martin Associates Ltd., Toronto, 1976, p. 28. Blackstone's legal interpretations influenced British and American law for nearly two centuries.

[14] *Report of the Royal Commission on the Status of Women in Canada*, p. 336.

[15] For a summary of their lives, see Carlotta Hacker, *Those Indomitable Lady Doctors*, Clarke, Irwin & Company, Toronto, 1974, especially pp. 26–35.

[16] See Wendy Mitchinson, "The WCTU: For God, Home and Native Land: A

Study in Nineteenth-Century Feminism," in Linda Kealey, ed., *A Not Unreasonable Claim: Women and Reform in Canada, 1880s–1920s,* The Women's Press, Toronto, 1979.

[17] But they ultimately served to undermine women's political potential. See Bacchi, *Liberation Deferred.*

[18] Quoted in Deborah Gorham, "The Canadian Suffragists," in Matheson, ed., *Women in the Canadian Mosaic,* p. 26. See also Gorham's study of "Flora MacDonald Denison: Canadian Feminist," in Kealey, ed., *A Not Unreasonable Claim,* pp. 47–70.

[19] Quoted in Gwen Matheson and V.E. Lang, "Nellie McClung: 'Not a Nice Woman,' " in *Women in the Canadian Mosaic,* p. 5.

[20] Nellie McClung, *In Times Like These,* introduction by Veronica Strong-Boag, Toronto: University of Toronto Press, 1972, p. 48.

[21] Gwen Matheson and V.E. Lang, pp. 11–12.

[22] See Candace Savage, *Our Nell, A Scrapbook Biography of Nellie L. McClung,* Western Producer Prairie Books, Saskatoon, 1979, p. 89.

[23] See Sydney Sharpe, "Subsistence versus Subservience," in *Origins of the Alberta Métis: Land Claims Research,* Métis Association of Alberta and Native Council of Canada, Ottawa, 1978; and "Sex Roles and the Canadian Frontier," paper presented to World Congress of Sociology, Toronto, 1975.

[24] Sylvia Bashevkin, *Toeing the Lines: Women and Party Politics in English Canada,* Second Edition, Oxford University Press, Toronto, 1993, p. 5. Bashevkin provides a useful chart giving the dates when the franchise was granted, when women were allowed to hold office, and when the first woman was elected in each jurisdiction. For the enfranchisement dates in the provinces see Appendix 1.

[25] For a short but informative synopsis, see *The Persons Case,* published by the Alberta Women's Secretariat, Oct. 1989.

[26] See Cleverdon, *The Woman Suffrage Movement in Canada,* pp. 143–55. For biographical sketches, also see *The Persons Case.*

[27] Tremblay, "Gender and Society: Rights and Realities," in Thomas, ed., *Canada and the United States,* p. 273.

[28] Sherrill MacLaren, *Invisible Power,* Seal Books, Toronto, 1991, p. 66.

[29] Bashevkin, *Toeing the Lines,* p. 12.

[30] Reprinted in a *Toronto Star* centennial edition, June 15, 1992. The reporter wrote that "Miss Macphail's voice took a low and quiet note that was pleasing to hear" when she was "spoken to this morning over the long-distance telephone."

[31] Agnes Macphail, "Men Want to Hog Everything," *Maclean's,* Sept. 15, 1949, quoted in Bashevkin, *Toeing the Lines*, p. 1.

[32] Margaret Stewart and Doris French, *Ask No Quarter: A Biography of Agnes Macphail*, Longmans Green, Toronto, 1959, p. 74.

5/ WIDOWS TO WARRIORS

[1] For a detailed account of the lives and trials of early women politicians, see Alison Prentice et al., *Canadian Women: A History*, Harcourt Brace Jovanovich, Toronto, 1988, pp. 276–85.

[2] Robertson, *More than a Rose*, p. 222.

[3] The other Conservative woman was Margaret Aitken, MP for York-Humber, Ont., from 1953 to 1962. Jean Casselman Wadds was elected in a by-election in 1958.

[4] From an interview with Sylvia Bashevkin, Apr. 16, 1993. Quoted in Bashevkin, *Toeing the Lines*, p. 87.

[5] Translation from *La Presse*, quoted in Gertrude J. Robinson and Armande Saint-Jean, with the assistance of Christine Rioux, "Women Politicians and Their Media Coverage: A Generational Analysis," in Kathy Megyery, ed., *Women in Canadian Politics: Toward Equity in Representation*, Vol. 6 of the Research Studies of the Royal Commission on Electoral Reform and Party Financing, Dundurn Press, Toronto, 1991, p. 139.

[6] Interview with Jean Pigott, June 3, 1993.

[7] Author conversation with Ellen Fairclough, June 15, 1993. She did not consent to an extended interview because, she said testily, "Everybody's writing a book about women in politics."

[8] Quoted in MacLaren, *Invisible Power*, p. 103.

[9] Ibid.

[10] Told by former New Democrat MP Dawn Black in an interview with the author on June 9, 1993. The late Ms. Jewett was the Liberal MP for Ontario's Northumberland riding from 1963 to 1965. In 1979 she was elected for the New Democrats in B.C.'s New Westminister-Coquitlam riding, and served until 1988.

[11] When LaMarsh supported Joe Greene in her Niagara Falls riding after retiring in 1968, she got a surprise. "I received a pleasant note from Trudeau, saying, 'We all miss you,' and thanking me for supporting Greene. It was very gracious, and much appreciated, as it was the only thanks I got for my support from any source." See *Memoirs of a Bird in a Gilded Cage*, p. 349.

[12] After LaMarsh died in 1980 of cancer, at age fifty-five, the CBC's "Take Thirty" TV show broadcast a revealing and affecting montage of clips and interviews. The quotes are taken from a tape of this show, which was made available to me by University of Alberta historian Cathy Cavanaugh. The "Take Thirty" show concluded with a moving interview of the late CBC broadcaster Barbara Frum, who grew up on the same street as LaMarsh in Niagara Falls and became a close friend. Frum gently suggested that LaMarsh made her own choices in life quite consciously and turned down several opportunities to marry. The one thing LaMarsh never wanted, Frum said, was pity—although the taped interviews suggest that LaMarsh felt some for herself.

[13] LaMarsh, *Memoirs of a Bird in a Gilded Cage*, p. 304. This remarkably honest and unaffected book remains one of the best ever about Canadian politics. LaMarsh is at her most effective when she turns her laser-sharp intelligence and wit to the lot of women in political life.

[14] Quoted in Bashevkin, *Toeing the Lines*, pp. 21–22.

[15] Penney Kome, *Women of Influence: Canadian Women and Politics*, Doubleday Canada, Toronto, 1985, p. 82.

[16] Prentice et al., *Canadian Women*, pp. 346–47.

[17] MacLaren, *Invisible Power*, p. 79.

[18] *Report of the Royal Commission on the Status of Women in Canada*, "Terms of Reference," p. vii.

[19] Interview with Céline Hervieux-Payette, June 2, 1993.

[20] *Report of the Royal Commission on the Status of Women in Canada*, p. 355.

6/ REGIMENTAL MASCOTS

[1] Interview with Monique Bégin, May 22, 1993.

[2] Recounted in Christina McCall-Newman, *Grits, An Intimate Portrait of the Liberal Party*, Macmillan of Canada, Toronto, 1982, p. 113.

[3] See Janine Brodie with Celia Chandler, "Women and the Electoral Process in Canada," in Megyery, ed., *Women in Canadian Politics*, p. 5. This volume contains excellent charts and graphs that illustrate women's participation in politics.

[4] See the Sheila Copps and Marcel Prud'homme discussion in "Minutes of Proceedings and Evidence of the Special Committee on Electoral Reform," Jan. 26, 1993, p. 8:135.

[5] Interview with Sharon Orr, June 11, 1994. Orr is now executive vice-president of marketing with the Canadian Association of Broadcasters.

[6] McCall-Newman, *Grits,* p. 378.

[7] "Minutes of Proceedings and Evidence of the Special Committee on Electoral Reform," part of *The Royal Commission on Electoral Reform and Party Financing,* Issue No. 8, Tues., Jan. 26, 1993, pp. 8:131–32.

[8] Interview with Monique Bégin, May 22, 1993.

[9] Interview with Jean Chrétien, June 21, 1993.

[10] Interview with Monique Bégin, May 22, 1993.

[11] Interview with Iona Campagnolo, May 3, 1993.

[12] Interview with Maude Barlow, Nov. 22, 1993.

[13] Interview with Céline Hervieux-Payette, June 2, 1993.

[14] Interview with Iona Campagnolo, May 22, 1993.

[15] Interview with Flora MacDonald, June 7, 1993.

[16] See Rosemary Brown, *Being Brown: A Very Public Life,* Random House of Canada, Toronto, 1989.

[17] Interview with Joe Clark, Apr. 4, 1993.

[18] Interview with Peter Raymont, Jan. 27, 1994.

[19] See Jeffrey Simpson's classic account of this strange passage in Canadian politics, *Discipline of Power: The Conservative Interlude and the Liberal Restoration,* Personal Library, Toronto, 1980.

[20] MacLaren, *Invisible Power,* p. 244.

[21] Patrick Nagle of Southam News, one of Canada's best and most experienced political journalists, believes that the controversy fixed Clark's image so solidly that he never had a chance to recover.

[22] Interview with Audrey McLaughlin, Apr. 4, 1993.

[23] For an excellent in-depth account of women's efforts in the constitutional debate, see Penney Kome, *The Taking of Twenty-Eight: Women Challenge the Constitution,* Toronto, The Women's Press, 1983. Shorter descriptions appear in her *Women of Influence,* pp. 123–38, and in Prentice et al., *Canadian Women,* pp. 400–404.

[24] Gwen Brodsky and Shelagh Day, *Canadian Charter Equality Rights for Women: One Step Forward or Two Steps Back?* Canadian Advisory Council on the Status of Women, Sept. 1989, p. iv.

[25] Copps, *Nobody's Baby,* p. 86.

[26] Tremblay, "Gender and Society: Rights and Realities," in Thomas, ed., *Canada and the United States,* p. 271.

[27] Janine Brodie, *Women and Politics in Canada,* McGraw-Hill Ryerson, Toronto, 1985, p. 127.

7/ BORN-AGAIN BRIAN

[1] Interview with Brian Mulroney, Feb. 10, 1994.

[2] For a lively account of Mulroney's relationship with Mila, see "Mila, the Movie," in Robertson's *More than a Rose,* pp. 394–408.

[3] Quoted in Kome, *Women of Influence,* p. 187.

[4] Interview with Janis Johnson, June 28, 1993. In 1990, Mulroney made Johnson a senator.

[5] Kome, *Women of Influence,* p. 146.

[6] Blais-Grenier, Mulroney's first environment minister, was demoted to the Tory back benches after being accused of misusing travel expenses. Afterward she accused the government of receiving kickbacks. She languished in the back benches until being defeated in the 1988 election. See especially MacLaren, *Invisible Power,* p. 109.

[7] Interview with Barbara McDougall, Jan. 24, 1994.

[8] Quoted in Charlotte Gray's insightful profile of McDougall, "A Woman's Place," in *Saturday Night,* May 1987.

[9] Lists of appointments supplied by Marjory LeBreton, 1993.

[10] Interview with Marjory LeBreton, July 25, 1993.

[11] *Beneath the Veneer: The Report of the Task Force on Barriers to Women in the Public Service.*

[12] Interview with Joe Clark, Apr. 3, 1993.

[13] Interview with Mary Collins, Apr. 14, 1993.

[14] MacLaren, *Invisible Women,* p. 127.

[15] Young, "Fulfilling the Mandate of Difference," p. 22.

[16] *Toronto Star,* Feb. 29, 1992.

[17] Lise Gottell and Janine Brodie, "Women and Parties: More than an Issue of Numbers," in Hugh G. Thorburn, ed., *Party Politics in Canada,* Prentice Hall Canada, Scarborough, 1991, p. 66.

[18] Interview with Judy Rebick, June 24, 1993.

[19] Kome, *Women of Influence,* pp. 181–82.

[20] From notes for a speech by Sheila Copps to the International Women's Day Brunch, held in Edmonton, Mar. 3, 1993.

[21] Interview with Brian Mulroney, Feb. 10, 1994.

8/ TRADITIONAL MAN

[1] Interview with Iona Campagnolo, May 4, 1994.

[2] Interview with Joyce Fairbairn, May 7, 1994.

[3] Her experience is similar to those of many women who say they feel very comfortable with Chrétien. He manages to be courtly without being condescending.

[4] Interview with Aline Chrétien, Feb. 23, 1994.

[5] For an excellent overview of the Chrétiens' private life, see E. Kaye Fulton with Christina Wolaniuk, "A Very Private Lady," in *Maclean's*, Apr. 18, 1994.

[6] Interview with Jean Chrétien, June 21, 1993.

[7] Speech by Joyce Fairbairn to the Winning Women group in Calgary, May 7, 1994.

[8] Interview with Joyce Fairbairn, May 7, 1994.

[9] Interview with Sharon Carstairs, June 9, 1993.

[10] Interview with Anne McLellan, June 2, 1994.

[11] Besides Augustine, the female parliamentary secretaries were: Mary Clancy (Halifax), Citizenship and Immigration; Marlene Catterall (Ottawa), Treasury Board; Dr. Hedy Fry (Vancouver), Health; Albina Guarnieri (Toronto), Canadian Heritage; and Susan Whelan (Windsor), daughter of former minister Eugene Whelan, National Revenue. See *The Globe and Mail*, Dec. 7, 1993. Female cabinet secretaries were Sheila Finestone (Montreal), Multiculturalism, status of women (Canadian Heritage); Ethel Blondin-Andrew (Western Arctic) training and youth (Human Resources); and Christine Stewart (Northumberland) Latin America and Africa (Foreign Affairs). See *Calgary Herald*, wire service story, Nov. 5, 1993.

[12] The Calgary business community led this lobbying effort in early 1994, and by March the government was talking about "reviewing" the sale of the government's remaining 70 per cent stake in Petro-Can. See *The Globe and Mail*, Mar. 1, 1994.

[13] Interview with Chaviva Hosek, Feb. 19, 1993.

[14] This story was recounted to the author by one of the women who attended the meeting.

[15] Interview with Brian Mulroney, Feb. 10, 1994.

[16] Interview with Barbara McDougall, Jan. 24, 1994.

[17] See Susan Kastner, "The Valley Girl and the Separatist," *Toronto Star*, Sept. 26, 1993.

[18] Heather Bird, "Back to the Drawing Room," in *Homemaker's Magazine*, March 1994. The fascinating fact about the birth of the Bouchards' child was first revealed by Quebec journalist Michel Vastel in the magazine *L'Actualité*.

[19] Letter to the editor, *Calgary Herald,* Oct. 14, 1993. The letter was signed by Valerie Clark and forty-one other female members of the Reform Party. "Each and every one of us has exactly as much power in the party as we want," they said, "and if we want more, it is openly available to us. The men in the Reform Party are quite accustomed to dealing with strong, independent women."

[20] Speech by Senator Joyce Fairbairn to the Winning Women group in Calgary, May 7, 1994.

[21] Jan Brown, "Changing the Gender Agenda of Politics," in *Canadian Parliamentary Review,* summer 1994.

[22] Interview with Sandra Manning, Mar. 25, 1994.

[23] Interview with Sandra Manning, Oct. 25, 1993.

[24] Interview with Preston Manning, Mar. 18, 1994.

[25] Interview with Deborah Grey, May 28, 1993.

9/ THE GREAT DIVIDE

[1] See political journalist Sheldon Albert's shrewd analysis in the *Calgary Herald,* Mar. 19, 1994.

[2] Interview with Val Meredith, Feb. 28, 1994.

[3] Quoted by Deborah Gorham, "The Canadian Suffragists," in Matheson, ed., *Women in the Canadian Mosaic,* p. 25.

[4] Brodie with Chandler, "Women and the Electoral Process in Canada," in Megyery, ed., *Women in Canadian Politics,* pp. 12–13. English philosopher Thomas Hobbes (1588–1679) was one of the earliest and most influential theorists of classical liberalism. John Locke (1632–1704) expounded a theory of individual rights that heavily influenced democracy in Britain, Canada, and the U.S. Some analysts feel that Locke was really an advocate of women's equal authority who was wilfully misinterpreted by his contemporaries. See Rosemary Agonito, "John Locke," in Rosemary Agonito, *History of Ideas on Women, A Source Book,* Perigee, New York, 1977, pp. 103–4.

[5] Iona Campagnolo told me on May 3, 1993, that Inman, later a Liberal senator, recounted this story when she was in her nineties.

[6] Interview with Catherine Callbeck, June 21, 1993.

[7] Correspondence from Lise Bacon to author, July 20, 1993.

[8] Interview with Grace McCarthy, Mar. 19, 1993.

[9] Recounted in Fife and Warren, *A Capital Scandal,* p. 212.

[10] Quoted in P.T. Rooke and R.L. Schnell, *No Bleeding Heart: Charlotte Whitton, A Feminist on the Right,* University of British Columbia Press, Vancouver, 1987, p. 190.

[11] Whitton made the remark in the Susan B. Anthony lecture at the University of Rochester in 1947, the year of the death of her companion of twenty-five years, Margaret Grier. When Whitton passed away in 1975, she was buried beside Grier and her friend's headstone was amended to read: "dear friend to Charlotte Whitton, 1896–1975."

[12] Interview with Iona Campagnolo, Mar. 15, 1994.

[13] See Marci McDonald, "Rebel with a Cause," in *Maclean's,* Apr. 4, 1994.

[14] For the best account of the Tyabji–Wilson fiasco, see Ian Gill's perceptive and witty article "The leader, his wife, his fiancée, and the press," in *Chatelaine,* June 1993.

[15] *The Globe and Mail,* Mar. 5, 1994.

[16] Interview with Judi Tyabji, May 17, 1993.

[17] Quoted in *Calgary Herald,* wire service story, Apr. 22, 1994.

[18] Brodie, *Women and Politics in Canada,* pp. 83–91.

[19] Interview with Diane Ablonczy, Jan. 11, 1994.

[20] Interview with Lyn McLeod, June 22, 1993.

[21] Interview with Alexa McDonough, June 8, 1993.

[22] Interview with Céline Hervieux-Payette, June 2, 1993.

[23] Interview with Pat Carney, April 1, 1993. Also recounted in Copps, *Nobody's Baby,* p. 87. Copps is often said to be a relentlessly partisan politician who believes Tories are the source of all evil, but in her book she gives full credit to Carney and other women. In conversations with the author, she has been equally generous to other opponents, including the NDP's Audrey McLaughlin.

[24] Interview with Janis Johnson, June 28, 1993.

[25] Interview with Evelyn Gigantes, June 24, 1993.

[26] Interview with Jodi White, Jan. 25, 1994.

[27] Interview with Brian Mulroney, Feb. 10, 1994.

[28] Margaret Thatcher, *The Downing Street Years,* HarperCollins, Toronto, 1993, p. 23.

[29] The "Politicians in Pumps" Seminar with Sharon Carstairs, Margaret (Joe) Commodore, and Barbara McDougall, and chaired by Stevie Cameron at the Canadian Association of Journalists (CAJ), Nov. 13, 1993.

[30] Interview with Sharon Carstairs, June 9, 1993.

[31] Related by *Calgary Herald* columnist Don Braid.

[32] Interview with Sheila Copps, Mar. 7, 1993.

[33] Interview with Jean Chrétien, June 21, 1993.

10 / THE LAST GATEKEEPERS

[1] Thirty per cent of female Reform candidates won, as opposed to only 24 per cent of male candidates.

[2] For a lucid examination of this phenomenon, see Gottell and Brodie, "Women and Parties: More than an Issue of Numbers," in Thorburn, ed., *Party Politics in Canada*.

[3] Bashevkin, *Toeing the Lines*, p. 68. She cites a study by Harold D. Clarke and Allan Kornberg.

[4] Interview with Jean Chrétien, June 21, 1993.

[5] LaMarsh, *Memoirs of a Bird in a Gilded Cage*, p. 36.

[6] Megyery, ed., *Women in Canadian Politics*, p. 4. This volume contains many excellent charts, graphs, and statistics on women's participation in politics.

[7] See Brodie with Chandler, "Women and the Electoral Process in Canada," in Megyery, ed., *Women in Canadian Politics*, p. 33.

[8] Interview with Marjory LeBreton, July 25, 1993.

[9] *Report of the Royal Commission on the Status of Women in Canada*, p. 339.

[10] Interview with Dawn Black, June 9, 1993.

[11] Interview with Judy Rebick, June 24, 1993.

[12] Lynda Erikson and R.K. Carty, "Parties and Candidate Selection in the 1988 Canadian General Election," in the *Canadian Journal of Political Science*, XXIV:2, June 1991, p. 348.

[13] From her speech to a symposium on the participation of women in politics, organized by the Royal Commission on Electoral Reform and Party Financing, Oct. 31, 1990.

[14] Interview with Peter Lougheed, Nov. 12, 1993.

[15] Gottell and Brodie, "Women and Parties: More than an Issue of Numbers," in Thornburn, ed., *Party Politics in Canada*, p. 63.

[16] See especially *Toronto Star*, "Rising to the Challenge," Mar. 14, 1993, p. B-1. Dozens of equally laudatory articles appeared during the campaign, praising the parties for their efforts.

[17] Interview with Deborah Grey, May 28, 1993.

[18] Interview with Jean Chrétien, June 21, 1993.

[19] Interview with Janis Johnson, June 28, 1993.

[20] Interview with Barbara McDougall, Jan. 27, 1994.

[21] Bashevkin, *Toeing the Lines,* p. 75.

[22] See column by Gerald Caplan, *Toronto Star,* Jan. 5, 1993.

[23] Still, there are Icelandic descendants like Janis Johnson who find the traditional parties better avenues for their feminist goals.

11/ CLOSER TO HOME

[1] Interview with Frances Lankin, July 3, 1993.

[2] Interview with Bob Runciman, May 11, 1994. The allegations of rape at the Bell Cairn training centre were never proven, but a provincial inquiry found that abuse and harassment were rampant in Ontario's corrections ministry. In one case, staff felt free to watch pornographic movies in a government lounge without fear of reprisal. Judge Inger Hansen, of Ontario Court, Provincial Division, scolded the government for allowing a "poisoned work environment." She wrote: "The Ministry's culture . . . perpetuated a work environment in which individuals were at risk of harassment and intimidation." Corrections Minister Allan Pilkey and his senior civil servant were removed, and the Bell Cairn school was closed. See *Toronto Star,* Jan. 15, 1993.

[3] See Sydney Sharpe's Women's View column, *Calgary Herald,* Apr. 11, 1993; and *Edmonton Journal,* Apr. 4, 1993.

[4] Interview with Evelyn Gigantes, June 24, 1993.

[5] Document summarizing NDP action on women's issues prepared by Barbara Donaldson in Marion Boyd's office, Mar. 22, 1994.

[6] *Toronto Star,* Dec. 6, 1993. An excellent article by Howard Levitt, a Toronto-based employment lawyer and author of *The Law of Dismissal in Canada,* outlines the responses of business to various laws passed by the Ontario NDP.

[7] Interview with Evelyn Gigantes, June 24, 1993.

[8] Interview with Marion Boyd, Aug. 28, 1993.

[9] Interview with Lyn McLeod, June 22, 1993.

[10] Documents provided by Penny Priddy's office, May 1994.

[11] Interview with Anne Edwards, May 11, 1993.

[12] Lise Bacon was Quebec deputy premier in former premier Robert Bourassa's government.

[13] *Moosomin World-Spectator,* Jan. 12, 1993.

[14] Interview with Janice MacKinnon, June 15, 1993.

[15] Interview with Lynda Haverstock, May 8, 1993.

[16] Government of P.E.I. information, 1994. Interview with Charles A. MacKay, May 18, 1994.

[17] Interview with Catherine Callbeck, June 21, 1993.

[18] Interview with Alexa McDonough, June 8, 1993.

[19] Interview with Sharon Carstairs, June 9, 1993.

[20] Figures supplied to the author by Lise Bacon, former deputy premier.

[21] See Stephen Clarkson and Christina McCall, *Trudeau and Our Times,* Vol. 1, McClelland & Stewart, Toronto, 1990, pp. 231–34.

[22] Interview with Francine Pelletier, May 3, 1993.

[23] *Montreal Gazette,* Apr. 24, 1993.

[24] Correspondence from Lise Bacon to the author, July 20, 1993.

[25] Nellie Cournoyea was minister of health, minister of energy, mines and petroleum resources, minister of public works, and the minister responsible for NWT Power Corporation.

[26] Rosemary Allerston, "The Northern Dream is Reborn," *Up-here: Life in Canada's North,* Vol. 8, No. 6, Dec. 1992/Jan. 1993, p. 4. *Up-here* is a glossy, lively magazine full of well-written articles about the North.

[27] Tony Penikett, probably the most able NDP leader in the country, announced his intention to step down in mid-1994. His NDP government was defeated in late 1992.

[28] Margaret (Joe) Commodore was a participant in the Canadian Association of Journalists seminar "Politicians in Pumps," Nov. 13, 1993.

[29] See Marina Devine,"Northerner of the Year: Rosemarie Kuptana," *Up-here,* Dec. 1992/Jan. 1993, pp. 12–17, 39–40.

[30] Interview with Aline Chrétien, Feb. 23, 1994.

12/ BEYOND THE GILDED GHETTO

[1] Interview with Joyce Fairbairn, May 7, 1994.

[2] See Prentice et al., *Canadian Women: A History,* p. 354.

[3] See Witt et al., *Running as a Woman,* p. 6. The authors trumpet the figure as a great triumph because it rose in 1992 from only 6 per cent in the previous election. Meanwhile, female representation in the elected Senate rose from 2 per cent to 6 per cent (six out of 100 senators).

[4] Melissa H. Haussman, "The Personal is Constitutional: Feminist Struggles for Equality Rights in the United States and Canada," in Jill Bystydzienski, ed., *Women Transforming Politics,* Indiana University Press, 1992, p. 114.

[5] Quoted in Kome, *Women of Influence,* pp. 178–79.

[6] Interview with Sunera Thobani, Nov. 11, 1993.

[7] Linda Trimble, "A Few Good Women: Female Legislators in Alberta, 1972–1991," in Catherine A. Cavanaugh and Randi R. Warne, eds., *Standing on New Ground: Women in Alberta,* University of Alberta Press, Edmonton, 1993, p. 89.

[8] Interview with Pam Barrett, May 21, 1993.

[9] Quoted in Young, "Fulfilling the Mandate of Difference," p. 7.

[10] *Chatelaine,* June 1993, p. 4.

[11] There were nine male cabinet ministers and nine women, including Bruntland as prime minister. See Anderson, *The Unfinished Revolution,* p. 249.

[12] Young, "Fulfilling the Mandate of Difference," p. 7.

[13] Interview with Glenda Simms, Nov. 18, 1993.

BIBLIOGRAPHY

BOOKS AND ARTICLES

Agonito, Rosemary. "John Locke." In *History of Ideas on Women: A Source Book*, edited by Rosemary Agonito. New York: Perigee, 1977.

Allerston, Rosemary. "The Northern Dream is Reborn." *Up-here* 8, 6, (December 1992/January 1993).

Amer, Elizabeth. "Icelandic Women Inspire." *Feminist Action*, September 1988.

Anderson, Doris. "Editor's Column." *Chatelaine*, May 1972.

—————. *The Unfinished Revolution: The status of women in twelve countries*. Toronto: Doubleday Canada, 1991.

Bacchi, Carol Lee. *Liberation Deferred? The Ideas of the English-Canadian Suffragists, 1877–1918*. Toronto: University of Toronto Press, 1983.

Barnes, Julian. "The Maggie Years." *The New Yorker*. November 15, 1993.

Bashevkin, Sylvia. *Toeing the Lines: Women and Party Politics in English Canada*, Second Edition. Toronto: Oxford University Press, 1993.

Beard, Mary R. *Women as a Force in History*. New York: Collier Books, 1962.

Bird, Heather. "Back to the Drawing Room." *Homemaker's Magazine*, March 1994.

Brodie, Janine. *Women and Politics in Canada*. Toronto: McGraw-Hill Ryerson Ltd., 1985.

Brodie, Janine and Celia Chandler. "Women and the Electoral Process in Canada." In *Women in Canadian Politics: Toward Equity in Representation*, edited by Kathy Megyery. Volume 6 of the Research Studies, Royal Commission on Electoral Reform and Party Financing. Toronto: Dundurn Press, 1991.

Brodie, Janine and Jill McCalla Vickers. *Canadian Women in Politics: An Overview*. Ottawa: Canadian Research Institute for the Advancement of Women, 1982.

Brodsky, Gwen and Shelagh Day. *Canadian Charter Equality Rights for Women: One Step Forward or Two Steps Back*. Ottawa: Canadian Advisory Council on the Status of Women, September 1989.

Brown, Jan. "Changing the Gender Agenda of Politics." *Canadian Parliamentary Review*, Summer 1994.

Brown, Rosemary. *Being Brown: A Very Public Life*. Toronto: Random House of Canada, 1989.

Burt, Sandra. "Legislators, Women, and Public Policy." In *Changing Patterns: Women in Canada*, edited by Sanda Burt, Lorraine Code, and Lindsay Dorney. Toronto: McClelland & Stewart, 1988.

Chrétien, Jean. *Straight From The Heart*. Toronto: Key Porter Books, 1985.

Clarkson, Stephen and Christina McCall. *Trudeau and Our Times*, Volume 1. Toronto: McClelland & Stewart, 1990.

Cleverdon, Catherine L. *The Woman Suffrage Movement in Canada*. Toronto: University of Toronto Press, 1974.

Cohen, Andrew. "Kim Campbell's Strange Trip." *Saturday Night*, September 1993.

Copps, Sheila. *Nobody's Baby*. Toronto: Deneau, 1986.

—————. Submission to House of Commons. "Minutes of Proceedings and Evidence of the Special Committee on Electoral Reform," January 26, 1993.

————. "Women in politics: for a better democracy." Opening speech for *Symposium on the Active Participation of Women in Politics.* Royal Commission on Electoral Reform and Party Financing, October 31, 1990.

Crosland, Susan. "Yes Ms. Prime Minister." *The Sunday Times of London,* reprinted in *The Globe and Mail,* July 10, 1993.

Devine, Marina. "Northerner of the Year: Rosemarie Kuptana." *Up-here* 8, 6 (December 1992/January 1993).

Erikson, Lynda and R.K. Carty. "Parties and Candidate Selection in the 1988 Canadian General Election." *Canadian Journal of Political Science,* June 1991.

Fife, Robert and John Warren. *A Capital Scandal: Politics, Patronage and Payoffs — Why Parliament Must be Reformed.* Toronto: Key Porter Books, 1991.

Fife, Robert. *Kim Campbell: The Making of a Politician.* Toronto: HarperCollins, 1993.

Financial Post. *Directory of the Government of Canada.* 1991–93.

Flexner, Eleanor. *Century of Struggle: The Women's Rights Movement in the United States.* New York: Atheneum, 1968.

Fulton, E. Kaye and Mary Janigan. "The Real Kim Campbell." *Maclean's,* May 17, 1993.

Fulton, E. Kaye and Christina Wolaniuk. "A Very Private Lady." *Maclean's,* April 18, 1994.

Gill, Ian. "The leader, his wife, his fiancée, and the press." *Chatelaine,* June 1993.

Gorham, Deborah. "The Canadian Suffragists." In *Women in the Canadian Mosaic,* edited by Gwen Matheson. Toronto: Peter Martin Associates Ltd., 1976.

Gottell, Lise and Janine Brodie. "Women and Parties: More than an Issue of Numbers." In *Party Politics in Canada,* edited by Hugh G. Thorburn. Scarborough: Prentice Hall Canada, 1991.

Government of Alberta, Women's Secretariat. *The Persons Case.* 1992.

Graham, Ron. "The Campbell Gamble." *Report on Business Magazine,* September 1993.

Gray, Charlotte. "Woman of the Year: Kim Campbell." *Chatelaine*, January 1994.

——————. "A Woman's Place." *Saturday Night*, May 1987.

Hacker, Carlotta. *Those Indomitable Lady Doctors*. Toronto: Clarke, Irwin & Company Ltd., 1974.

Haussman, Melissa H. "The Personal is Constitutional: Feminist Struggles for Equality Rights in the United States and Canada." In *Women Transforming Politics*, edited by Jill Bystydzienski. Bloomington: Indiana University Press, 1992.

Hunter, Diane, Julie Johnston and Anne Tingle. *The Campaign Book*. Calgary: Winning Women, A Political Skills Group. n.d.

Istona, Mildred. "We Are Women, Hear Us Roar." *Chatelaine*, June 1993.

Kaminer, Wendy. "Feminism's Identity Crisis." *The Atlantic*, October 1993.

Kanowitz, L. *Women and the Law: The Unfinished Revolution*. Albuquerque: University of New Mexico Press, 1969.

Khosla, Punham. "Review of the Situation of Women in Canada, 1993." Toronto: National Action Committee on the Status of Women, July 1993.

Kome, Penney. *The Taking of Twenty-Eight: Women Challenge the Constitution*. Toronto: The Women's Press, 1983.

——————. *Women of Influence: Canadian Women and Politics*. Toronto: Doubleday Canada Ltd., 1985.

LaMarsh, Judy. *Memoirs of a Bird in a Gilded Cage*. Toronto: McClelland & Stewart, 1968.

Lloyd, Trevor. *Suffragettes International: The world-wide campaign for women's rights*. London: Library of the 20th Century, 1971.

MacLaren, Sherrill. *Invisible Power*. Toronto: McClelland-Bantam, 1991.

Maillé, Chantal. "Primed for Power: Women in Canadian Politics." Ottawa: Canadian Advisory Council on the Status of Women, 1990.

Marsh, James H., editor. *The Canadian Encyclopedia*, Vol. II. Edmonton: Hurtig, 1985.

Matheson, Gwen and V.E. Lang. "Nellie McClung: 'Not a Nice Woman.'" In *Women in the Canadian Mosaic*, edited by Gwen Matheson. Toronto: Peter Martin Associates Ltd, 1976.

McCall-Newman, Christina. *Grits: An Intimate Portrait of the Liberal Party.* Toronto: Macmillan, 1982.

McClung, Nellie. *In Times Like These.* Introduction by Veronica Strong-Boag. Toronto: University of Toronto Press, 1972.

McDonald, Marci. "Rebel with a cause." *Maclean's*, April 4, 1994.

McLaughlin, Audrey with Rick Archbold. *A Woman's Place: My Life and Politics,* Toronto: Macfarlane Walter & Ross, 1992.

Mitchinson, Wendy. "The WCTU: For God, Home and Native Land: A Study in Nineteenth-Century Feminism." In *A Not Unreasonable Claim: Women and Reform in Canada, 1880s–1920s,* edited by Linda Kealey. Toronto: The Women's Press, 1979.

Newman, Peter C. "Kim Campbell." *Vancouver* magazine, May 1993.

Noble, Barbara Presley. "The Debate Over *la Différence*," *The New York Times*, August 15, 1993.

Ontario Institute for Studies in Education. *The Women's Kit.* Toronto, n.d.

Prentice, Alison et al. *Canadian Women: A History.* Toronto: Harcourt Brace Jovanovich, 1988.

Riley, Susan. "Ms. Representing Feminism: The Troubling Ascent of Kim Campbell." *This Magazine*, May 1993.

Robertson, Heather. *On the Hill: A People's Guide to Canada's Parliament.* Toronto: McClelland and Stewart, 1992.

——————. *More than a Rose: Prime Ministers, Wives, and Other Women.* Toronto: Seal Books, 1992.

Robinson, Gertrude J. and Armande Saint-Jean, with the assistance of Christine Rioux. "Women Politicians and their Media Coverage: A Generational Analysis." In *Women in Canadian Politics: Toward Equity in Representation*, edited by Kathy Megyery. Volume 6 of the Royal Commission on Electoral Reform and Party Financing. Toronto: Dundurn Press, 1991.

Rooke, P.T. and R.L. Schnell. *No Bleeding Heart: Charlotte Whitton,*

A Feminist on the Right. Vancouver: University of British Columbia Press, 1987.

Rowbotham, Sheila. *Women in Movement: feminism and social action.* New York: Routledge, 1992.

Savage, Candace. *Our Nell: A Scrapbook Biography of Nellie L. McClung.* Saskatoon: Western Producer Prairie Books, 1979.

Sawatsky, John. *Mulroney: The Politics of Ambition.* Toronto: Macfarlane Walter & Ross, 1991.

Sharpe, Sydney and Don Braid. *Storming Babylon: Preston Manning and the Rise of the Reform Party.* Toronto: Key Porter Books, 1992.

Sharpe, Sydney. "Election '93, Part 1." Chatelaine, May 1993. "Election '93, Part 2." *Chatelaine,* June 1993.

—————. "Northern Light." *West,* April 1990.

Simpson, Jeffrey. *Discipline of Power: The Conservative Interlude and the Liberal Restoration.* Toronto: Personal Library, 1980.

Stewart, Margaret and Doris French. *Ask No Quarter: A Biography of Agnes Macphail.* Toronto: Longmans Green, 1959.

Thatcher, Margaret. *The Downing Street Years.* Toronto: HarperCollins, 1993.

Tremblay, Manon. "Gender and Society: Rights and Realities." In *Canada and the United States: Differences that Count,* edited by David Thomas. Peterborough: Broadview Press, 1993.

Trimble, Linda. "A Few Good Women: Female Legislators in Alberta, 1972–1991." In *Standing on New Ground: Women in Alberta,* edited by Catherine A. Cavanaugh and Randi R. Warne. Edmonton: University of Alberta Press, 1993.

Ullyott, Kathy. "See Jane Run." *Flare,* October 1992.

Vickers, Jill McCalla and Janine Brodie. "Canada." In *The Politics of the Second Electorate: Women and Public Participation,* edited by Joni Lovenduski and Jill Hills. London: Routledge & Kegan Paul, 1981.

Vickers, Jill McCalla. "Feminist Approaches to Women in Politics." In *Beyond the Vote: Canadian Women and Politics,* edited by Linda Kealey and Joan Sangster. Toronto: University of Toronto Press, 1989.

Vickers, Jill, Pauline Rankin, and Christine Appelle. *Politics As If Women Mattered*. Toronto: University of Toronto Press, 1993.

Wilson-Smith, Anthony with Glen Allen and Luke Fisher. "Closing the Gap." *Maclean's*, June 7, 1993.

Witt, Linda, Karen M. Paget, and Glenna Matthews. *Running As a Woman: Gender and Power in American Politics*. Toronto: Maxwell Macmillan Canada, 1994.

Woodley, Barbara. *Portraits: Canadian Women in Focus*. Toronto: Doubleday Canada, 1992.

Young, Lisa. "Fulfilling the Mandate of Difference: Cross-Party Co-operation Among Women in the Canadian House of Commons." Paper prepared for the annual meeting of the Canadian Political Science Association at Carleton University, June 6–8, 1993.

GOVERNMENT OF CANADA DOCUMENTS

Elections Canada.

"Number of Candidates," 1974–1988.

"Number of Women Elected in Parliament," 1988, 1994.

"Official Spending Limits for Political Parties and Candidates," 1993.

"Summary of Candidates Elected," 1974–1988.

"Standing of Parties," 1994.

"Women Candidates in Canadian General Elections," 1988, 1994.

"Women Candidates and MPs in Canadian General Elections," 1994.

Government of Canada. *Report of the Royal Commission on the Status of Women in Canada*. Ottawa: Information Canada, 1970.

Government of Canada. *Beneath the Veneer: The Report of the Task Force on Barriers to Women in the Public Service*. Ottawa: Minister of Supply and Services Canada, 1990. Vol. 1, "Report and Recommendations"; Vol. 2, "What the Numbers Told Us"; Vol. 3, "What the People Told Us;" Vol. 4, "Annotated Bibliography."

House of Commons debates. *Hansard*. June 7, 1985, p. 5528; June 30, 1987, p. 7867; October 29, 1987, p. 10532; December 14, 1987, p. 11760; March 18, 1988, p. 13906; June 6, 1988, p.

16167; June 8, 1988, p. 16167; July 4, 1988, p. 16999; December 19, 1989, pp. 7216–17; February 22, 1990, p. 8693; September 18, 1991, pp. 2299–2300.

Library of Parliament. *Compilations. No. 15e.* Ottawa: Information and Technical Services Branch, June 1994.

Minutes of Proceedings and Evidence of the Special Committee on Electoral Reform, January 26, 1993, p. 8:135.

"Report of the Special Advisory Committee to the Speaker: Recommendations for Amendments to the Standing Orders on Unparliamentary Language and the Speaker's Authority to Deal with Breaches of Decorum and Behaviour." June 22, 1992.

NEWS ACCOUNTS

The Calgary Herald. January 29, April 11, April 17, April 18, May 19, October 25, November 5, December 8, 1993, February 28, April 10, April 22, 1994.

The Edmonton Journal. September 21, October 24, December 26, 1992; January 16, February 13, March 3, March 10, March 20, March 27, April 4, May 29, June 6, June 9, June 10, October 24, 1993. Columnist Liane Faulder, March 20, 1993.

The Globe and Mail. January 27, February 9, February 13, March 12, March 17, April 6, June 3, September 10, September 11, September 14, September 18, October 9, December 7, December 10, December 18, 1993; January 19, February 10, February 17, February 23, February 25, March 1, March 5, March 9, May 21, 1994.

The Montreal *Gazette*, April 24, 1993. Columnist William Johnson, March 19, 1993.

The Moosomin World-Spectator, January 12, 1993.

The Toronto Star. January 6, 1991; February 29, May 24, May 28, June 15 (Centennial Edition), June 20, 1992; January 15, June 8, September 26, October 11, November 13, December 6, December 7, 1993.

The Vancouver Sun. March 16, March 18, March 23, April 7, July 31, 1993. Columnist Mia Stainsby, Oct. 3, 1991.

The Los Angeles Times, April 21, 1981.

Frank magazine, November 25, 1993.

Maclean's, "The Number Two," December 6, 1993.

CBC Newsworld broadcast on April 15, 1993.

CBC "Take Thirty." Special on Judy LaMarsh, 1980.

Canadian Association of Journalists seminar, "Politicians in Pumps," chaired by Stevie Cameron. Panelists: Sharon Carstairs, Margaret (Joe) Commodore, and Barbara McDougall, Winnipeg, November 13, 1993.

INDEX